What's Worship Got to Do with It?

What's Worship Got to Do with It?

Interpreting Life Liturgically

CLÁUDIO CARVALHAES

With a prelude by PAUL GALBREATH
and a postlude by JANET R. WALTON

CASCADE *Books* · Eugene, Oregon

WHAT'S WORSHIP GOT TO DO WITH IT?
Interpreting Life Liturgically

Cascade Books
An Imprint of Wipf and Stock Publishers
199 W. 8th Ave., Suite 3
Eugene, OR 97401

www.wipfandstock.com

PAPERBACK ISBN: 978-1-6203-2971-9
HARDCOVER ISBN: 978-1-4982-8523-0
EBOOK ISBN: 978-1-5326-4501-3

Cataloguing-in-Publication data:

Names: Carvalhaes, Cláudio, author. | Galbreath, Paul, prelude. | Walton, Janet, postlude.

Title: What's worship got to do with it? : interpreting life liturgically / Cláudio Carvalhaes ; prelude by Paul Galbreath ; postlude by Janet Walton.

Description: Eugene, OR : Cascade Books, 2018 | Includes bibliographical references and index.

Identifiers: ISBN 978-1-6203-2971-9 (paperback) | ISBN 978-1-4982-8523-0 (hardcover) | ISBN 978-1-5326-4501-3 (ebook)

Subjects: LCSH: God—Worship and love. | Christian life.

Classification: BV176.3 .C36 2018 (print) | BV176.3 .C36 (ebook)

Manufactured in the U.S.A.   NOVEMBER 8, 2018

To
Jaci C. Maraschin, Janet R. Walton and Paul Galbreath,
my liturgical trinity!
From them I learned most of what I know about liturgy
and without them it would be impossible for me to be here.

Gratitude

Some of the people who blessed me with their love and care and support in the production of this book: Paul Galbreath, Janet R. Walton, John C. Webster, Andrew Foster, Ken Sawyer, Gene LeCouteur, Jacob Martin, Mrinalini Sebastian, Dean Thompson, Katie Bombalurina Mulligan, Kerri Allen, Stephen Ray, Paul Myre, and Wabash Center for Education; Daisy Machado, Lutheran Theological Seminary at Philadelphia, McCormick Theological Seminary, and Union Theological Seminary.

I also want to thank Dr. Gregory Lee Cuellar and Mrs. Nohemi Cuellar for allowing me to have the drawings from immigrant and refugee children at the borders of Texas and Mexico in the incredible social, artistic, pastoral, and justice work they do with these kids. It is called the Arte de Lágrimas Refugee Artwork Project. I say something more at the introduction.

A special thanks to my wife, Katie, and my kids, Libby, Cici, and Ike, for their patience and love during the final months preparing this book.

Contents

Acknowledgments

Chapter 1 is a reprint of Cláudio Carvalhaes, "Worship—Loving Madly." *Liturgy, Special Issue: Liturgy, Culture, and Race* 29 (2014) 55–62. All rights reserved. Republished by permission of the copyright holder.

Chapter 2 is a reprint of Cláudio Carvalhaes and Paul Galbreath, "Easter: Imaginative Figurings for the Body of Christ." *Interpretation: A Journal of Bible and Theology* 65 (2011) 5–16. All rights reserved. Republished by permission of the copyright holder.

Chapter 7 is a reprint with changes of Cláudio Carvalhaes, "Louder Please, I Can't Hear You: Voices, Spiritualties and Minorities." *Reformed World* 57 (2007) 45–57. All rights reserved. Republished by permission of the copyright holder.

Chapter 8 is a reprint with changes of Cláudio Carvalhaes, "'Gimme de kneebone bent'—Liturgics, Dance, Resistance and a Hermeneutics of the Knees." *Studies in World Christianity* 14 (2008) 1–18. All rights reserved. Republished by permission of the copyright holder.

Chapter 9 is a reprint with changes of Cláudio Carvalhaes, "Praying With the World at Heart." *Dialog: A Journal of Theology* 52 (2013) 313–20. All rights reserved. Republished by permission of the copyright holder.

Chapter 10 is a reprint with changes of Cláudio Carvalhaes, "A Pregação na Liturgia da Igreja, na Liturgia do Mundo e na Liturgia do Próximo." *TEAR: Liturgia em Revista* 1 (2012) 48–57. Centro de Recursos Litúrgicos (CRL) e Grupo de Pesquisa Culto Cristão na América Latina, Programa de Pós-Graduação em Teologia da Escola Superior de Teologia, São Leopoldo, RS, 2012.

Chapter 12 is a reprint with changes of Cláudio Carvalhaes, "And the Word Became Connection: Liturgical Theologies in the Real/Virtual World." *Liturgy* 30 (2015) 26–35. All rights reserved. Republished by permission of the copyright holder.

Prelude

One of the great insights of liturgical studies over the last couple of decades has been a growing awareness of the liturgical diversity in the life and practice of the early church. Increasingly, the recognition of the distinct practices of early Christians in different communities in the ancient world stands in stark contrast to the demands by many in the contemporary liturgical guild to identify a liturgical core that can be preserved and promulgated in the liturgies of churches of diverse historical and theological lineages.

During the twentieth century, the emergence of the liturgical renewal movement (coupled with the ecumenical movement) pressed scholars to search for and establish a reducible core shared by the church.[1] In the mid-twentieth century, the classic work of Dom Gregory Dix in *The Shape of the Liturgy* provided a nearly evangelical interpretation of a transhistorical liturgical core. Dix's thesis on the historical foundation of the mass and its preservation through history and culture continues to hold influence on the development of liturgical resources that seek to preserve an ecumenical and historical common ground.

Recently, the work of Paul Bradshaw has challenged the dominance of Dix's hypothesis.

> So seductive has been the picture painted by Dix that it has tended to blind us to its shortcomings and thus mislead us. . . . For the truth is that there is no really firm evidence that primitive Eucharistic practice ever did conform to the sevenfold shape of the Last Supper, whereas there are signs of the existence of early Christian ritual meals that do not seem to relate themselves to this event or to be patterned according to its model.[2]

1. Interestingly, the search for a liturgical core mined the riches of early church history to establish a prototype which was then promulgated through the production of worship books and resources in mainline Protestant denominations.

2. Bradshaw, *Eucharistic Origins*, vi.

Bradshaw's methodical critique of Dix's historical reconstruction of a unilinear transmission of the mass has been joined by a growing body of work that underscores the significance of other cultural influences on the meal practice of early Christian communities, especially the Greco-Roman banquet. In particular, the work of Dennis Smith and Hal Taussig has strengthened the understanding of the diverse influences on the development of Eucharistic practices in the early Christian movement.[3]

Similar patterns have emerged in the research around baptism that underscores the diversity of practices in different parts of the ancient world. The New Testament includes a variety of images, formulas, and patterns for baptism. As with communion, Christians adapted ritual elements from surrounding cultures in diverse ways. Christian baptism was influenced by the ritual practices of other religious traditions as well as by Roman bathing customs.

There is a growing recognition among scholars that as the Christian movement spread across the Roman Empire, baptismal practice took on the unique features of local communities. Liturgical scholar Bryan Spinks concludes his analysis of the documents from the first three centuries, "The different ritual patterns found in the early Christian evidences mirror secular bathing customs."[4] For example, some Christian communities used incense; others, ritual lamps and torches. Anointing before and/or after bathing quickly became a customary part of baptism. Local communities of Christians, however, likely followed regional, cultural habits in their choices about when to anoint the individual and in other actions associated with bathing customs that became part of the baptismal liturgy. Over time these ritual elements were given theological interpretations. For example, oil's use for sealing and preservation is interpreted as the Spirit's work of redeeming us, and a lighted candle is for illumination, just as Christ's light leads us out of darkness. After surveying the biblical images of baptism, liturgical scholar Bryan Spinks concludes,

> The New Testament is both the fulcrum from which emerges all theological reflection on baptism and all Christian baptismal rites, and the touchstone, or "norming norm" against which they may be tested. However, the books of the New Testament

---

3. Smith and Taussig published a brief examination of their thesis in *Many Tables*. Since that time, they have separately published major works on the influence of Greco-Roman meals on the development of early Eucharistic practice. See Smith, *From Symposium to Eucharist*, and Taussig, *In the Beginning Was the Meal*.

4. Spinks, *Theologies of Baptism*, 35–36.

present neither a single doctrine of baptism, nor some arche-
typal liturgical rite.[5]

While the grip of Dix's hypothesis about the development and preservation of Eucharistic prayer is finally beginning to recede, a more nuanced
approach that argues for the recognition and priority of universal elements
throughout the history of Christian worship has taken its place. Gordon
Lathrop follows a similar trajectory as Dix's work in arguing for a universal
shape of the liturgy, which Lathrop identifies as the *ordo*. Lathrop discovers
an implicit grounding of this fourfold pattern (gathering, word, thanksgiving, sending) in Scripture itself. Lathrop proceeds to move beyond merely
recognizing these transcultural elements to arguing for their priority over
contextual practices and local customs.

> We need to require local traditions . . . to take second place
> to thanksgiving at table and the shared holy meal. We need to
> require local traditions to circle around and serve the central
> matters of our communion, the word and sacraments that bear
> us into the very life of the triune God. The church is always lo-
> cal, but the local reality must be broken open toward the one
> who holds all localities together and so is the ground of our
> *koinonia*.[6]

Such an approach presumes a universal core to the thanksgiving at table.
Like Dix, Lathrop claims a divine mandate for a liturgical *ordo* that comes
as God's gift to the church. Lathrop quotes from the Ditchington Report
(which he helped write): "The pattern of this gathering and sending has
come to all the churches as a common and shared inheritance. That received
pattern resides in the basic outlines of what may be called the *ordo* of Christian worship . . ."[7]

The question must be asked whether the cost of suppressing diversity
to promote a kind of unity of enforced Christian liturgical practice is true
either to the life and witness of early Christian practice or to the needs and
expectations of diverse Christian communities in the twenty-first century.
It is precisely at this point that liturgical scholars and worship leaders have
so much to learn from this collection of essays from Cláudio Carvalhaes.

The remarkable thing about this collection of essays is not simply that
they point to the diversity of liturgical practices that the Church needs to

---

5. Spinks, *Theologies of Baptism*, 12.

6. Lathrop, *Holy People*, 127. I am not sure whom Lathrop is referencing with the
pronoun "we."

7. Lathrop, *Holy People*, 125.

embrace as a way of making room for Christian faith to respond to the particular and distinct needs of local communities of faith. The truly remarkable thing is that the essays foreshadow a way that Carvalhaes's liturgical theology is diverse in its own right (*in esse*). This is not simply a contrast to the insistence on uniformity by some in the liturgical guild. This is an embodied witness to a pluriform exposition of liturgical theology in the life of one extraordinary scholar. From theology to politics to gender identity to race to philosophy to postmodernity, Cláudio Carvalhaes shows a dexterity and fluency rarely exhibited in this age of micro-specialization. He does so not to create a single trajectory or to establish a "correct" way of doing liturgical scholarship. He does so to expand and expose the narrow ways in which we have become accustomed to thinking and operating.

Some readers will be frustrated by the lack of a single trajectory and a singular thematic argument in this collection. Personally, I find this approach refreshing since it opens up and alludes to multiple possibilities for ways to move forward and embrace truly diverse liturgical agendas and audiences. Readers will discover their own favorite essays in this monograph. My own favorite is the astonishing essay "Gimme de kneebone bent," which combines liturgical scholarship, postcolonial criticism, postmodernity, and gender theory in a way that I had never considered previously. Here the call for full, embodied participation by all in worship opens up the possibility for the assembly to demand and take its rightful place. No longer can order and rules be handed down and enforced by a hierarchy that seeks to impose a single way in which participants can properly worship God. Instead, those in leadership roles are invited to open up space so that all can respond and contribute in ways that enrich the congregation.

I invite you to partake of this smorgasbord of essays from one of the most creative thinkers of our times. But be forewarned that this collection is not for the faint of heart. Your preconceptions and practices will be shaken and challenged. The end result, however, is to inspire your theological and liturgical imagination to reach out to discover new ways in which worship moves beyond the narrow confines of the walls of our church buildings and begins to encompass all of life.

Paul Galbreath
Professor of Theology, Union Presbyterian Seminary

Introduction

My wish is that you may be loved to the point of madness.

—André Breton

The liminality of ritual is the power of transcendence, of no-saying, of expressing what society and culture deny, of unmasking pretension, of elevating persons and things of "low degree," of "putting down the mighty from their seats" (Luke 1:52–53). It is the power Shakespeare called imaginative, to "give to aery nothing a local habitation and a name."

—Tom F. Driver

The Presbyterian congregation of Morro Doce, a neighborhood in the outskirts of São Paulo, Brazil, was made up of people living inches above utter poverty. The church had a deep commitment to its own people and the larger community. They took care of each other in many ways. By the third month I was there as a pastor they couldn't pay my salary. When the congregation realized it, they started to cook and buy basic things for my house and my family. Every Sunday night after the evening service when I got on the bus to head home, I always carried several bags of goodies, food for the whole week. During the week, people would be at each other's houses caring for their kids when the parents needed to go to work. The very few who had cars came to church and left loaded with twice as many people than their cars could carry. Every Sunday morning, the kids were at the bus stop waiting for me screaming with joy and expectation. Sunday afternoon, I would visit families; I was always received with a banquet.

When I came as pastor, the congregation met in a small, rented room. After six months, we wanted our own building. To buy a piece of land and build four walls and a roof would cost us about five thousand dollars. We started saving as much as we could. However, we didn't make much progress. Every month there was a more urgent need for a member of the church. One Sunday, a family from the favela, whose six kids came to church every week, asked us if we could help them redo their fallen roof. All of our small savings and the money of almost our entire budget went to that roof. Not long after that, most of our kids got lice in school. We had to provide a haircut to almost all of our kids and make arrangements for the families to go to the drugstore and get the necessary soap and medicine for their kids. Every Sunday, eighty percent of our money went to that need. Then we realized that almost all our kids didn't have breakfast on Sundays because there was no school. Then we started using the money to pay for breakfast and the church would be crowded every Sunday morning. Even the local bus driver knew that Sunday at 8 a.m. he would have his bus loaded with kids from the favela coming to our church.

Nonetheless, the church was happy to even imagine a new building where we could offer more services to the community. We did everything to raise money, from pizza night to yard sale, ice cream and cakes, clown evenings, clothing, etc. But due to the constant needs of the congregation, we could never save enough money. At the end of three hard years raising money for the building, we had less than $100 saved. Everything in that congregation, including the budget, was geared towards the immediate needs of the people and the community around them. No one even went hungry there!

Our liturgical life changed in relation to the needs of the community. We had a proper reformed liturgical order for every Sunday but I soon realized that it was the life of the people that would give shape to the liturgy in ways that happened organically. One day we would spend more time praying for each other than doing anything else because the needs were such that everybody needed prayer. One day when I was preaching, I asked an elder to tell a story of his experience living in Argentina, since he was the first member to go abroad in a mission from his work. His story was so funny that the whole congregation started laughing so hard I couldn't finish the sermon. In the midst of loud laughing we barely had breath to sing the last hymn. Of course, not everything went smoothly; we had problems, too. Nevertheless, empowered for its daily life by the priorities of the liturgy (work of the people) at Morro Doce congregation I saw a community (church-world-neighbor) empowered.

What I am trying to do in this book is to give voice to the possibilities of communities to make a difference to the people who worship together and to the communities around them. With this book I invite conversations about different approaches to our own lives and our liturgies, and about how our ecclesiologies, civil life, and worship services are all intertwined and interconnected. This book is a series of imaginings, sometimes surely idealized, that offer ways to think and plan our liturgies differently and do things differently.

Lex Agendi: The Law of Agency

This book hopes to be an alternative to the understanding of liturgy as the work of God on behalf of the people (*Gottesdienst*) where just some privileged scholars have a say in what we are to pray, sing, or do, and with that, define what life is all about. No! Liturgy is indeed the work of the people, who together bring their resources, wisdom, and experience as we mutually learn with one another. We do this with scholars joining different forms of knowledge for that specific context we live in. In that way, there is no dismissal of the academic knowledge from all kinds of scholars, but there is a shift in the relationship. Scholars are not telling us from hierarchical places what they have received from God and people are only to say "Amen" to their divine wisdom as if they are safeguarding God, faith, and our lives in some form of liturgical order or understanding. Instead, we tell each other what the will of God might be and how we should have this gathering as we create worlds and faith possibilities.

In that way, liturgists and liturgical theologians should be "organic intellectuals" in a Gramscian sense,[1] organic theologians who open up organic liturgies, rather than organizers of religion and keepers of tradition. That means that ideas and praxis must go hand in hand, always being concerned with both a certain anti-intellectualism that dismisses ideas and the academic life that is not connected to the streets and to social movements. It is the local situation that demands our attention and knowledge. In that way, the liturgical theologian is demanded to make an oath of allegiance with those who suffer and bring all of the possible sources of power to engage these situations, even if beyond the scope of our beliefs. Life comes first and traditions come after, as a way to sustain the lives of those who suffer; if these sources of tradition don't pass the ethical test of protection of life in gruesome situations, no tradition is worth living. The very handling of the

---

1. Valeriano Ramos Jr. explains the role of the organic intellectual in Gramsci: "Thus, the organic intellectual 'gives his class homogeneity and awareness of its own function, in the economic field and on the social and political levels.'" In addition, their interests are, "more nearly identical with those of the dominant classes [they identify with] . . . than the traditional intellectuals." Ramos, "Concepts of Ideology, Hegemony, and Organic Intellectuals."

past must be careful when placing it with the present. As liturgical theologian Jaci Maraschin said,

> The liturgical moment is always a kind of center where the memory of the divine lived in the past, faces the challenges and the exigencies of what is to happen. If the gathering emerges from tradition but does not close itself to this tradition, its very nature is to be open to what has not yet happened, and turns tradition into a model for the future with the clear presupposition of a criticism. That is why the judgment of the present proceeds from the celebration of what happened in the times of liberation and it is animated by the hope of what might happen because of our commitment to this common decision . . . But what kind of gatherings do we have now? Assemblies eaten away by the commitment to the powers of this world and captive of the social system, political and economic in which we live. That is why, in general, the liturgical gatherings become tiresome, devoid of the vital element that would make them exulting in joy and interpreters of reality.[2]

The liturgical theologian, more than holding tradition, interprets reality through rituals with the people. More than keepers of cultural assertions recoded as liturgies received from God, the liturgical theologian must combine the roles of prophet, the priest/pastor, and the scholar. We do not only have to work together to choose the order of our worship that fits our current situation, but more, we need to make connections of our faith and the world in which we live in order to face larger agents of death. Liturgy is not a political party or a political party event. However, since it holds and shows God's power in the world, liturgy is a local counter-power to the global movements of power that dismantle the basic social systems of life. By affirming God's *imago Dei* and equality for all under God's justice and love, our rituals go against the market and the needs of economic organizations that pipe the flow of wealth to some people and leave the vast majority of the world population without minimal access to the sources of good. With the clash of these many horizons, the rituals of our worship must respond to the lack of glory in the world by stretching horizons of hope, faith, justice, and liberation so communities of excluded people, praying to God for their own liberation and the liberation of the world, can continue to believe that people, especially poor people, like some forms of just societies, must be defended.

2. Maraschin, "Libertação da Liturgia," 133, 138.

Along with Nathan D. Mitchell, I believe that we are not only "participants in Christian liturgy but as agents in an evolving human history, as citizens of the world—a universe—whose magnitude and complexity challenge many of our traditional (and comforting) conjectures, about the relation between God, people and planet."[3]

Thus, religious rituals, and in our case Christian rituals, cannot be canned liturgical theologies, even if they claim to be *theologia prima*. Liturgical knowledge aims to create, share, and construct knowledge together, from the wisdom of our own communities with the thousand traditions of Christianity and other religions, and not as fossilized rituals we keep by talking in circles only to find inner meanings that reconfirm what we already know.

Liturgical knowledge, like any other knowledge, is a form of power, with its paradoxes and ambiguities, which goes against the desire to keep the class structures of churches. The call from our worship space is to abandon the allegiance to the middle and upper classes and go work with people on the margins of our brutal society. Thus, the crux of the shaping and formation of this liturgical knowledge must be aware of the sources used, the positions taken, the memories chosen, the actions done, and the relations and partnerships engaged in these meetings as paramount to what we want to think and do about our (liturgical) lives together. My hope is that this book will foster heterogeneity of rituals, a plurality of possibilities for life, and not a singular thought/belief that we must be faithful to, or else perish. In other words, I hope that we will be able to do liturgies that will consider different local sources, multiplicities of languages and perspectives that will entail different sets of questions and needs for different localities, bringing different life experiences into consideration so we can create different worlds, different racial, class, gender and social intersectionalities through a vast array of locally situated liturgies.

While not offering something as definite as how to do worship "properly," I hope that by shuffling resources, references, and unexpected juxtapositions, we will learn to be critical of our forms of doing liturgies and writing liturgical theologies. As we do it, we don't need to either necessarily set ourselves with the keepers of the tradition or with those who dismiss any traditional form of worship by doing whatever they want for the sake of the new. In other words, we will go against worship forms that reflect the rigidity and righteousness of proper worship orders as well as the self-congratulatory rituals of cultural self-absorption and entitlement. Perhaps we must create something in between, something that helps us place ourselves in the midst

---

3. Mitchell, *Meeting Mystery*, xii.

of those who are hurting and generate social disciplinary subjects who will tackle the imbalanced forms of common living and fight against the norm of patriarchalism and its hierarchical, heterosexual structures, go vehemently against the racism that breaks the backs of our people, queer our forms of gender and sexualities, and displace forms of *imago Dei* that associate God's goodness with certain economic gains in life.

The Rituals/Liturgies of the World, of the Church, and of the Neighbor

Within Christian rituals we are indeed entangled in liturgical knowledges that create worlds and forms of life and living. The world, the church, and our existential life are all implicated and intertwined in our prayers, songs, and celebration of the sacraments. It is at this encountering of many waters that this book is located, as a fragile ecumenical interreligious boat, trying to navigate life and death bursting from all these places. In Nathan D. Mitchell's spellbinding book *Meeting Mystery*, we learn about this liturgical encounter:

> Christian ritual, prayer and sacrament occur at the confluence of three distinctive yet essentially interdependent liturgies: the "liturgy of the world," the "liturgy of the church," and the "liturgy of the neighbor" . . . The Christian community never celebrates its liturgies for itself; it celebrates them in and for the world, for the life of the world.[4]

The *liturgy of the world* encompasses the whole network of connections between countries and the globalized conditions of human life through movements of political systems and nation-states, capitalism and free-trade agreements, militarism, drugs, agribusiness, local and global religions, immigration, labor, and so on.[5] The *liturgy of the church* entails the sources and histories of many traditions that we Christians in the twenty-first century need to deal with in an expansive ecumenical frame and its continuing explosions of identities. The *liturgy of the neighbor* has to do with the ways in which the existential and confessional forms of my neighbors' lives are respected and cherished, which includes the multiplicities of religions.

The liturgy of the neighbor is about communities of people and forms of common living within communities that shape the individual and social

---

4. Mitchell, *Meeting Mystery*, xiii.

5. For a good introduction to the notion of globalization, see Appadurai, *The Future as Cultural Fact*.

life in various ways. In these three liturgies, social markers of class, culture, religion, gender, and sexualities operate within forms of power. Life and death are being created, negotiated, dismissed, abused, and empowered.

The connectivity of these three liturgies is the way of thinking at the border. These liturgies and this form of border thinking are fundamental components to the formation of different liturgical assemblages, connecting local sources, diverse groups and ethnicities, and forms of life, feelings, and subjectivities that foment different forms of marginal thinking, thinking that comes from those from the underside of history. This inner-outside circularity of liturgies reflects, challenges, engages, and transforms social realities that end up doing the same things to liturgy.

These intersectionalities and connections imply a multiplicity of sources, symbols, and perspectives coming from below, from local contexts in constant relation to global forces. In this way liturgies are not repetitions of unmarked universal truths, but only ritualized social forms that "produce localities," that is, that enhance forms of power within groups who live together. In this way, the liturgy of the world can only be thought, considered, and ritualized if done in constant tension and relation with the local context of the liturgy of the neighbor, whose body and *oikos* pertain to a certain liturgy of the church(es). The relation between the world/global and local/church–neighbor must be put in perspective. Ajun Appadurai explains the local in relation to the global:

> I stress locality because, in the end, this is where our vitally important archives reside. Localities—in this world, and in this argument—are temporary negotiations between various globally circulating forms. They are not subordinate instances of the global, but in fact the main evidence of its reality. . . . The local is not merely an inert canvas upon which the moving space of globalization is painted, but the local is itself a constant and laborious work in progress, so that the production of locality is fundamental and never completed site of human action.[6]

This movement wants to name what is thought of as universal and show it as what it has always been—regional. In that sense, it wants to debunk the power of coloniality with border thinking. Walter Mignolo defines coloniality:

> What "coloniality" unveiled is the imperial dimension of Western knowledge that has been built, transformed and

---

6. Appadurai, *Future as Cultural Fact*, 69, 116.

disseminated over the past 500 years. "Coloniality of knowledge and of being."[7]

While this work hints on the work of decoloniality, it also fails miserably. In many cases, instead of producing an "epistemological disobedience" as Mignolo says, it ends up reinstating a re-westernization of the liturgical ontological structure, failing to do the work of delinking its connections. In any case this is a work in progress.

The chapters in this book are placed under these three liturgies with the hope that we will point to some of the issues of these immense complexities, hoping to show that they are fully intertwined and cannot be thought/lived without the other. How we organize these liturgies and therefore our faith and our lives is our task. Expanding the understanding of juxtaposition offered by Gordon Lathrop,[8] the idea is to juxtapose not only what is within a given shape of liturgy but also the many liturgical things we call holy with what is there but goes without being spoken, namely, prayers with race, baptism with economic inequality and civil disobedience, Eucharist with agribusiness and immigration, songs with social freedom, and so on.

These amplified forms of juxtaposition call us to engage the places between the altar/table and the world, asking for what has been silenced, denied or simply not spoken, thus hidden, and not visibly clear to the formation of society but gives full rise to racism, economic disparities, social exclusion, and an eclipse of the poor in most of our liturgies.

In these juxtapositions, we are heightened by the connectivity of what is called the *lex orandi, lex credenda,* and the *lex agendi-vivendi* of the church, that is, the connections between the laws of prayer, belief, life, and ethics. The wrestling with these laws altogether is not to find out what comes first but rather how one may live, incite, expand, and respond to the other. As Mitchell says,

> The slogan *lex orandi, lex credendi* does not, then, offer as much light as it may seem to promise. In spite of the tension between them, doxology and doctrine remain a cozy *ménage à deus*, each partner in the pair defining itself in terms of the other. But the deeper question is not whether faith controls worship, or vice versa, but whether either of them can be verified in the absence

---

7. Mignolo, *Geopolitics of Sensing and Knowing.*

8. "The thesis operative here is this: Meaning occurs through structure, by one thing set next to another. The scheduling of the ordo, the setting of one liturgical thing next to another in the shape of the liturgy, evokes and replicates the deep structure of biblical language, the use of the old to say the new by means of juxtaposition." Lathrop, *Holy Things,* 33.

of a *lex agendi* (a rule of action or behavior), an ethical imperative that flows from the Christian encounter with a God who is
radically "un-God-like," a God who, in the cross of Jesus and in
the bodies of the "poor, the hungry, the thirsty, the naked, the
imprisoned," has become everything we believe a God is not.
The ethical imperative implied by the phrase *lex agenda* breaks
apart our comfortable "faith and worship" duo by introducing
that subversive element of *indeterminacy.*[9]

This claimed indeterminacy neither does away with the ethical imperative nor with beliefs and faith, but rather, it establishes an ethical caution to
the liturgical ways in which we believe and hold the sacred, and how rituals
relate, or not, to the lives of others, to the living of bio-systems and to senses
of justice, solidarity, and peace.

In some ways, this book wants to point back to the revolutionary kernel
of Christianity and its connection with the poor. It hopes to connect with
a Jesus that had no possessions and was never concerned with the holding of power, or endowments or budgets, but who lived in the midst of the
people. We have misplaced Jesus's movement by making it into an institutional church that has become a rich class operating a wealth operation that
supports a certain high class and the larger inequalities of the world, many
times mirroring the economic systems of society. The Christian church has
failed in so many ways.[10] It has, in many instances, sided with the powerful,
with economic systems of profit, fought more for power and money than it
has to struggle on the side and in the trenches of the poor, the immigrants,
the refugees, the homeless, the incarcerated populations, battered women,
abused and abandoned children, people with disabilities, the rural small
workers, and so on.

In times such as these, we must recall what and where are our allegiances and heighten our ethical awareness to make sure that we don't
retreat to our own bubbles of religious–class identities and the protection
of our own social privileges. In times such as the ones we are living, we
are called to use the potency we have received from God and in prophetic
ways fight against that which produces death, re-creating forms of living
that honor everyone but fundamentally those who are in weary situations
and who hold onto their lives by a thin line. It is in times such as the ones
we are living that we have our rituals: to teach us to fight and to meditate, to
struggle and to pray, to discern what to learn, and how to replace hatred and

9. Mitchell, *Meeting Mystery*, 39.

10. See Mattson's "American 'Christianity' Has Failed."

confusion with love and acceptance. In times such as the ones in which we are living our rituals can create a spirituality that gives life!

Our rituals have immense power! Rituals create and enact worlds. Worship services are liminal spaces where people, things, and the world can be transformed. Tom F. Driver defines ritual in expansive ways and helps us see our liturgical practices in ways fundamental to our understanding of worship and the potential transformation of the world. He says,

> A religion is a praxis, a certain way of acting in the world, and this is established through a certain way of acting ritually . . . Ritual refuses to recognize clear lines of demarcation between the psychological, the socio-political and the material worlds . . . [ritual can transform] a total situation by means of an enactment undertaken with strong subjective desire and producing an effect upon a number of subjects and objects together. It is, in short, a reordering of a totality. . . . Theodore Jennings has pointed out that one reason rituals change is that they not only transmit ancient knowledge but also assist the discovery of new knowledge. Ritual is neither a detached contemplation of the world nor a passive symbolization of it but is the performance of an act in which people confront one kind of power with another, and rehearse their own future . . . Ritual is the work of beings who are characterized by their capacity to perform and hence to fabricate a social world that is not simply given to them but is compounded of desires and actions that are subject to moral evaluation.[11]

If we gain an expanded notion of what rituals can be and do, we gain new forms of thinking about society and its transformation. Fundamental to the notion of ritual is its ability to transform people, and especially the poor. Driver says it powerfully:

> Ritual is better understood from a vantage point created by a "preferential option for the poor." That is to say, we cannot well appreciate the power of ritual unless we see its usefulness to those in need, especially those who, having little social power and, being the victims of injustice, have a need for the social structure to be transformed.[12]

---

11. Driver, *Liberating Rites*, 169, 173, 176, 186, 188, 190, 191.

12. Driver, *Liberating Rites*, 167.

Conclusion

Trying to capture the whole book in one sentence, this present work intends to do what I began in my book *Eucharist and Globalization*[13] and to continue to pursue it. This is what liturgical theologian Don Saliers so beautifully described as "to interpret life liturgically."[14] The measurements of human life, what we consider life, and how we claim and protect life are all there in our worship services!

This book has three parts: "Liturgy of the Church," "Liturgy of the Neighbor," and "Liturgy of the World." Each part addresses different aspects of these three liturgies while weaving everything together. Formation and information, thinking and practicing, mind and body, spirit and reality, pain and sorrow, joy and glories, sweat and prayer, tears and praise are all connected from different perspectives. The book intentionally blurs different language styles, uneven chapters and the so-called autonomous lines of these discourses. I write as an organic intellectual, a pastor, and an artist. Between the many voices inside of me, there is my own attempt to make sense of my own self, the faith I received and the world that needs to be transformed.

Lastly, but most fundamentally, you will see throughout the book, drawings from immigrant/refugee children of various ages and countries. Every month, Dr. Gregory Lee Cuellar and Mrs. Nohemi Cuellar go to a bus stop at the border of the United States and Mexico and ask children to draw what they saw on their journey, what they felt crossing the border. The children can either keep the drawing or give it to them. In the process, there is conversation and connection, and some form of gentle healing is offered. The pictures are breathtaking and show the pain and sorrow of children who should never have to go through this situation. They are a cry out in the desert to an unjust and merciless system that involves various forms of trafficking, violence, slavery, sex abuse, drugs, militarization, economics, and social and political forces that, as always, affect the most vulnerable of our world. The parents of these kids are just trying to find a safe haven for themselves and their beloved ones. I would do the same if my kids were going hungry or in danger. The brutality of unequal immigration policies in this country come back with a vengeance to these now dilacerated, brutalized, and traumatized kids. Dr. and Mrs. Cuellar are like a balm of Gilead in the very little they can do to offer pastoral care to these families but also to

13. Carvalhaes, *Eucharist and Globalization*.

14. Saliers, "Afterword: Liturgy and Ethics Revised," in *Liturgy and the Moral Self*, 214.

show how evil the immigrant system is. From a PDF they provided to me, they describe their work:

> For this project, the goal is to collect art pieces created by refugee Central American children and youth crossing over the Texas-Mexico border. Their art pieces will contribute to the real-life human story behind the current border crisis. From these art creations, the unheard voices of the refugee children will be brought to the fore in the form of multiple public art exhibits. Our goal is to help bring awareness to the refugee children's plight.

Surely, these pictures are the most beautiful and important part of this book. In some ways, this book serves mostly to offer sustenance to the light shed on the lives of these kids and put them at the center of our beliefs, worship, and community life. Bring this art to your church, create a discussion, and consider these kids as if they were your own.

Part I: Liturgy of the Church

1

Worship
Loving Madly

Faith is not a question of the existence or non-existence of God. It is believing that love without reward is valuable.

—Emmanuel Lévinas

Look
What happens
With a love like that,
It lights the whole sky.

—Hafez of Shiraz

Christianity was never intended to be a system or a structure of belief in the modern sense; it originated as a disposition of the heart.

—Diana Butler Bass

Love is not a vague feeling or an abstract idea. When I love someone, I seek what is best for them. If I begin to take the love of Christ seriously, then I will work toward what is best for my neighbor. I will seek to bind up the wounds and bring about healing, no matter what the cost may be.

—Billy Graham

In a world where faith is often construed as a way of thinking, bodily practices remind the willing that faith is a way of life.

—BARBARA BROWN TAYLOR

Let your religion be less of a theory and more of a love affair.

—G. K. CHESTERTON

The soul of the soul of the universe is Love.

—RUMI

Amanece en mí la belleza del asombro,

El asombro de un amor.
Cada día es un hoy de Dios
Aunque piense que no soy digno.

—BROTHER ROGER, TAIZÉ

In his *Confessions*, Augustine asks, "What do I love when I love my God?"[1] His question is not about what to believe when we believe in God but about what we love when we love an invisible and intangible God. His answer is moving:

> But what do I love when I love you? Not the beauty of any body or the rhythm of time in its movement; not the radiance of light, so dear to our eyes; not the sweet melodies in the world of manifold sounds; not the perfume of flowers, ointments and spices; not manna and not honey; not the limbs so delightful to the body's embrace: it is none of these things that I love when I love my God. And yet when I love my God I do indeed love a light and a sound and a perfume and a food and an embrace—a light and sound and perfume and food and embrace in my inward self. There my soul is flooded with a radiance which no space can contain; there a music sounds which time never bears away; there I smell a perfume which no wind disperses; there I taste a food that no surfeit embitters; there is an embrace which no satiety severs. It is this that I love when I love my God.[2]

1. Augustine, *Confessions* X.7.
2. Augustine, *Confessions* X.7.

What did Augustine love when loving God? His answer employs negation by way of affirmation. Indeed nothing related to God's creation is involved—not food, not his body, not his body embracing somebody else's body—and, yet, all of it. For our purposes here, we can add to Augustine's question: what do we love when we love both God and our neighbors in the act of worship? What experience in our inner selves, in nature, and culture do we love when we love both God and neighbors in the act of worship? Is it not a deep interconnectedness with both our God and God's creation, an inter–intra–relation that produces an ecstasy not unlike what Augustine described? Is it not such an expanded notion of love that we must grasp when considering what worship can or should be? Augustine's profound and intimate question makes us connect the love of God with the entire world and compels us to define what love might mean and what to be human is all about.

Octavio, "El río (The river)"

Octavio is three years old, and he came from Guatemala. When asked to recall something of his trip, he began to draw aggressive strokes with the marker. This symbolized the vicious river he and his group had to endure on their journey.

How is this love and our sense of humanity connected to worship? We can look around the globe and see how love has been enacted in various communities' liturgies in order to reinvent our ways of loving in our worship services and communities. For Christianity, worship is one of many acts of love; however, worship is a privileged place to learn, live, and rehearse this love. Inside of the worship space, the whole world is challenged and reordered—or should be. There is nothing more pressing, more urgent and more needed in our world today than to love one another. Everywhere we go we are confronted with this demand to love. The worship space is where we fix, re-orient, re-learn, and find better ways to love.

The word "worship" comes from the Middle English word "worshipe, worthiness, honor."[3] In other words, to worship is to ascribe worthiness, or honor, to somebody or something. Thus, if I am to follow what Jesus himself affirmed as the greatest commandment, I can only worship God if I, at the same time, love my neighbor.[4] This means that my love of God is equally measured by my love of others. In this regard, there is no distinction between giving honor/praise to God and ascribing honor to other human beings—although we do have distinctions of quality, format, and shape in our worship to God and our loving one another. Our honoring of God is different, but not higher, than the ways we love another person because God can only be known in and through others. If worship is to honor God and my neighbor, this also means that I must care for my neighbor in ways that I would care for Jesus.

Such worship is daunting if not impossible because it requires that I pay attention to all aspects of the life of my neighbor, as I give myself completely to God and care for others as I care for Jesus in my life. If worship involves this kind of (radical) love, it will only be by the grace, mercy, and love of God that we will be empowered to do it. To put it more concretely, then, in rendering glory to God, I must check to see if my neighbors have health insurance. While I sing alleluias, I have to know if my brothers and sisters have a roof over their heads. While I am eating the bread and drinking the wine, I need to be on the lookout for those who are hungry. While I am singing the *Kyrie*, I must also confess my profound lack of commitment to care deeply for the well-being of my neighbors, especially the poor. While I see my sister being baptized, I must also ask after the conditions of the earth, God's creation, God's body. While offering myself to God in my local

3. See etymology in The Free Dictionary: "Worship" from Middle English worshipe, *worthiness, honor,* from Old English weorthscipe : weorth, *worth*; see worth + -*scipe, -ship,* at http://www.thefreedictionary.com/worship.

4. Matt 22:36–40 and 1 John 4:20–21.

sanctuary, I must consider if my sisters and brothers in other places and those with other religious commitments have the means not only to survive, but to thrive.

When worship enacts love in these ways, my worship goes beyond my personal desires and is not centered on my individual wants. As we learn what love is all about, we learn to seek together for the common good. We enter into a corporate love; we are part of a body of love and a loving body, living with one another and the whole ecological system in more mutual and just ways. Thus, I worry less about myself in worship and more about my sisters and brothers and about how we together are caring (or not) for the world and all its creatures. I express care for my neighbors, as they care for me. I will care for the earth as the earth feeds and nourishes and gives me all I need.

The Economic Turn

In attempting to answer Augustine's question, "What do I love when I love my God?," we must make a turn towards economics because it is the economic system that governs our communal life as well as our sense of ecclesia and our worship—and divides us by class and race and other marks of difference. It is when we tackle economics that we can think about how fully we act out expressions of love of God and others. We are embedded in a larger economic structure that delimits our relationships with neighbors near and far, especially those whom the economic system places at serious disadvantage. As Jesus himself pointed out, "Truly I tell you, just as you did not do it to one of the least of these [the hungry, the thirsty, the stranger, the prisoner], you did not do it to me".[5] From this perspective, when we worship, pay taxes, or struggle for a better world, we must have the sick, the naked, the imprisoned, and the hungry in front of our eyes and at the center of our hearts. Everything must work towards the least of these, because that is where Jesus is, that is who Jesus is. And so, in our daily life as well as in our lived worship, our embodied love of God and of others, we must engage economic systems because everyone is immersed in them, whether we like it or not.

Our task, or love-ethic as Christians, is to return to God what belongs to God. The earth/land belongs to God and all the wealth of the world that comes from the land belongs to God. No one can hold or keep anything as private property for his/her own enjoyment without caring for the least of

5. Matt 25:42–46.

these! Loving God and our neighbors therefore includes criticizing, changing, and even impeding models of society that exclude the vast majority of people. When we think about economics, we are thinking about a complicated structure of forces, and, as we think, we must keep in our hearts the suffering and exclusion of the poor.

That a handful of people control what should in principle be common to all people is just plain wrong! God gave us all—not just a few of us—the fertile earth and its fruits to feed everyone. Those of us who are relatively secure often do not think about these resources because we have easy access to them. However, if our family members could not drink water because a private company, with the support of the government, would not let them drink it, we would think about these things quite differently. Our faith is fundamentally a communal, rather than a private, faith. Our task is to take the land back for God—which means, for everyone. Scripture says: "Is anyone thirsty? Come and drink—even if you have no money! Come, take your choice of wine or milk—it's all free!"[6]

Faith, which entails the love of both God and neighbor, must be seen to be deeply related to both the economic and ecological systems in which we live. Our ferocious consumerism and greed are affecting people everywhere and our faith must respond to that suffering by offering a new model of society that can be actually lived in our parishes. When we disassociate our worship life from the ways we organize our society, we lose the prophetic voice of our liberator and end up playing with ritual modes of self-gratification.

Christians work from the perspective that we are called to care for others and, so, in any economic system the basic question must be: where is the love for the least of these? If there is no justice for the poor, we are failing to love God and thus our worship will be empty. Instead, our worship has to remind us of the love of God and that love points us to the devastating ways we are organizing our lives and creating soaring inequality. Politics and economics go hand in hand, and our eyes must be turned to this intersection. Economic inequality creates all sorts of social inequalities and undermines democracy by making politics a game that only the rich can play. The rich, then, play to their own advantage both domestically and internationally (e.g., through a combination of large businesses and financial organizations like The World Bank, The International Monetary Fund, The Club of Paris) and to the disadvantage of the poor.[7] As Warren Buffet pointed out, "There's

---

6. Isa 55:1.

7. As Joseph E. Stiglitz, a Nobel Prize winner in economics, wrote of the 2012 US presidential campaign, "The word inequality wasn't heard often—indeed, given the attention focused on the 1 percent by the Occupy Wall Street movement, the absence

class warfare, all right, but it's my class, the rich class, that's making war, and we're winning."[8]

As Christians we cannot let this class win, for God has sided with the poor. Jesus was born in a borrowed manger, became a fugitive immigrant, never owned anything, and was always on the side of the least of these.[9] As Christians, we must stand with those with whom Jesus stood. Martin Luther King Jr. put it this way:

> I choose to identify with the underprivileged . . . I choose to identify with the poor . . . I choose to give my life for the hungry . . . for those who have been left out of the sunlight of opportunity . . . I choose to live for and with those for whom life is one long, desolate corridor with no exit sign. This is the way I'm going. If it means suffering a little, I'm going that way. If it means sacrifice, I'm going that way. And if it means dying for them, I'm going that way, because I heard a voice saying, "do something for others."[10]

What do I love when I love my God when I sit idly by as billionaires rule my life and the life of the people? A naïve and unchecked faith is ill-prepared to worship God in Spirit and in Truth. We are each other's keepers! Our faith must lead us to more equitable ways of sharing God's resources. One of the gifts of having grown up in a Calvinist tradition is that we are always suspicious of power and we must continuously attend, criticize, and put pressure on the system to ensure that it contributes to the well-being of all and especially of the poor. In this context, we in the church should join *los indignados* from Spain, the people of Tariq Square, the Occupy Wall Street movement, and the numerous others grassroots movements that fight for the common good and offer resistance to an economic status quo that favors the rich at the expense of virtually everyone else. Worship, too, can be a time and place where we together can be suspicious of how the powerful game the system and can practice modes of resistance to make it work to the benefit of all.

---

of attention to the issue might seem surprising—until one remembers that much of the $2 billion spent on the campaign was raised (by both parties) from persons in the 1 percent—and one wouldn't want to offend them" (*Price of Inequality*, xvii).

8. Quoted in Stein, "In Class Warfare, Guess Which Class Is Winning."

9. Matt 1:1—2:23; Luke 1:1—2:40; John 1:1–14; Luke 9:58; Matt 25:31–46 NRSV.

10. King, "The Good Samaritan."

Worship and Our Common Life

Our common life, including our religious ways of living in community, is deeply implicated in the ways we organize our life economically. We cannot disassociate our prayers and singing from the economic system that defines who we are and how we worship and how we get to church and, even, to which church we belong. Our religious life is trapped in our cultural–economic ways of living. Nonetheless, for the most part, we are often clueless about the rules of economy. From our pulpits, sacramental practices, and praise we have not done much to challenge the unjust structures of the economic system, but, instead, have silently agreed that consumerism—the private accumulation of possessions—is the measure of our lives.

We both live and worship in self-centered enclaves. Our public worship is, in actuality, private. It belongs to a denomination and a social class and those who do not belong cannot come in. Churches have clear rules and boundaries in worship that communicate forcefully who can be part of it. Our liturgies maintain the same class structures that we see in our society. Very rarely do we see people of different economic or cultural or racial backgrounds worshiping together and even more rarely do we see worshiping communities working to break the structures of economic class differences.

As much as many of us are afraid of words like socialism or communism, there is a need for the church of Jesus Christ to rediscover the potentialities of socializing our lives since the current individualistic economic model is clearly not working. As Karl Marx writes, "Accumulation of wealth at one pole is at the same time accumulation of misery, agony of toil, slavery, ignorance, brutality, mental degradation, at the opposite pole, i.e., on the side of the class that produces its own product in the form of capital."[11] Our Christian middle/upper-class churches, seminaries, and Christian organizations have maintained the class wars in our society by supporting the market and by refusing solidarity with foreigners, members of ethnic and racial minority groups, and people of lower classes. Now this church is dying along with the class structures, which it both supports and depends upon, because it is unwilling to breakthrough economic class differences and welcome those it is has excluded.

Our worship is already tainted by inequality. By keeping this unequal hierarchical economic power structure, our alleluias end up confirming the evil economic system that is in place. But we can and must resist and change! It will be challenging but we can move step by step towards more just ways of being church. For instance, we might begin by looking at the way we

11. Marx, *Capital*, 1:709.

determine salaries. Our love for one another should never allow for the differentiation of salaries. Why do we tolerate a disparity in salaries among those who work in churches, seminaries, and other Christian organizations? Why do we, as the church of Christ, say "amen" to inequitable compensation structures in which a few people make hundreds of thousands of dollars while large numbers of pastors are barely able to scrape by? Why don't we see such inequality as evil? How can such inequality coexist with love?

We as the church of Jesus Christ are heirs of a message that offers life for all and promises everyone a place within, without any need to fight for it. In order to live into this promise the liturgical movement must become a revolutionary movement. We must promote ways of worshiping that embody the promises on which we depend: that God is maker of earth and heaven, the owner of all land and sea and sky—and that we as God's servants must provide for all, which means that we all have social, economic, and ecological responsibilities and must be mutually accountable. Our worship must contribute to the re-structuring of societies around common sharing and democratic participation, where people decide what to do and we all have limits to our personal resources.

What really matters here, what we must hold dear to our hearts, is that if we continue to be isolated from the poor, including in our worship services, we will continue to die. What we learn from the gospels is that when the poor die, Jesus dies too. When one goes hungry, Jesus goes hungry too. As Christians, we have a preferential love for the least of these because Jesus had preferential love for them, too.

Further, if we understand that everyone is created in the *imago Dei*, then we will pray for one another and raise our voices to promote equality, solidarity, and the sharing of lives and goods. And, in worship, we will rehearse a new society of justice, solidarity, and love every Sunday, every day. For the love we received from God is a social love that must transform our societies! Ours is a shared love of God that creates an "elucidating responsibility"[12] and makes miracles happen! Ours are the mutual possibilities to feed each other, to create alternative models of cooperative economics and democracy in which all people's economic and political rights are preserved!

God's Love Infuses and Transforms Our Lives

God's love binds us together as one Body and both demands that we pursue justice, peace, and solidarity and empowers us to do so. Similar to the

12. Heschel, *Moral Grandeur and Spiritual Audacity*, 262.

African sense of *Ubuntu*, we will depend so deeply on each other that we will stick together and care deeply for the other. This may feel daunting until we learn what God's tough love is all about. Tough love is to learn to give and to share, learning to hold dear in our hearts that God's abundance is not in one's possession but in one's giving and providing for somebody else. God's tough love is illustrated forcefully in the story of God's provision of manna in the wilderness—if you take just enough there is plenty for all; if you take more than your share you end up with rot and mold. Of course, many Christians have already learned this—but such Christians seem most often to be those who have been marginalized or downtrodden—like the social and economic solidarity among the Black churches, which survive and thrive in the midst of a white-supremacist US. It is well past time for all of us to hold dear in our hearts that God's provision only comes through each other. In this walk together, we have to do what the Apostle Paul promotes; we must learn "to wait for each other."[13]

It is often said that the opposite of love is fear, but greed, complacency, and laziness oppose love as well. Love gives and does not hold back. Love wants others to realize their full potential rather than promoting oneself. Love works hard and keeps at it instead of waiting for someone to come serve us. Love demands investment in others—the giving of time, money, attention, care, talents, and gifts. These elements are at the heart of our theologies and a lazy person cannot do it. A lazy person only cares for his/her own comfort, sensations, needs, and world. S/he wants others to work for them, like the owners of corporations who live off the profits produced by the toil of their workers. A lazy person cannot love because love demands constant work, which can only be sustained by the grace of God. Our public service to God will look like the work of Sisyphus, endless movements of pushing the rock up the mountain just to see it roll down again. In other words, it will take an enormous amount of work to move an inch of justice against the miles of greed and destruction that have permeated our society. Yet move we must—and move we can—because of God's love for us.

13. 1 Cor 11:33 NRSV.

Angel, "Sin fronteras (Without borders)"

Angel is ten years old, from El Salvador. In this picture he drew himself in outer space. He is smiling in his spaceship, flying freely through a borderless universe.

One way to promote small moves towards justice in relation to the economic system is socially responsible investing. Even as we press for more substantive changes in the market, we can make investment decisions based on social as well as economic indicators as we select companies in which to invest. We may choose alternative investments, such as companies which are not listed on the stock market—community development banks, cooperatives, micro-financing firms, and the like, which may produce a lower interest yield but are doing some real good among the poor. There are several good examples such as the Oikocredit, which began in conjunction with the World Council of Churches as the Ecumenical Development Cooperative Society and concentrated on funding cooperatives among the poor throughout the third world.[14] Instead of simply maximizing profit in the market, these strategies create possibilities for communities of faith to go around the system and are based on values of solidarity, mutual trust, and deep relation with the earth. Here are just a few examples:

- Cooperative banks give credit so that those who save can support those who need access to money. These cooperatives do not pursue large profit margins and so fees can be much lower than those offered by the private market. One of these cooperatives, En Comun de la

14. See http://www.oikocredit.coop/ and http://oikocreditusa.org/.

Frontera, A.C.,[15] in Nogales, Mexico, helps people start small businesses. Currently they have 1,618 poor people participating, men and women who can get a small credit to open a tortilla stand or a shop to sell their handcrafted art and so on. Most borrowers pay back their loans with almost no interest in a couple years.

- Barter-based cooperatives that do not rely on legal currency are cropping up. For instance, in Spain, Portugal, or Greece, people are trading hours of work with one another without the Euro.[16]

- Agri-ecological cooperatives, such as the Landless Workers Movement in Brazil, are modeling new ways to own and use land. One of them, called Copavi, a settlement in the south of Brazil, just celebrated twenty years where twenty families farm 106 acres of land and share a dignified life together.[17]

Conclusion

There are so many other examples that can inspire us if we really want to live beyond the Market. As the church of Jesus Christ, we must support, enhance, and initiate alternative economies throughout the world. We must support and promote justice and reconciliation rather than exploitation and division. And we must do this in worship as well as in our daily and institutional lives. Gathered to break open God's word and to share a meal, we practice that it is possible to offer love, to forgive, to share resources. Our task is to love the unloved. In worship, as those whom God calls Beloved— even before we learned to love God, even while we were estranged—we learn that we are loved and so can love others. In worship, we all learn both to give and to receive love. This empowerment of love enables the community to care for each other and to be responsible for one another in material ways. As long as I maintain that to love is impossible, I can easily slip away from my responsibilities. But in worship, I see and feel and hear and taste that love is possible—and so my own love of others is both possible and necessary. Moreover, the love I come to know in worship, God's love, is tough: experiencing divine tough love helps me move away from the sort of sentimental love that comes wrapped up in niceness, tolerance, paternalism, and philanthropy.

15. http://www.microcreditsummit.org/council/2052/en-comun-de-la-frontera.html.

16. See Cha, "Spain's Crisis Spawns Alternative Economy."

17. Quental "Copavi, no Paraná: 22 anos de produção solidária."

Grounded in the life, death, and resurrected life of Jesus Christ that is embodied throughout our worship, an empowered love will go beyond expressions of charity or niceness. Such a love will strengthen our desire to care for each other and for neighbors, promote a materiality that will divide possessions, set a table on which we can share a truly common meal, prepare prayers that place us in solidarity with the poor and afflicted around the globe, put nourishing food in people's stomachs, visit those who are sick and those in prison, listen with compassion to those abused and silenced, wash each other's feet, ensure that all have access to health insurance, raise a communal outcry to God for the refugees as we process around our sanctuaries to feel what it means to wander without a home in which to rest, and stretch our hands towards the world to craft justice and embrace suffering. In this way, our worship reframes our understanding of God, of each other, of how we should relate economically and politically, of our bodies, and of the world—that we might go and act . . . until all who are marginalized are included and all who are hungry are fed.

We can now return to Augustine's question and answer that the ways in which we relate, connect, care, and honor our neighbor are the ways we love, praise, and serve God—a God who is never only mine but ours, a God we will never fully know but who we will honor and worship as our collective action of love. The enactment of our liturgical gestures will empower each other's sense to become the subject of our own history. Our liturgical gestures will be marked by a vast array of cultures, ethnicities, and sexualities—and they will provoke the mixing up of social classes until our distinctions disappear. Our stories are stories of love woven in God's love story in Jesus Christ. In our liturgies, we will provide a transition space for a social world of common care to emerge. Through our liturgies, we will start to rewrite the history of the world as a love story, one person and one community at a time. In our worship, we will love madly—as God so loves the world.

2

Easter

Imaginative Figurings for the Body of Christ

Cláudio Carvalhaes and Paul Galbreath

The development of Easter as a fifty-day season in the church year was an extended historical process that allowed central theological themes to find their place as a part of this central celebration in the life of the church. Careful attention to the embodiment of these themes in our Easter celebration can foster the work of renewal in our own diverse communities of faith.

Easter Sunday: the sanctuary is filling up while the brass section is warming up. The minister walks into the sanctuary to check on things one last time. A pitcher of warm water sits by the half-filled font ready for the baptism of three infants and two adults. The table is set with bread and wine. The Bible is marked and the sermon is ready to be preached.

The minister is excited and weary from the services during the last three days—Maundy Thursday, Good Friday, and the Easter Vigil. He nods to the young man sitting in the second pew who was baptized last night. As he looks around the sanctuary, he recognizes many of the Easter Sunday visitors dressed in their new clothes. He has not seen many of them since the Christmas Eve service. He knows that for some of them the service fills the time slot between the morning Easter egg hunt and the special brunch at the tennis club. As he looks around the sanctuary, he wishes that the celebration of Easter would be more than a social, cultural observance. He longs for the good news of the resurrection of Christ's body to take root in this sanctuary.

What will it take for the Church to reclaim the Easter story and to live in light of it? Are there clues from the history of the Church and from the work of liturgical scholars that can guide us to a more lasting and robust celebration of Easter that will nurture our Christian lives? In this article, we offer biblical and historical research on the development of the liturgical calendar and the lectionary as a basis for imaginative readings of ways in which diverse congregations in vastly different locations can reclaim the celebration of Easter as a season that shapes our faith.

Historical Developments

In the early Jewish-Christian communities, the celebration of Easter began deeply rooted in its connection to the Passover calendar. From its inception, the celebration of Easter was connected to Jewish *Seder* practices. In a review of first-century CE Seder rituals, Larry Hoffman underscores the fluidity of practices that co-existed at the time. Hoffman characterizes the Seder as "sacred theater" and outlines the rudimentary elements that were needed for the celebration: a table with food; open-ended questions to prompt conversation; a general (but not necessarily textual) rendition of Exodus 12; and a time of praising God, usually in the form of psalms.[1] Furthermore, Hoffman argues that Greco-Roman meal practice in the symposium provided a venue that gave shape to the Seder, which maintained an early emphasis on a shared meal and spontaneous conversation. Such a pattern served as a liturgical template for the development of Easter rituals while embedding them in practices that provided other layers of meanings.

The nature of early Christian celebrations of Easter has been characterized as unitive due to the association of resurrection with the broader account of Jesus's incarnation, life, and death. Kenneth Stevenson suggests that "it would never have occurred to Christians living then to have had a Holy Week at all. For them it was sufficient to celebrate the death and resurrection of Jesus in one fell swoop."[2]

While scholars frequently use the language of the unitive nature of Easter to emphasize the way that it was inextricably connected to other services, this should not imply uniformity in the assemblies' gatherings. Hence, development of Easter practices can be seen as a complex merging

1. Hoffman, "Passover Meal in Jewish Tradition," 13.

2. Stevenson, *Jerusalem Revisited*, 5.

of elements of the Greco-Roman banquet, Jewish Seder practices, and the shared memories of Jesus's final days in Jerusalem.

Thus, even the language of Easter itself, known as *Pascha*, meaning "passing through," began to carry a double memory of the Exodus 12 text of the Israelites' passing through the Red Sea as well as the story of Jesus's passing from death to new life. Through associative, typological, and figurative readings of Hebrew Scripture, Christian communities developed interpretations and ritual actions that further distinguished the Christian meal practices from those of their neighbors. Karl Gerlach demonstrates how homiletical reflection on Exodus 12 gave rise to narrative re-interpretation and ritualization within the context of a Christian assembly. Gerlach concludes, "As Christian authors view Exodus 12 as a narrative frame for stories about Christ and the Church, the paschal night provides a liturgical space for these stories to be told."[3]

Such a shift in ritual interpretation is accompanied by a growing controversy over the appropriate time for this celebration. For some Christian communities, the connection of the events of Holy Week to the celebrations of Passover (and their subsequent reinterpretation) required that the primary gathering coincide with the Jewish liturgical calendar, which fixed the date as Nissan 14/15 (known as *Quartodecimans* because of their allegiance to meeting on the 14th day of Nissan). Over time, other communities (for a variety of reasons) recognized the Sunday following Nissan 14/15 as particularly appropriate for the emphasis on Christ's resurrection, which had been a central theological rationale of the Sunday weekly assembly by Christians. The intense struggle over the differing dates for the celebration of Easter led Constantine to issue a decree directing churches to observe Easter on the same date.

J. Gordon Davies describes the liturgical developments around the celebration of Holy Week as characterized by a move from the symbolic to that

---

3. Gerlach, *Ante-Nicene Pascha*, 402. To cite but one example of this development, consider this excerpt from the paschal homily of Melito of Sardis from the late second century:

> The scripture from the Hebrew Exodus has been read
> And the words of the *mystery* have been plainly stated,
> How the sheep (probation) is sacrificed
> And how the People is saved
> And how pharaoh is scourged through the *mystery*.
> Understand, therefore, beloved,
> How it is new and old,
> Eternal and temporary,
> Perishable and imperishable,
> Mortal and immortal, this *mystery* of the Pascha . . .
> (Gerlach, *Ante-Nicene Pascha*, 62)

of historical commemoration. The goal was to provide a model of the life of Christ that was accessible to the burgeoning numbers of Christians who joined the church in the post-Constantinian time.[4] According to Davies, the developments around the celebration of liturgical time in the fourth century served the primary purpose of providing a ritual narrative that invited participants to walk into these accounts. A closer examination of the accounts of these celebrations suggests a more nuanced approach. While the fourth-century celebration of Holy Week in Jerusalem did make use of certain geographical locations (e.g., Mount of Olives and Golgotha), other locations were surprisingly ignored. Paul Bradshaw notes that "no attempt was made to locate the Eucharistic celebrations on Holy Thursday at the supposed site of the Last Supper."[5] Stevenson refers to this development as "rememorative." History and symbolism are blended together in ways that make the rituals and narratives accessible to participants.[6] In the process, Easter began to take on its own emphasis.

Accompanying this transition is the growing tendency to associate baptism with Easter. At the end of the second century, Tertullian recommends Easter as a primary time for baptisms to occur. The ritual actions themselves provide a reframing and re-interpretation of biblical texts. A service that places the reading of Exodus 12 alongside baptism suggests links between the two that otherwise might go unnoticed. In his examination of homilies from ancient Syria, Gerlach notes the preferred status of baptismal typology in spite of attempts to develop Eucharistic themes.[7] Increasingly, the celebration of a collection of unitive events around Jesus's death and resurrection that were marked in widely diverse ways in early Christian communities began to receive separate attention and were associated with particular occasions and designated services.

Over time, the increasing frequency of baptism as part of the celebration of Easter shaped Lent as a time of intense preparation for those who were presented as baptismal candidates. In some parts of the church where catechumens prepared for two to three years, the time leading up to their baptisms brought a heightened sense of anticipation.[8] The journals of Egeria provide a sketch of this process in Jerusalem in the fourth century CE.[9]

4. Davies, *Holy Week*, 12–17.

5. Bradshaw, "Easter in Christian Tradition," 3.

6. Stevenson, *Jerusalem Revisited*, 9.

7. Gerlach, *Ante-Nicene Pascha*, 405ff.

8. A few recent attempts have picked up on this historic connection between Lent and baptism. See Stan Hall, RLM, Vol. 1998 and Paul Galbreath, "Ash Wednesday" (2010).

9. Wilkinson, *Egeria's Travels to the Holy Land*.

A more important development, though, in terms of Easter as a liturgical season, was the designation of a period of services to reflect on one's baptismal experience at the Easter service. The acceptance and transformation of Pentecost from a Jewish harvest festival occurring fifty days after Passover by early Jewish and Gentile Christian communities provided a period of time that took on increased importance. The book of Acts already portrays a theological reinterpretation of this festival by associating it with the emergence of the church as a result of the work of the Holy Spirit. Already by the second century CE, Christian observance of Pentecost had moved in a distinctly different direction form its Jewish antecedents. Martin Connell notes,

> Unlike the Jewish feast, which marked the day of Pentecost alone, the Christian practice, when it first appears, marked a *quinquagesima*, a period of "fifty days" including and following the feast of Easter.[10]

The shift in calendar to marking this lengthy period of time was accompanied by a shift in tone that focused on the days as a time of prolonged celebration with daily gatherings increasingly taking on Sunday practices, including a ban on fasting. These developments brought together a prolonged period of mystagogical reflection on baptism during the season of Easter with the theological notion of the church's birth celebrated on Pentecost as the culmination of the great fifty days. Craig Satterlee has chronicled this approach to post-baptismal reflection in his work on the sermons of Ambrose of Milan. "Thus, the purpose of mystagogical preaching was to 'explain' to the neophytes or newly baptized 'the meaning and nature of the liturgical actions in which they have participated: baptism and Eucharist.'"[11]

Accompanying these developments in separating the paschal events into distinct festivals was the growing importance of pilgrimage especially to Jerusalem and the association of events with particular historical sites. Such a process leads Martin Connell to conclude,

> The span of the first five or six centuries of the Christian faith seems to indicate a general movement from the integrity of *quinquagesima* to its dissolution in late antiquity and the early Middle Ages, perhaps as a result of the same tendency to historicize the life of Jesus of Nazareth in liturgical celebration that also brought Holy Week into being.[12]

---

10. Connell, "From Easter to Pentecost," 94.

11. Satterlee, *Ambrose of Milan's Method of Mystagogical Preaching*.

12. Connell, "From Easter to Pentecost," 105.

In the midst of this process of liturgical adaptation, Anscar Chupungco has challenged us to note other influences at work. Chupungco underscores the cosmic claims of Easter and the theological possibilities of linking Easter to the cycles of nature. Following the spiritual and allegorical linking of spring with Christ's passion, Chupungco concludes that, "Easter is a spring feast in every respect, from its origin and development to its ritual expressions. As a result there is a kind of symbiosis between the Christian feast and springtime. The qualities of one have been absorbed by the other."[13] In churches in the northern hemisphere, the celebration of the season of Easter retains ties to the return of spring and the renewal of the earth. By contrast, churches in the southern hemisphere experience these cosmic cycles in ways that the season of Easter becomes a promise to accompany them on the seasonal journey through fall and winter. From either perspective, it is important to note the development of Easter as it relates to our relationship to the earth.

In sum, these insights from the historical development of the season of Easter are presented in order to highlight certain theological themes that took place in different settings in the life of the early church: diverse ways of gathering around table, extending Easter as a season of fifty days, celebrating baptisms and reflecting on lives shared together, linking Easter with the rhythms of the earth. In light of their historical significance, we have developed three imaginary narratives of the ways in which the celebration of the season of Easter could be marked today.

---

13. Chupungco, *Shaping the Easter Feast*, 36.

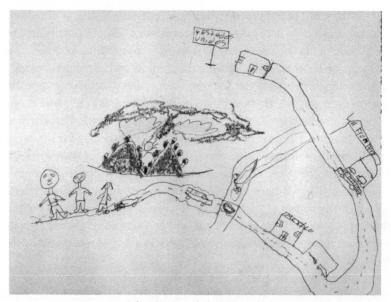

Julian, "Mi jornada (My journey)"

Julian is thirteen years old, from Guatemala. In this picture, he drew his journey experience to the Texas-Mexico border. In the center is his homeland, which is the only scene in color. He, his father, and his five-year-old sister, Dianna, walked six days before catching a ride to the Guatemala-Mexico border. After crossing the Suchiate River by raft-boat, they traveled by bus to the Texas-Mexico border. They crossed and were detained at a detention facility for several days. They were finally released and taken to the McAllen [Texas] Central Bus Station.

Scenes from Congregational Life

Congregational Rebirth in the United States

When you ask any of the old-timers how new life came to Grace Presbyterian Church, they all point to the same starting place. It began the spring that there was a hole in the roof of the sanctuary. For years the congregation had been slowly declining. They had watched the neighborhood around the old church building change as well. Crime had increased and the old houses surrounding the church seemed to be decaying. Many of the members of the church moved out of the neighborhood to the suburbs and while some continued to drive in to the city for Sunday morning services, it looked to be only a matter of time until the church would close its doors for good. The congregation had tried adding new services and offering programs. They might work for a while, but they never seemed to last. As the congregation grew smaller and smaller, all they could do was to gather for the regular services. When torrential rain came that spring, a leak began in the sanctuary and threatened to change the place that they gathered for worship. So the congregation took the last of the church's endowment to pay a roofer to patch up the roof.

The roofer told them that he would start working on the roof during Holy Week and that the sanctuary would be closed. When the session began to plan the Good Friday service, they looked for a different place to meet. Given the obstacles that they were facing, their young pastors encouraged them to try something new. They would walk through the neighborhood and have a service of readings from the Passion Story at places where violence in the neighborhood had taken place during the last year. Amidst darkened skies, a small group of about twenty people met outside the old sanctuary at noon. They looked up to the sky and saw the roofing crew pounding nails. Slowly they made their way to the street to the first gathering place. Late in December, a young boy had been killed by gunfire from a drive-by shooting while playing in his living room. The group from the church stopped in front of the house and began to sing, "Were you there when they crucified my Lord?" An elder read of Jesus praying in the Garden of Gethsemane. And then they moved on to the next stop. In front of a small grocery store, they gathered at the place where an older woman had been robbed. The force of the blow on her head had caused her to fall and she was injured so badly that she died several weeks later. Quietly the church group sang again, "Were you there when they crucified my Lord?" Tears filled their eyes as the Gospel was read.

After two hours of walking through the neighborhood, they returned to the church. The group was tired, but they promised to meet for an Easter service on Sunday morning. When they gathered three days later, the pastor stood up and announced, "This morning, I have asked a few of our members to speak about the service we held on Friday." One by one, they told about how deeply they were moved by what they had seen and felt as they walked around the neighborhood. Then the pastor spoke, "We cannot stay inside the walls of this church any longer. This morning we are unlocking the doors of this church and we are committing ourselves to working for justice in this community. May the Spirit of God breathe new life into us as we go forth. Christ is risen indeed. Alleluia!"

The change did not come about magically. Day after day, they gathered for a small meal and began to walk around the same streets of the neighborhood. On Fridays, they began serving a meal at the church for homeless people in the neighborhood. On Mondays, they worked in the community garden planting, watering, and weeding. On Wednesday afternoons, they volunteered as tutors in the elementary school. Every Saturday morning, they picked up the trash in the school yard down the street.

Starting that season of Easter, each Sunday service included reports on the church's involvement in the neighborhood and an open invitation to bring friends and neighbors to help with the work. At the end of each Sunday service, they gathered around the baptismal font and prayed for God to strengthen them and bless the work that had begun.

Slowly but surely, Grace Presbyterian Church began to grow.

Eucharist and Baptism during Easter Sunday in Mexico

It was Easter morning. After picking up people in various places around town, we traveled in two big vans for about two hours from Nogales into a small village in the countryside of Mexico. We arrived at a place where people were already waiting for us. The place was decorated with colorful banners and handmade paper crafts. It was a piece of land with fruit trees, a small house with a room, a kitchen and a bathroom where the pastor lived by himself, a large unfinished church building without doors or windows, and what seemed to be a small swimming pool. After being welcomed and sharing *la paz del Señor*, everybody started to prepare the fire, set the table, in order to start to eat. Tortillas and wine were placed among the food. At a point the pastor said, "*Oremos, hermanos y hermanas*" (Let us pray, brothers and sisters) and he prayed thanking God for that special day that we were celebrating the resurrection of Jesus Christ. After he prayed he said, "Today is special for us! As Christians we remember the life, death, and resurrection of Jesus Christ. And to celebrate that vividly we are going to have the Lord's Supper and baptism! Around the table we eat and share the life of Christ and our lives together . . . *y no nos podemos olvidar de eso*" (and we can't forget that). He went on talking about the ways in which Christ transformed his own life. Then he said, "We are here because of Christ . . . remember that last night when Jesus ate with his disciples . . ." and he went on to say the words of institution, breaking the tortillas, and pouring the wine. "*Mira, la comida de Dios para nosotros*" (Look, the food of God for us.) He then shared the tortillas and the wine with all of us and we ate and drank around the table.

We continued our Eucharistic meal with fried chicken, tortillas, chili, tomato, lettuce, crema, and guacamole. Background music played and children, adults and dogs were all fed. After we ate we were called to sit under a tree instead of moving to the empty church building. We started singing as if the service were continuing without any break. Testimonies were offered, songs were sung, and several Bible passages were read. The pastor then preached, saying how important it is for us to get together on Easter day, because on that morning Jesus was resurrected and was alive and that day was very special. "*Tenemos que celebrar hermanos y hermanas!*" (We must celebrate, brothers and sisters). No death could hold Jesus down and Jesus's life is what keeps us going. "*Vamos desde los días de los muertos hasta el día de los vivos*" (We go from the day of the dead to the day of the living). He also said how many times in our lives we die and resurrect, and the fact that we were eating together on that very special day was because of Jesus's death and resurrection. "*No es verdad hermana Maria, no es asi mismo hermano Jorge?*" (Isn't it true, sister Maria; isn't it like that, brother Jorge?).

He then started to talk about baptism as a new life out of death and how the Christian church around the world has always done that, how we become part of God's world family and how we now, through the love of God in Christ, have a deep sense of belonging. He invited us all to the tiny swimming pool, and once we were all gathered there he said, "This water is our water reservoir. Here we pour the water that comes to us during the week and also save the water when it rains. But now, our water reservoir is going to be our baptismal font, our Jordan River where our brothers and sisters will be baptized. *Hay mucha agua para nosotros!* (There is lots of water for us!). "Our lives are marked by the waters of our baptism and the remembrance of our baptism sustains and continues to transform our lives. *Jesus es la agua de la vida, hermanos y hermanas!*" (Jesus is the water of life, brothers and sisters).

He knelt, and moving the waters with his hand he said, "Through the waters God seals us with God's love and today we remember this love in Jesus's death and resurrection for us." He stood up and brought one candidate at a time into the water. There, with the help of two deacons he asked questions pertaining to the candidate's faith. After that they were immersed in the water and when they came out, there was an explosion of applause and praises among the community, with people shouting, "*Gracias a Dios que esta vivo, somos una familia!*" (Thanks to God who is alive, we are a family).

After the candidates were baptized we sang a song and a baptismal certificate was given to each of the new members. During that process, the pastor said, "When you go to the consulate to get your visa to go to the United States, they will ask for your birth certificate. Now you can bring your baptismal certificate because they will accept that, too. You are now born into God's love and belong to God's family." We prayed and sang once more while the new members received hugs from everybody. We sang, "*Pues si vivimos, para el Señor vivimos, somos del Señor, somos del Señor.*"

Then the pastor invited us back to the table to continue eating while the kids went to the water reservoir/baptismal tank that now became their swimming pool. He then blessed us, saying, "Brothers and sisters, what a joyful day today. We ate together, we celebrated Jesus's life, death, and resurrection, and we participated in the baptism of our family members. Now, our kids are playing in the water. The water of our baptism is the water of our lives, the waters that quench our thirst, that wet our lands and give us food, and that give us life, joy, and new life. This Easter, let us remember that we belong to the water, gift of God to the world, and through the waters of our baptism, we belong to Jesus Christ, gift of God for the transformation of the world. Go in peace under God's resurrected son, preserve the water and keep your faith, Amen."

Eucharist and Pilgrimage in Guatemala

It was Easter day. It was six o'clock and this church, built by indigenous Guatemalan people, was filling up. The smell of incense filled the air. People were gathering at the sanctuary and making conversation as they prepared for the service. Children were already running around playing with each other. The band got their space and people started winding down their conversation. A man came to the microphone and said, "*Buenos días, hermanas y hermanos*" (Good morning, brothers and sisters). "We are here today very early in the morning to remember the day when the women went to Jesus's tomb just to find out that the tomb was empty. Alleluia! We are here at this Easter Sunday to celebrate that the tomb is empty, that the women saw Jesus resurrected, and that Jesus conquered death forever. Praise be to God!" He prayed and invited people to sing.

After a time of singing hymns and *coritos*, people sat down and the pastor started to preach from the pulpit: "*Hermanos y hermanas*, in the midst of the life that Jesus gave to us, we must remember our brothers and sisters who died trying to cross the desert looking for a better life for their families. We must remember those who are still on their way and we haven't heard from them anymore. We must remember those who cannot come back and those who have no means to try for a new life. We must remember the families that stayed here and are fractured by the absence of a mother, a father, a son, or are going through illness without means to be treated. As we remember Jesus Christ, the way he passed from life to death and back to life again, the Passover is very important for us too. Because like the Hebrews in Egypt, who were trying to find a promised land, we too are trying to pass over the desert both ways to keep our families fed and alive. Sometimes the *crossing* of the desert for us is like the *cross* of Jesus Christ, *crossing* from death to life, being *crossed* by so many border fences, injustices, and with a high price to pay. The sacrifice of Jesus becomes our sacrifice as we also try to search for more just ways to live. *Ai hermanos y hermanas*, we all belong to Jesus, who *cross*ed so many borders and distances, hatreds and antagonisms, self-righteousness and arrogance. In Jesus, a migrant himself, we understand ourselves. It is through his cross and the *cross*ing over so many borders that his life, death, and resurrection entails, that we understand our attempts to cross whatever prevents us from having a dignified life.

"Let us not forget that Easter was only possible because of Good Friday! So, if you are *cross*ing the desert alone or with your family in the future, among bandits and robbers, and drug dealers, don't forget that we must keep the promise of Easter and the hope of a new life! Let us pray for all of those who are passing/crossing over places and doing it for the love of their families. Let us pray that God gives them and us, *cross*er people, a promised land as well, be it here, in our pilgrimage, or anywhere else . . ."

He paused, took a breath, and said, "Let us pray . . ." As the people started to pray, the space was filled with loud prayers and, soon, overflowing tears. For about an hour, people prayed alone, then together, then alone again, standing, shouting, jumping up and down, crying quietly on bent knees, and supplicating God's mercy and favor towards them and their families. We could hear several people praying for children without fathers and mothers, and for those who were deported and had nothing else to do in their homeland; for kids who learned about gangs in the US, were deported back to their countries, and started violent gangs; for women raped and abused by *coyotes* (people who lead migrants across the border) and border patrol police along the desert . . . We could hear about split families, torn down by the lack of jobs, threatened by people who lend them money to cross the desert but had to come back home without any success, couples estranged by such a long time without seeing each other . . . The prayers made the building become heavy and after a while the movements started to slow down.

As the prayers started to lose intensity, people sat down and remained seated in the pews. A deep silence took over the worship space and the whole congregation didn't say a word or make a move . . . After what seemed to be a very long time, the pastor came to the Eucharistic table and helped by two women, uncovered the bread and the wine for the Eucharist. The pastor said, "*Hermanos y hermanas, hay alguien aquí que quiera dar un testimonio?*" (Brothers and sisters, is there anybody here who wants to give a testimony?). People were so tired that, very surprisingly, silence was kept intact. From the table the pastor continued, "Don't give up! God has given us life! God has provided for the journey. Look and see, we have food for the journey! Especially at this Easter day, as we eat and drink this food, we *must* remember and never forget that life is bigger than death! No matter what you or your family is going through, or where you might be in your pilgrimage, there is promise of life for you to keep going. Today is the Easter of our Lord Jesus Christ and because of Jesus, it is our own Easter as well!

"Like the women who went to the tomb, we are called to go there and see that our Lord is risen! Let us keep going brothers and sisters. We cannot stop or we will die before our time like so many of our people! Here at this table are the signs and the promises of our new life, life always renewed to us. Like Jesus with his disciples and friends, it is the eating and drinking together that helps us continue our journey. Here we stop and renew our strength, here we stop and find rest, here we stop and gain new perspectives, here we stop and are reminded that we are not alone, that God almighty is with us and that the church of Jesus Christ, God's family, is with us, here in Guatemala, in El Salvador, in Honduras, in Mexico and in los Estados Unidos.

"As we are about to eat this bread and drink this wine, remember the powerful life, and death, and resurrection of Jesus Christ. Jesus fought against the injustices of his time and was killed. Now, in Jesus's memory, get your portion of strength, and renewal, and transformation, and go back to the road trusting that God in Jesus, through the work of the Holy Spirit, will walk with you, will be part of your pilgrimage, and will give you a new Jerusalem, a promised land here and also when you die. See, we can still be thankful for God's love in our lives can't we? Let us do this: as you take a piece of this bread, give it to somebody else and receive it from somebody else as a gesture of our life together, of our dependence on each other, as a reminder that we are not alone and that he is here in our midst through each other." And raising the bread he said, "On the night when Jesus had his last supper with his friends . . ."

Conclusion

These figurings of the church of Jesus Christ in different places show the diversity of situations where people are celebrating Eucharist, each place with its own specificity and a different reading on the season of Easter. Since its inception, Easter is the weaving of God's story in our story, and our story reshaped by the story of God. Easter is not an isolated event but a culmination of the past, present, and future presence of God in history. At Easter, creation is reclaimed, our past is redone, our present is firmly grasped, and our future holds a promise. In Easter we celebrate not only Jesus's resurrection but also Jesus's life and death, because resurrection only makes sense in light of the ethical ways Jesus lived his life. In Christ, Easter becomes a political project to the world, as it embraces the world with prophetic admonitions and promised transformation.

Grace Presbyterian Church finds its way back when they reach out to others. The many signs of a dwindling church have its claws deeply entrenched in their souls and a sense of helplessness carries the scent of death. However, it was Easter time that provided new life to this congregation. Instead of ending in the cemetery, their journey took on another route and new life came upon then. Where there was death, now there is a stubborn sense of newness.

The Mexican Baptist church shows us that life is interconnected in deep ways. No compartmentalization of the congregation, no separation between Christian education, testimonies, drinking water, baptism and fun, preaching, the pastor's house, the worshiping tree, tortillas, guacamole, crema, grape juice, hymns, *coritos*, and life together. In this community, drinking water became the baptism font as a way into Easter and then back to the place of play for children who are nurtured by the community. Citizenship and baptism are understood as the same and the nation-state and church family are closely connected, for better or for worse. Easter time is about families connecting, new people joining, and the world gathered around the dining table and the baptismal font/reservoir/pool.

The Guatemalan Pentecostal church seems to be the only place where people can go and feel the world as bearable. The weight of disgrace crushing people's lives is so pervasive that life is always at risk of being taken away in a heartbeat. In the midst of death, of rupture, of brokenness, Easter is this "brute flower of desire"[14] that forces life into the midst of this people who instead of nihilism choose the painful path of believing that life is still stronger than death. In a world that forbids them the luxury of living simply with their families, that does not allow them to live with a minimum assurance of help/providence, that prevents them from moving, and that insists in keeping them without social/economic choices, Easter becomes the place of safety, a country of radical belonging without borders and walls where dreams of a just society and family reunion can be nurtured.

In these figurings of the churches of Christ in times of Easter, we can notice the following:

(1) Easter goes from being a celebration on a given Sunday of the calendar to becoming a way of living. The development of celebrating Easter as a season of fifty days marks the understanding of Easter as not simply a point in time, but a journey on which we go. Ultimately,

---

14. Veloso, "O Quereres."

Easter saturates the entire liturgical calendar/life as it is repeated every Sunday. No matter when we are celebrating, it will always be Easter.

(2) Yet, Easter never comes without the wrestlings of life and the brutalities of Good Friday. The early historical celebration of Easter held closely to the inherent relationship between death and life. Sundays arrive only after the announcements of death along the way, the Tenebrae of Wednesdays, the anguishes of Maundy Thursdays, the desperation of Good Fridays, and the numbness and revolt of Saturdays. Then and only then, we are able to figure out what Easter Sunday is all about.

(3) Easter links together a basic sacramental pattern for the life of the church. A meal gathering and the welcoming of new brothers and sisters through the waters of baptism are basic to the Easter celebration.

(4) Easter then provides a framework to live in the world by the ways in which Christ lived. There is the proclamation of a new and alternative way of living in God's kin-dom, with the beatitudes, the parables, the harsh demands to love your neighbor, to share food, feelings, and belongings with those excluded. This new way of living is always pressing against injustices, class divides, and the status quo. Even if our culture has made Easter a cultural event, tamed from the challenges and exigencies that Easter entails, we are nonetheless required by Easter to pay attention to the things God and God's kin-dom requires of us that were demonstrated in the life of Jesus.

(5) Easter brings a sense of becoming, not only in a figurative way but very concretely: it starts social processes of liberation, of justice, of transformation, freedom, and dignity; it reunites people; it prevents evil from destroying lives; and it teaches us to share our belongings and to pay attention to others' lives.

(6) Easter prompts people to probe for a sense of gratitude and to offer thanksgiving as a way of maintaining balance with the difficulties of life.

(7) Easter is about a "dangerous and liberating memory"[15] of Jesus that becomes a source of continuous hope and social transformation for all and especially for the crucified people.

(8) Easter is the unbelievable promise and possibility of life in a world where death spreads everywhere.

15. "*memoria passionis, mortis, et resurrectionis Jesu Christi* . . . a dangerous and liberating memory, which badgers the present and calls it into question . . . [and] compels believers to be in a continual state of transformation in order to take this future into account." Metz, *Faith in History and Society*, 88–89. Italics in original.

3

Baptism

Promises, Breaks, Demands, Rebellion, and Hope

This is the role of the church: to free people.
—Martin Luther King Jr.

Frank and I didn't pray. It didn't occur to us. We had swum in religion all our lives and had not gotten wet.
—Lidie Newton, a character in Jane Smiley's novel *The All-True Travels and Adventures of Lidie Newton*

Any religion that professes to be concerned with the souls of men [and women] and is not concerned with the slums that damn them, the economic conditions that strangle them, and the social conditions that cripple them is a dry-as-dust religion.
—Martin Luther King Jr.

Introduction

It was very early on a Sunday morning when a van took us from Nogales in Mexico to a small town whose name I have forgotten in the midst of the

Nogales deserto. When we arrived, we could see a church building and in the back a large yard with trees and a pool filled with water. The pastor lived in a small house with a kitchen, bathroom, and a bedroom. Upon arrival, everybody started to work: in tasks familiar to them, men started to take some water from the pool and get some chairs for the elderly people to sit around the big tree, under its shadow where the service would happen, while many children were already running around the yard and laughing loudly. Some women had been preparing food, but there was good also brought by each family. The pastor welcomed us as people arrived and everybody got ready for the service. My Spanish teacher, a very simple man who earned his money singing poetry on local buses in Nogales, was the lead singer with his guitar. We all joined in singing with the birds around us adding their voices. We sang hymns from dusty torn hymnals and other *coritos* into the air to the glory of God. There were testimonies and prayers filling the songs with joy. Soon the pastor preached and announced the names of the people who were going to be baptized, and each said a word about their reasons to be baptized.

We moved away from the sheltering tree to the pool next to it. One by one, the five baptismal candidates descended into the pool and were baptized while the congregation cheered and celebrated as each came out of the water. All along people were singing and offering praises and prayers that filled the thick hot air of the desert. After the newly baptized people were a little dry the pastor gave to them a baptismal certificate, which was to serve as a document for them to get papers and their passport. The certificate had the appearance of an official paper with the stamp of the congregation and signatures of the pastor and other church officials. The baptism documented a new identity. The certificate had other purposes that complicate this story. With the baptism certificate, people could claim their civil identities and belonging. After the service was over, the kids got into their bathing suits and jumped into the pool. We spent the day eating, singing and celebrating the embodied promises and ambiguities of this tiny portion of God's realm.

It was in that worship service in the desert of Nogales that I received the gift of the rich complexity of baptism. Baptism is not only and solely a function of the church, not only the liturgy confirming the gospel, but a connected symbol to the sacred wisdom of the whole life of the community. The old spoke to the new and the new spoke the old in new ways, in expanded forms of juxtapositions made by the people. The pool had three purposes: it was the water reservoir for the local community, gathering the rain that served for planting, cooking, and bathing; it was the baptismal font for baptisms; it was also the swimming pool for kids to have fun, and it was shared by the congregation. For that community, the baptizing pool was a reservoir of memory, of meaning, of fun, of survival. It was the very source of their survival, their fun, and their faith. Water for this church comes before, during, and after the religious ceremony. The sermon connects sacrament with life. The whole worship was the whole life re-presented, performed, hoped, and fully lived.

What this church can offer us is a deep sense of relation with God's creation, a deep connection with an ecological thread of life. It was the holy water that gave meaning to the words spoken around the water. The ritual didn't need to be elevated or the waters made holy. Instead, the community went down to the already holy waters for the people to be baptized. Symbols of life and faith were not juxtaposed as if the holy had to somehow invade the "profane" to make it value something, but rather the intertwined sacramental symbols of life and faith were rightly blended in that community pool.

Linda Gibler cites the use of water in the Easter Vigil:

> Blessed are you, Ever-Present God,
>
> Creator of the Universe,
>
> Through you we have the gift of water for baptism.
>
> This water of Stars, Earth, and Life you give
>
> To bring us into the fullness of life in you.
>
> This is the water over which your Spirit hovered at the Beginning,
>
> The water that cleansed the Earth in Noah's day
>
> Through which the Israelites passed unharmed
>
> In Moses' Day
>
> And in which Jesus was baptized.
>
> This is the water Jesus calmed,
>
> The water he turned into wine in Cana
>
> And that flowed from his side on Calvary[1]

Baptism Unites

Baptism is God's gift of grace, mercy, forgiveness, and love to the church. God's gift to the world! In baptism, God forgives our sins and issues a constant call to us to forgive each other following the pattern of Jesus's prayer. In this gift, we receive the unconditional love of God through the life of the church in Christ. It is God's gift, unconditionally given to all, that shows everyone is equally valued in God's eyes, without distinction in ability, gender,

1. Gibler, *From the Beginning to Baptism*, 12.

color, class, language, origin, or ethnicity. Also, the whole earth gets wet with the waters of baptism and becomes God's body. Then, earth, neighbor, ourselves, all carry in itself the *imago Dei*! Baptism is then a way to become fully ourselves in the whole vast *oikos* body of God.

Baptism has to do with our immersion and union with the life of Christ, and our lives with one another and with the earth. We are buried and raised with Christ to walk in newness of life. We are commanded to live an ethical and moral life that mirrors Christ's life. As we are united with God in Christ, nothing can take away this love from us. We are united with our sisters and brothers into the church and beyond it, too, since God's gift in Jesus is for all. Baptism becomes an eternal seal, an everlasting stamp of God's love on us that should change the way we live, the way we consider things, the way we relate to one other, and to the planet.

In baptism, God pours out the Holy Spirit on us.[2] Baptism is the beginning of a new chapter in the story of a whole life in which God's love precedes the actual baptism. The Christian life and its promises will continually come to us in many ways by the power of the Holy Spirit. We will need the constant outpouring of the Holy Spirit to discern our times, our leaders, and the government. The more fascist the political scene the harder we must use the power that the Holy Spirit gives us. It is thus fundamental to know that at the beginning of our baptismal life we have all we need to live our lives fully and face the powers of death in our world. The sanctification process in one's discipleship happens through ongoing discernment about these resources and the use of them through the power of the Holy Spirit.

Baptism is one of the many ways God is sacramentally present in the world, and so it is connected with the sacrament of the Eucharist/Lord's Supper/Communion. The Eucharist is a place to remember where we come from, whose we are, and the commitments made during our baptism for the rest of our lives. Around the expected sacraments of baptism and Eucharist, God moves in unexpected ways. God's itinerary is varied, and so baptism can also lead us to the table and sometimes the table will lead us to baptism.

Baptism is a "showing of a doing,"[3] an expression of God's showing and doing something new in us and in the world, something profound, to the point of redemption and transformation, a loving regard for the world, and for people to be loved, deeply loved. In this way, it has to do with a constant word and act of God in the life and liturgy of the one who received this love, in the life and liturgy of the church and of the world.

---

2. While some people will distinguish the baptism of water from the baptism of the Spirit, others will say that the baptism of water is the baptism of the Holy Spirit.

3. Driver, *Liberating Rites*, 91–98.

In baptism, we learn that the Christian church is a global community of local communities, united as the body of Christ. Just as it is our challenge to care for those who come from Mexico, Ethiopia, Bangladesh or any other country when they are living near us, it is their shared vow and demand to care for us when we are near them. In baptism, we are reminded that we have a citizenship beyond our passport. A document from the early church put it this way:

> For Christians cannot be distinguished from the rest of the human race by country or language or customs. They do not live in cities of their own; they do not use a peculiar form of speech; they do not follow an eccentric manner of life . . . They live in their own countries, but only as aliens. They have a share in everything as citizens, and endure everything as foreigners. Every land is a foreign land . . . They busy themselves on earth, but their citizenship is in heaven. They obey the established laws but in their own loves they go far beyond what the laws require. They love all men, and by all men are persecuted. They are unknown and still they are condemned; they are put to death, and yet they are brought to life. They are poor and yet they enjoy complete abundance. They are dishonored and in their very dishonor they are glorified; they are defamed and are vindicated. They are reviled, and yet they bless; when they are affronted, they still pay due respect. When they do good, they are punished as evildoers . . .[4]

Baptism brings about a new rationality, a new identity, and a new understanding of what being human is all about. It gives a place to belong, an ever-expanding sense of identity, and a way of being in the world. This can be translated into an expanded sense of humanity, a conception of life that extends itself to a multiplicity of eco-biological systems and forms of living, and a new ethical living to see and acknowledge our connections with a variety of forms of life. Baptism is a great social equalizer. Baptism carries a harsh ethical demand. Maxwell Johnson writes,

> Indeed, baptism into Christ—like death itself, the central Pauline metaphor for baptism—is the "Great Equalizer." It transcends all such distinctions and, as such, provides us with a perspective and foundational basis from which we might address any and all forms of racism, classism, and sexism.[5]

4. "Letter to Diognetus," in Richardson, *Early Christian Fathers*, 11.
5. Johnson, *Rites of Christian Initiation*, 452.

As we are united in Christ, we participate in the whole of God's creation. Baptism has to do with individual, social, ecological, and cosmic regeneration, salvation, and redemption. This new life in Christ brought about by God in baptism is a way of walking through the waters of our baptism daily, with its commitments, its connections, and its demands. Like in that little town in the desert of Sonora, Mexico, we should still be damp from baptism when we join the celebration. As Maxwell Johnson says of the church, it is as "those who always walk wet in the baptismal waters of their origin."[6]

Baptism Divides and Disrupts

Baptism, for almost every Christian church, is a sacrament, a sacred mystery that happens in the lives of those who enter into the life of Christian communities. In baptism, Christians go through a rite of passage. By the grace of God in Jesus Christ, they become someone else, newly marked by God's unconditional love. Baptism issues a radical transition, to the point of a break. Christians go from participating in an old order of things to belonging to another, new, radically different world order, the order of God's love where everyone, baptized or not, carries the *imago Dei*.

Some writers are aware of the divisive and disruptive side of baptism. Dietrich Bonhoeffer knew the radicalness of baptism, to the point of saying that in baptism we literally break from the world by dying to the sinful, dreadful, and disconnected patterns of human existence and by finding a way for the heart to get out of oneself and live for another. Bonhoeffer says, "The break with the world is absolute. It requires and causes our death. In baptism we die together with our old world."[7]

Only through an absolute "break from the world" can Christians work from a place of love and for the planet where life is connected with all its multiplicities. In our baptism in Christ, in God's love, we lose many ties that condition us into anything that takes away the possibility of life in its fullness! The grace of God in baptism demands us to abandon a life that is complacent with any form of oppression and assumes a radical posture against all forms of evil, just as Bonhoeffer relinquished his life to fight against death.

The whole ritual of baptism enacts a fundamental break. In the history of the church, we see how baptism was developed from a variety of views and practices. From the Greek, the verb *Baptisein* means to immerse, to

6. Johnson, *Rites of Christian Initiation*.

7. Bonhoeffer, *Discipleship*, 208.

dip. Christian baptism comes from a variety of theological understandings and also a variety of practices. Some sources will say that the practices and meanings of baptism came from Jewish practices Christians based on rituals of cleansing and purification, one that Jesus did and told us to do.[8] In John 3:5 baptism is understood as a new beginning through the language of new birth. In Romans 6:3–11 there is a deep unification with Christ through Jesus's death, burial, and resurrection. The immersion of the new believer copies this movement of dying and resurrecting in Christ through the waters. In the following three centuries, the church added several elements to the rite. Some of those included,

- *Catechesis*, teaching the tenets of the faith to newcomers that could last up to three years;
- *Vigils*, fasting and abstinence from sex to prepare the body for the special event;
- *Anointing* of the head or the entire body both before the event in preparation and after the event to seal the new believer in the life of Christ;
- *Laying on of hands*;
- *Insufflations*, which is breathing into the face of the baptismal candidate. This was done in conjunction with either an exorcism or the conferral of the Holy Spirit based on John 20:22 where the risen Christ "breathed on them and said to them, 'Receive the Holy Spirit.'";
- *Opening of the ears through spittle* (known as the *effeta*) to help believers hear the word of God;
- *The renunciation of Satan* and exorcism, which symbolized purification and the change of ownership from the Devil's control to God's kingdom, care, and protection;
- *Repetition of prayers*; while churches used different patterns, preparations and formulas to baptize, they all took great care to ensure that new believers understood the implications of their new faith.

All of these aspects can be seen through Bonhoeffer's prism of breaking with a certain past and order of things into a new past, present, and future that now belong to God. Cleaning the body was the cleansing of the mind and the soul, once owned by anything that was not God. There is an explicit renunciation of an old life into an explicit affirmation of a new belonging to God and a new world order. In baptism, a new world is possible!

8. Matt 3:16–17; 28:19, NRSV.

Bonhoeffer's break is ritualized in the form of death present in the immersing of one into the waters and back to life. In the baptismal rite of passage, we break from the allegiances of the old world, led by and filled with evil forces that destroy life, that keep pushing us against each other, that bring the worst of ourselves to our relationships, that make us live out of feelings of fear, greed, hatred, and envy. In the ritual of baptism, we break from a world that is grounded in a kind of anthropology that places the *human kind* above all other *kinds of life*. Reborn into the newness of life, we start seeing that all forms of life, be it in animals, soil, birds, seeds, air, and so on, are multiple kinds of life that must be esteemed with the same respect, and lived in deep relation and solidarity for the sake of the life of the world. In baptism, we break from an *eco/oikós* made of exploitation of the earth, without any consideration for the many cycles of life, and turn to an *oikós* where everybody can live. In baptism Christians break with an *eco-nomos* that places development above and beyond any limit and serves only to feed greed and envy into an eco-system where the *nomos*, i.e., the law, is organized for all living creatures. Thus, the vision of baptism needs to be fully enacted in our lives.

For a short moment where we go through a liminal movement, we receive the grace of God to break with the world as we know it, and that fills us with a sense of loss, of nihilism, of no-nomos, of not belonging anywhere and to anyone. Breaking with what we thought defined us before, with that which gave us a name, identity, and a sense of life in the world, we feel like our whole world is crumbling down. And we die. However, when we come back to life, immediately after our shattered world, after this breaking, an opening happens, a new sense of potency in life is received in ways that we never felt before. This potency is the presence of the Holy Spirit that will enable us to live the fullness of this world from now on. If before we lived lives shackled to all kinds of oppression, now we are completely transformed, we have received freedom, life in fullness.

A new reasoning is now necessary for there is a mission to create, engage, and follow. Jesus's baptism is God sending Godself to the world in flesh, bones, desires, feelings, and needs. From that moment, Jesus's ministry starts. Jesus has to honor God and this sending: he has to live off its challenges and so many trials that the end of his life was the cross and death. The same trajectory has been repeated throughout the world by people, communities, and other forms of life that radically lived Jesus's message. They start from a break with the world and a stubbornness to live life in fullness that faces all the obstacles and evils of this world.

Thus, baptism is such a radical decision in one's life that it must be pondered carefully. Baptism disrupts our ways of living and breaks our ties with the world we knew. There is a baptismal case of a family who wanted to be Christian and did the whole *catechumenate* in order to be baptized. They seriously studied what baptism meant and the call God was issuing for a new life. On Saturday, just before their baptism, they called the pastor and said "we are not ready, baptism is about strong commitments and we need to think this over for a little longer." The pastor was very happy and said, "You understood baptism fully. You are ready! But let me know if you want to continue when you are ready." In a time where pastors baptize anyone in order to gain new "members," this family understood what was at stake in this rite of blessing and transformation.

Baptized into Community: The Task of Freedom

The ritual of baptism can only be performed if the assembly is present. There can't be private baptism, for the rite is a public announcement that God has called someone to live life in fullness. After baptism, from now on, this new member will receive what s/he/they needs to live. Detached from the lure and promises of commodified happiness of this world, the baptized learns that happiness is already here, in God and now in him/her/they, placed there by the Holy Spirit, already received. Now s/he/they can live a life in which even fear bends its knees before God.

The new life found in God's love through grace and manifested through the waters can set us free! Jesus is the incarnation of God's freedom. He was free to move through life without being reduced solely to a certain religious identity. He was a Jew and he was free to move about other geographic areas, he was free to move within and beyond his own Jewish learnings, he was able to talk and engage with women and the lower caste of his society. He made the use of the freedoms of Jewish identity. He didn't have to protect any tradition if it didn't make sense. He criticized vehemently religious, economic, and social forms of living that oppressed people. He brought life to everyone he met. It is from this same freedom that we receive from God that we live.

Freedom in Jesus's ministry does not carry a petty sense of free personal choice, or the historical theological account of personal free will. The Samaritan didn't act because he had free individual will to help that person on the road. I borrow the definition of freedom from the Brazilian philosopher Vladimir Safatle to say that this was also Jesus's form of freedom, "the ability to recognize that which imposes itself on us as necessary."[9]

---

9. Safatle, "Por um colapso do indivíduo e de seus afetos."

Julian, "Mi casa y escuela (My house and school)"

Julian is thirteen years old, from Guatemala. In this picture, he drew his home and school. The turning of the time is captured by the sun and the moon. The clouds pour rain onto the lush hillside forest. The river flows with a boat and fish. Julian also drew his journey experience (see previous chapter).

The community of the baptized is grounded in "the ability to recognize that which imposes itself on us as necessary." Every question posed to us in our baptism has to do with a larger project of a kin-dom[10] of freedom that demands from us that we become aware of what we must do with the life we have received from God and the lives near us.

Jesus's sense of freedom is about living our lives into the contradictions, complexities, paradoxes, ambivalences within each of us, ambiguities of power, powerlessness and potential meaninglessness of our existence, with a very critical mind that makes sensible and ethical choices in relation to somebody else in order to figure out, every day, why we must continue to live. And to love. To be free is to be bound to somebody else, indeed *everybody* else!

From baptism, we realize that the gospel is the equalizer of people in society and in that way, everything in the church should be shared so that everyone can have enough to live and to live well. Like the church in the desert of Nogales, the water was not a private possession, nor was it used for profit. Instead it was a common source of life for all and the people were free to share it equally. In baptism, we offer a place for somebody to belong,

10. For a powerful view of what kin-dom means, see Isasi-Diaz, *La Lucha Continues*, 243–51.

we open our doors and borders, our love committed to somebody else and the whole earth is honored. In baptism, we widen widely the limits of our ecclesiology, expand the allegiances we make, make the whole eco-system our parish, broaden the commitments we are bound to, and reimagine what kind of world community we have. Michael L. Budde developed a deep sense of ecclesial solidarity in his *The Borders of Baptism*:

> When Christians take ecclesial solidarity as their starting point of discernment—political, economic, liturgical, and other-wise—it makes them members of a community broader than the largest nation-state, more pluralistic than any culture in the world, more deeply rooted in the lives of the poor and marginalized than any revolutionary movement, more capable of exemplifying the notion of "E pluribus Unum" than any empire past, present, or future. Seeing oneself as a member of the world-wide body of Christ invites communities to join their local stories to other stories of sin and redemption, sacrifice and martyrdom, rebellion and forgiveness, unlike any other on offer via allegiance to one's tribe, gendered movement of class fragment.[11]

To be baptized is to make an oath only to God, and to order our steps in such a way that we turn to God's preferences: each other, God's creation, and especially the poor. When baptism is fully enacted in my life, my limits and the possibilities of my life become directly related to somebody else. Thus, I cannot have it if you don't have it; I cannot eat if you can't eat; we cannot have full lives if the earth doesn't have a full life; I cannot live if the planet can't prosper. This ongoing process comes to our conscience when a person is baptized or a community member renews baptism vows. When they do that, Christians are reminded to confess their sins and announce that a new world is possible.

In this way, this sense of freedom is not only lived by the individual but also by the community in which the baptized was received. That means that the freedom of that assembly is the ability to recognize that whatever need that individual imposes on the community becomes a necessity, not a limitation, or an embarrassment.

Living through Baptism

Practically, that sense of freedom should mean that not a single baptized person should go hungry, or go without housing, or education, or health

---

11. Budde, *Borders of Baptism*, 4.

care! And that is because the baptized individual is baptized into a local and global family. The enactment of baptism in our lies is the enactment of a new society and a new form of living. I often tell my students this story: imagine someone here who has a daughter and she decides to go visit Brazil. When she gets there, she realizes that she lost everything on the airplane and she cannot go back to the United States for the next 10 years. What is she supposed to do? Besides holding on and not collapsing, she should walk around the streets of São Paulo until she can find a church. Imagine she discovers the Christian church where my family worships. What that little Presbyterian Church would have to do is to welcome her and find a family for her to be with, feed her, offer her all she needs to get her life together, protect her from the government if they want to throw her out and help her get documents, learn the language, have health insurance, and find a new job. All of this should be a demand to any church because she was baptized in the love of God and her community in the US promised to take care of her. For the promises of baptism made anywhere must be fulfilled everywhere.

Baptism is not only the performance of a religious rite, obedience to an ordinance, or the celebration of a sacrament. It is much more than that since in baptism God is building a new world, showing a new way to be in the world. It is the building of a new world in the face of evil. In this battle, the path is made of struggle, resistance, dissent, crucifixion, and resurrection. To be baptized is to carry the cross daily and be with those whose lives are threatened to be extinguished daily.

Living through baptism means to look at the world with baptismal lenses and to gain different anthropological views: we are not the most important thing on earth or in the universe. We are one form of life and this life only exists because it is in relation with other forms of life. God's grace is on us all. When I am dunked into water I realize that I am also water and part of so many other forms of life. In the chain of life, I am just one part of this expansive chain that must be respected: water, animals, plants, seeds, creatures and the billion forms of life that live in our universe. In this way, the new understanding I receive from baptism tells me that my life coexists with other forms of life. Baptism is thus the discovery of my coexistence with the whole universe through God's creation. In other words, baptism is the embrace of various forms of being human, a much larger sense of life, a belonging to an eco-system that is the source of our living.

Thus, our baptism in the name of the Trinity entails a movement of faith that points to a circularity of life that coexists only if in deep relation with all the various bio-systems of life. In fact, baptism is a bath into what life is all about, a communal (Trinitarian) work to defend and set forth life in its fullness everywhere. In that way, baptism is life coming first and religion coming after to protect and preserve life. This is what José Arregi's short definition of eco-liberating spirituality is about:

> An authentic spirituality, whether religious or not, is essentially ecological. An ecological spirituality is necessarily liberating and a liberating spirituality is necessarily ecological. And only an ecological and liberating spirituality is truly "spiritual" regardless of whether it is or is not coated in beliefs, norms and rites that we call religious.[12]

All of this is to say that the grace of God through baptism radically breaks with an anthropology that centers in the human-kind only and disperses its value and honor to multiple *kinds* of humanity. The Brazilian anthropologist Eduardo Viveiros de Castro says that the indigenous people of the Central and South Americas see different forms of humanity in everything. There are different levels of humanity to be dealt with. He says,

> If everything is human, we are not special; this is the point. And at the same time, if everything is human, beware of what you do, because when you cut a tree or kill a bug, you are not simply moving particles of matter from side to side, you are dealing with people who have memory, take revenge, strike back, and so on. As everything is human, everything has ears, all its actions have consequences.[13]

If we are to talk about diversity, we must talk about various forms of humanity and not only within a religious, market-oriented approach to humanity. Even a diverse engagement of cultures within a proclaimed multiculturalism is not enough because to engage in different understandings of *culture* is to still stay under the grid of a white way of thinking and talking about humanity and society. By challenging us with indigenous thinking, Viveiros de Castro challenges our theological anthropology and we have to respond to it. When new challenges and new neighbors are considered, it demands us to think of our faith, thinking, feeling, and practices, differently. Baptism has to do with life in its fullness and does not need to confine belief to a certain understanding of life just to protect tradition. On the contrary, the open conscience of our faith is to have the old to say of the new as the new witnesses to the old and breaks the old into new forms of living the traditions. Larry Rasmussen asks us a hard question:

---

12. Arregi, "The Spirit Who Moans in All Beings."
13. Castro, "Antropologia Renovada."

How do we do it with our neighbors, all our neighbors—human and other-than-human—when Earth is "hot, flat and crowded" and borders and walls no longer protect?[14]

Having our trust in God, the baptized do not fear to lose God's grace or be unfaithful. Rather, we humbly change and embrace the indigenous *perspectivism*[15] of various humanities and add to our faith a mutuality of humanity in plants, animals, humans and the whole bio-system of sustainability. In this way we are faithful to God and Jesus as we are faithful to life.

Still damp from the waters of our baptism we go from drought and the human devastation of the earth to a multilayered humanity project that will be beneficial to the planet. As Thomas Berry states,

> We need only see that our human technologies are coherent with the ever-renewing technologies of the planet itself. An indispensable resource in fulfillment of this task is the guidance of the indigenous peoples of this continent, for they have understood, better than we have understood, the integral relations of humans with this continent and with the entire natural world. . . . In more recent centuries we have been concerned with interhuman relations. Our future rests even more decisively on our capacity for intimacy in our human-Earth relations.[16]

Drinking from the eternal living waters of God, we can forge an intimate baptismal *perspectivism* lived through a deep and wet, eco-liberating spirituality. Fully connected with one another and the creation, hearing the pain and moans of creation, we begin to hear and see and feel and breath and taste and touch the ways in which the earth and its poor are living, the ways in which the wretched of the earth and the wretched earth are all intertwined with the devastating destruction of the planet.

This baptismal *perspectivism* can be seen in a powerful story of the Zionist congregation in Mucheke Township, Masvingo, Zimbabwe told by Larry L. Rasmussen in his spellbinding book *Earth-Honoring Faith: Religious Ethics in a New Key*:

14. Rasmussen, *Earth-Honoring Faith*, 5.

15. A term coined by Brazilian anthropologist Eduardo Viveiros de Castro. *Perspectivism* is a perspective from the indigenous populations. "Amerindian Perspectivism is a conception according to which the world is populated by other subjects, agents or persons, other than human beings, and who see reality differently from human beings" (32). "One of the theses of perspectivism is that animals do not see us as humans, but rather as animals." Castro, *Encontros*.

16. Berry, *Great Work*, xvii–x.

Bishop Marinda welcomes Bishop Moses, whose own green robe carries the logo of the African Association of Earthkeeping Churches across the back: an African farmer kneeling, planting a tree. Beneath the tree are the words of Colossians 1:17: "In Christ all things hold together."

"Bishop Moses" is a conferred title. It recognizes (and symbolizes) extraordinary leadership on the part of Inus Daneel, bringing the Shona people up from destitution through a grassroots movement of earth-healers. The ties to the soil of these subsistence farmers are strong. Fighters for independence from Rhodesia called themselves "Sons of the Soil." These ties found Christian voice in a cosmology of the whole community of life as framed liturgically. So tree-planting happens in the context of a Eucharist; seed dedication does as well. The first fruits of the harvest are gathered in a Feast of Booths celebration, itself borrowed from the Hebrew Bible. No cutting of trees alongside streams is allowed, in recognition of the living waters of life common to scripture, baptism, and the sacred groves of the ancestors. The young are trained in local horticulture and land preservation as their training in stewardship. All the earth of these granite hills has become the religious focus of a comprehensive guardianship, so much so that the people felt their work together needed a name—The African Association of Earthkeeping Churches (AAEC)—and a slogan: "Regaining the Lost Lands, Reclothing the Earth."[17]

This way of living liturgically is what baptism in Christ demands of us! Plants juxtaposed to confessions, birds juxtaposed to forgiveness, seeds juxtaposed to Eucharist, water juxtaposed to the living water of Jesus, eco-systems juxtaposed to the word of God!

All of this is at the heart of the notion of life and freedom that baptism presents to us! For the ideas of *perspectivism*, freedom, and mutual care in the baptized community have to do with a personal conversion that expresses itself in much larger ecclesio-political-earth life issues. Individually and communally, we must look at the world from this wet perspective and work to transform every aspect of life that is not living the potential of its fullness. Let me name some.

17. Rasmussen, *Earth-Honoring Faith*, 32–33.

Water Systems

The baptized should touch the water that baptizes her or the water that blesses him, or the water that she drinks or the water in which he bathes and ask: Where does this water come from? What is this faucet linked to? What are the rivers associated with this water that sustains this community? Who owns the fountain, the very beginning of these waters? What companies eject their garbage in its waters? More, what do plastic bottles do to the environment? But more than that, what are the economic-political interests that do not put a ban to the use of plastic? Why are big corporations able to go to local communities and pollute their rivers and dump their hazardous trash in their backyard and there is no punishment for these companies? Let us keep our baptismal promises!

When we look at the oceans, we see that human fishing is depleting forms of life and shifting the eco-system of the oceans. The use of rivers for private profit cannot be respected even if under the approval of the law. Any law. The fight of indigenous people in Standing Rock against private companies who want pipelines for oil through their lands is the plight of life lived in fullness! The oil was moved from white neighborhoods who disagreed with its presence and the project was taken to the indigenous people, a minority without the same power of the middle and upper classes. The privilege of white people is to ignore comfortably the discomfort their privilege costs others.

Private, multimillion-dollar international corporations invade water reservoirs of sacred indigenous lands to exploit them for private profit. The construction of two controversial oil pipelines, the Keystone XL and the Dakota Access in South and North Dakota and the *Belo Monte Dam*, a hydro-electric dam complex under construction on the Xingu River in the state of Pará, Brazil, are clearly signs of the unregulated power of corporations who own the State that passes law to protect the interests of capital. This means that indigenous people and their sacred lands do not matter, continuing to rip apart the mutual eco-system of our survival. To protect these rivers and the indigenous communities is to own one's baptismal oath!

In the 1980s, in a colonizing effect that the World Bank pushed in every country in Central and Latin America, Bolivia privatized its main national resources: railways, airlines, hydrocarbon industry and also its water sources. The cost of water skyrocketed and the people started to complain. With riots after riots and fighting against its own government, the people won the battle. The movie *Even the Rain* shows part of this battle.[18] In some

18. *Even the Rain.*

ways, the Bolivian people took back what belonged to them, making water be used for the supply of people and not for the profit of private corporations. Water today is the new gold! In the waters of our baptism, the water systems belong to God not to anyone! Because of that we can say that the water systems belong to all as we all belong to God! Given the precious condition of water, it is right and necessary that we stay wet from our baptism!

Land

The anthropologist Darcy Ribeiro tells the following story. "I tell you about a conversation I had with a very clever Indian, Chief Juruna. He asked me one day who invented paper, and I wanted to explain how to make paper with crushed wood. Juruna complained that he wanted to know about the real paper, the paper that made man a landowner of lands he had never seen and where a people lived for centuries."[19]

The history of colonial land theft and improper ownership of lands must be an ongoing question asked by the baptized. Why do we have private lands? And if we do, why are some people entitled to so much and the majority to nothing? The Landless Movement (MST) in Brazil is a movement for agrarian reform and sharing land among the Brazilian people. However, the media keep trying to disqualify their work, saying they are vandals, socialists, and unlawful people. The Brazilian government and congress, owned by the agribusinesses, keep on spreading hatred against small rural workers, and organizations such as MST, killing people who work for the protection of the land and agrarian reform. The Pastoral Commission of the Land (CPT) said that in 2015 fifty people were killed in land conflicts throughout Brazil and nothing was done to bring the killers to justice.[20] In the state of Pará, between 1964 and 2010, nine hundred fourteen rural workers, religious people, and lawyers were killed for questions related to the land.[21] Chico Mendes was known globally, and he was killed for protecting the eco-system.[22] The US Catholic nun Dorothy Stang was killed protecting the people and the land.[23] Just recently Isidro Baldenegro López, an

19. Ribeiro, "Duas Leis Reitoras."

20. http://www.mst.org.br/2016/04/14/impunidade-em-mortes-e-motor-da-violencia-no-campo.html.

21. http://www.cartacapital.com.br/sociedade/elas-marcadas-para-morrer-7816.html.

22. To learn more about Chico Mendes, see https://en.wikipedia.org/wiki/Chico_Mendes

23. To learn more about Dorothy Stang, see https://pt.wikipedia.org/wiki/Dorothy_Stang.

indigenous activist protecting the pine-oak forests of Mexico's Sierra Madre, was shot and killed.[24]

Our baptismal vows denounce agribusinesses that keep recolonizing countries, deforesting countries across the world, poisoning the land with agrotoxins, stealing the land from small farmers, contaminating rivers in small communities, and shifting natural courses of rivers into artificial ones in order to support fishing and agribusiness—for example, the forced changes in the San Francis River in Brazil, where the longtime river communities have been dismissed, evicted, and abandoned.

Associated with the land is the issue of housing. Again, the same questions have to be posed: why do some people live so well while others don't have a roof over their heads? Only a society that doesn't understand anything about baptism can have homeless people.

Economy

I want to stress one issue inside of the church that also reflects the gap between baptismal commitments of the Christian faith: disproportionate salaries. If we think about how churches structure the salaries of their employees, we will soon realize that a few people get lots of money while most of its pastors get small salaries. Why do some people in the major offices and tall-steeple churches get so much money and the vast majority of the pastors have to get by with whatever they can muster? Why do some pastors have a whole package and some are working less than thirty hours per week so they will not receive benefits? The community of the baptized should ask, "What is the principle that organizes these salaries?" "Why do male pastors get better salaries than women?" Why does this happen in a community that says everyone has the *imago Dei*? Because if all have the *imago Dei* everyone should have the same salary (varying on cost of living according to where people live)? Why are salaries so disparate in a community that calls itself baptized by Jesus Christ into the newness of a just and fair world? That is to be considered in seminaries and any other Christian institution. Why is it the pre-baptized world reigns mightily in our churches and we don't say anything? The *imago Dei* in us all demands us all to interpret it in a very material way and not only in a too easy, spiritual way.

Since there is no limit to the disparity inside of the church, there is no limit to the disparity in society. Unless our baptismal vows demand us to put limits to our greed, to our uneven understanding of the *imago Dei*, we

24. Malkin, "Isidro Baldenegro, Mexican Environmental Activist, Is Shot to Death."

will not see that happening in our society. Wendell Berry tells us about the theological contradiction of a life without limits:

> The problem with us is not only prodigal extravagance, but also an assumed godly limitlessness. We have obscured the issue by refusing to see that limitlessness is a godly trait. We have insistently, and with relief, defined ourselves as animals or as "higher animals." But to define ourselves as animals, given our specifically human powers and desires, is to define ourselves as limitless animals—which of course is a contradiction in terms. Any definition is a limit, which is why the God of Exodus refuses to define Himself: "I am that I am."[25]

Moreover, our sense of limitless faith and demanded entitlement have created believers who have become vicious consumers, treating God as an object of consumption or a guarantor of our consumerist form of living. When do we hear in our churches that we cannot have all we want? Or that we must restrain our way of living? Or give what we have? Berry continues:

> In keeping with our unrestrained consumptiveness, the commonly accepted basis of our present economy is the fantastical possibility of limitless growth, limitless wants, limitless wealth, limitless natural resources, limitless energy, and limitless debt. The idea of a limitless economy implies and requires a doctrine of general human limitlessness: All are entitled to pursue without limit whatever they conceive as desirable—a license that classifies the most exalted Christian capitalist with the lowliest pornographer.[26]

We are baptized into the "I am that I am" in whom we live and thrive. If God is my desire and my neighbor my limit, then what might God ask of us? This limitless life is opposed to the gospel, for God calls us in our baptism to share and to give. This sharing and giving is bound within the context of the community who embraced us in baptism. This baptism is an immersion into a local community and thus into the local economy and obligations of that neighborhood as well. In this way, baptized into the life of a local economy I must care for the ways they live. We must then search for better, more honest and fair ways in which we might live together. Wendell Berry gives us two organizational principles to do that: neighborhood and subsistence.[27] Neighborhoods supporting local farming and living off of the land can foster not only local commerce but also they can export the surplus

25. Berry, *What Matters?*, 42.
26. Berry, *What Matters?*, 43.
27. Berry, *What Matters?*, 192–93.

of their harvest and exchange their produce with other communities. In the church in Sonora, the planting and harvesting of the produce and the sharing of the water were what kept the community going.

Border Walls, Immigrants and Refugees

Any baptized Christian should challenge any borders of separation, recognizing the tragic early-modern roots of national narratives. Were the Christian churches to live their baptismal vows fully, they would all go to the borders between the southern US and Mexico and tear that wall down. In Christ, there are no countries to be banned, no people to be feared, no national identities or passports. That is all we need. The church would have to engage in civil disobedience holding immigrants in Sanctuary movements. It is an utter contradiction for presidents of the US to say that they are Christians while building walls and deporting immigrants. Their first commitment is to nation-states and so-called economic developments. The problem with immigration is not only a lack of immigration policies, but a whole reordering of world economic systems. If NAFTA were to be banned and fair economic relations with Mexico were to be considered beyond any form of free-trade systems, an enormous change of immigration flow would occur. Perhaps needy people without health and dental coverage in place would flow into Mexico, as many US citizens do by going to the border cities to buy produce or medicine or have medical or dental treatments. Raising up walls and deporting immigrants are clear signs of an unbaptized nation.

By the waters of our baptism any ban to prevent people from joining others will be denounced! If any people are defamed, we will speak glory into their names! We will go against any government administration that uses scare tactics such as "discriminatory legislation, economic deprivation, public defamation, administrative harassment, and social ostracism,"[28] for they are the same things Hitler did to the Jews. We will go against any law that disrupts families and communities.

It is at this time that the waters of our baptism should have drenched us into the fight against these demonic, inhumane movements, putting ourselves on the line, siding vividly (and sharing unmistaken baptismal vows) with those afflicted, with those who are suffering under the weight of defamation, destruction, violence, destitution, displacement, and inhumanity.

---

28. Yad Vashem, "Frequently Asked Questions," http://www.un.org/en/holocaustremembrance/docs/FAQ%20Holocaust%20EN%20Yad%20Vashem.pdf.

Healing and Learning

Fundamental to baptism is the healing of the person. Oil was a central aspect of early Christian baptism. Any baptized community should expand the local religious assembly's forms of healing to the whole society. That means that universal health care is a nonnegotiable demand of the baptized community. No one can go about their lives without having proper health care. This goes back to the common sources of our goods. We cannot privatize health for this is a common good! It is a demand to the political system to provide the best health care system for all the people. The same thing has to be said about education. Education is not for profit, for only a few, for those who have better GPAs. Indeed, it is a way to even out differences and give opportunities for life transformation to anyone. Thus, not to care for somebody else's body and learning process is, in concrete ways, to understand baptism in solely spiritual ways, detached from its necessary historical incarnation. No one should go without health care and education in any baptized assembly!

White Supremacy

Since baptism is gaining new clothes, spiritually and socially, we also gain a new identity. Not only that, it is a baptism into a new rationality, a new form of thinking. Burial in Christ means a change in ways of feeling and being in the world. That means we must develop new forms of thinking that delink us from the forms of colonial thinking that have prevailed for so long. Colonial thinking is a way of keeping the sources of our faith white and European, based on heterosexual patriarchy, sexism, racism, white supremacy, and hierarchy. Baptism can be a way of enculturating the baptized into asymmetrical forms of power that keep some people receiving more privileges at the expense of others who have to have less. Going against any form of privilege, baptism dismantles some ways of assimilating life from the perspective of one group over against others. In this way, baptism as a great equalizer goes from the idea and the ritual of healing and burying and being born again and cleansing into the practice of this ritual into our communities and society. The equalizing process promised and demanded in baptism continues as we change our minds and go through various conversions/*metanoias* and into work in the world. Thus, we engage in the struggle for LGBTQA people, with the plight of those with disabilities, with the needs of homeless people, into the streets to scream Black Lives Matter, into the protection of indigenous people's rights for their land and sovereignty, into the fight for women, into the protection of children, into the inclusion of the poor, into a recognition that baptism unites us with all who suffer and breaks our connections with the causes of suffering.[29]

People of Other Religions

Now one can ask: What about non-Christians. Aren't they also a part of the larger community of the beloved people of God? Do they carry the *imago Dei*? And the immediate response is an absolute "YES!" Baptism does not differentiate people's humanities and their intrinsic honor and value because of religious belonging. Through baptism, the baptized community now sees everybody under the same love and *imago Dei*. Before baptism, we would say, "Perhaps *this* person carries the *imago Dei* but not *that* person." However, because of baptism we say yes to this and affirm each person as a precious manifestation of God's love. My eyes cannot help but see them as carrying the same *imago Dei* that I do myself! No more, no less. There are plenty of examples of churches caring for non-Christians around the globe, where Christians have discovered the deepest meaning of baptism. Baptism sends us to whoever is in need without fear. Thus, if a Muslim, or a Hindu, or a Buddhist, or a Jew, or a person of any religious affiliation, or a nonreligious person goes inside any Christian church, they would have to receive the same treatment as any Christian believer. For they are, in the views of the baptized community, precious gifts sent to us by God, angels visiting us, real people living with us who are shining the glory of God! They are us in distinctive and insurmountable ways. They are people who bring us wisdom and other connections to the earth and an expanded way to be human.

Conclusion

Our baptismal vows and commitments stretch us into decisions that have to do with the whole well-being of the planet. Without the understanding of the Christian faith as deeply entrenched in the materiality of life, without the incarnation of Jesus Christ in our common living, our theological sense of baptism will be weak, partial, lacking, and vulnerable to the idols of our age. Our baptized lives show our allegiances and with whom we are siding. Thus, to end this chapter I will raise two major things baptism calls us to in life: memory and revolt.

---

29. See chapter 6, "Praying with Black People for Darker Times."

The subversive memory of Jesus is disturbing for the status quo, for those who hold power. Through baptism, the grace of God continues to transform the individual—her heart, body, and soul—and fills this child of God with an expanded mission towards transformation and love and care for all human-kind(s)! Following Lamentations 3:21, "But this I call to mind, and therefore I have hope," we bring to mind and remember moments, people, salvific historical events, and wisdom that can transform our time. The baptism of Jesus and our own baptisms are constant reminders of that which can bring us hope. Thus our fight is over spiritual and historical amnesia, lack of historical ground that detaches our discipleship from the very core aspects of our baptism. Baptism is the assurance that it is God who keeps us standing.

The memory of Jesus's baptism and our baptism is also the historical memory of global and local events in different contexts. Baptism connects us with sacramental movements of the Holy Spirit across the globe. In the waters of our baptism, we remember that we come from the womb of God and the waters of the world. Thus, one of our major demands is to keep the memory of the earth and our fundamental belonging to it. Once we lose our connection to the earth, we are fully colonized, we are puppets in the hands of corporations, we lose our sight to what really matters, and we yield our resources, joy, resistance, commitments, strength, and so on, to our oppressors. That is why the Christian sacraments are vital to our lives! They are made of water, bread and wine, soil, water, seeds, climate, environment, and elements. In our renewal of baptism, in baptizing new people, in always celebrating the Eucharist, we are always and fundamentally going back to the earth, to God's creation.

Wendell Berry reminds us of that so well:

> As local community decays along with local economy, a vast amnesia settles over the countryside. As the exposed and disregarded soil departs with the rains, so local knowledge and local memory move away to the cities or are forgotten under the influence of homogenized sales talk, entertainment, and education. This loss of local knowledge and local memory—that is, of local culture—has been ignored, or written off as one of the cheaper "prices of progress," or made the business of folklorists. Nevertheless, local culture has a value, and part of its value is economic. This can be demonstrated readily enough. For example, when a community loses its memory, its members no longer know one another.[30]

30. Berry, *What Matters?*, 143.

In our collective faith, our common gathering to worship God, we are re-minded that the "homo" in *homo sapiens* is related to humus, born of earth, soil, an earthly being, that connects all of our humanities. We are all linked with the earth, our common *oikos*. So we must remember where we come from and proclaim: from dust to dust, we belong to God! This is the Christian statement of faith, love, and hope!

In 2015, the Pastoral Land Commission (CPT) in Brazil celebrated a gathering with a document called "Memory, Rebellion and Hope." In it, poor people said the following:

> The families of the Earth will fight until victory! Occupy, Resist and Build . . . We have so much history to tell . . . of our people, dead and alive. We create memory to unite past and present, not to repeat history! But to radicalize it, going back to the roots of love for the earth and for the people of the earth. When we occupy the earth or when we are evicted, we are together! This hope is in our hands. In one, the struggle and organization— daily and rebellious—in the other, faith and passion—daily and rebellious. On the one hand we resist the system of death with struggle. On the other hand, we find that conquering land and territory and staying in them is not enough. The challenge is to build new people and new interpersonal, family, gender, genera- tion, social, economic, political relationships between different spiritualties and religions and with nature itself. Remembering struggles and resistances fuels our indignation and rebellion. It is right to rebel, it is legitimate and urgent. Because violence and destruction are not part of the past, but are lived in every corner of the country, with many faces and the same complicity of the authorities that should care for the good of the people. These fights extenuate and exhaust our communities. The rebellion is slowly emerging, born of the reality of oppression that chal- lenges the conscience . . . With the memory of our struggles and resistance we feed our rebellion . . . (and) hope is the persistence of rebellion! We also call on churches, institutions and organiza- tions to resume an urgent process of rebellion and mobilization for life, which includes the defense of the planet earth, our com- mon home, its waters and its biodiversity.[31]

31. CPT: Carta Final - Faz escuro, mas cantamos! https://www.cptnacional.org.br/ index.php/publicacoes-2/destaque/2723-carta-final-faz-escuro-mas-eu-canto.

The call to memory and resistance from the poor in Brazil is a call from the poor and from the screams of the earth everywhere. Our baptism does not serve any oppressive reality but instead calls us to dismantle systems that do not keep life lived in to its fullness! It is because of what God did in us through baptism that we can find ways out of no ways. Chris Hedges also adds his voice to the need for revolt, "There is no way within the system to defy the demands of Wall Street, the fossil fuel industry or war profiteers. The only route left to us, as Aristotle knew, is revolt."[32]

In baptism we give our lives to God! In baptism we say that we can only submit to God and the God of life! When we instead submit ourselves to the power of States, corporations and private sources we are submitting ourselves to that which is not God. We are betraying the God who baptized us in Christ through the Holy Spirit. However, in baptism we break with the submission of this world. Wendell Berry refigures this baptismal notion of insubmission in our communities in the US. He writes,

> We Americans are not usually thought to be a submissive people, but of course we are. Why else would we allow our country to be destroyed? Why else would we be rewarding its destroyers? Why else would we all—by proxies we have given to greedy corporations and corrupt politicians—be participating in its destruction? Most of us are still too sane to piss in our own cistern, but we allow others to do so and we reward them for it. We reward them so well, in fact, that those who piss in our cistern are wealthier than the rest of us. How do we submit? By

32. Hedges, "Let's Get This Class War Started."

not being radical enough. Or by not being thorough enough, which is the same thing.[33]

Heirs of a tradition of radical Christians, and servants of a God who in Jesus did not submit to anybody or anything but God, we must continue to enact, by the grace of God, the baptism we received once so we can live under the radical marks of this sacrament! Against what Martin Luther King Jr. called "dry-as-dust religion" we need a wet religion, a very wet Christianity! Stay damp, wet, drenched in the waters of our baptism!

---

33. Berry, *Way of Ignorance*, 21.

4

Season of Advent

Future and Past Happening in the Present

In the womb of Mary
God became human.
But in Joseph's workshop
God also made class.

—DOM PEDRO CASALDÁLIGA

Introduction

The season of Advent is the season where we prepare ourselves to receive something bigger than us, something beyond our senses, our cognition, our very thinking. We cannot fully prepare, or be fully present, for it is always beyond us. In fact, we run the risk of not getting it, of not feeling it, of not being struck by its awe and wonder. On the other hand, we can get stuck in so much preparation until we realize that the time of its arrival is already gone. This is the season of Advent.

In the Advent season, we live through the season that points to Christmas and Epiphany. The first part is the waiting/anticipation/longing for the arrival of God, Emmanuel. Then we go through Christmas Eve where we celebrate the wonder of God with us, and the third part is the Twelve days of Christmas at the end of which we begin celebrating Epiphany, God coming to us. We could use the words of John Caputo to define Advent as the "insistence of God" to come to us.[1]

The historical components of the tradition we have today were composed from a myriad of events throughout history. The church took the celebration of Jesus's birth (which surely would belong to prior times) and associated it with the time (and perhaps themes) of celebration of other festivals such as the pagan festival of the Unconquered Sun. From these original mixed compositions, we have the season of Advent that must be interpreted every year in new light, and darkness, with new hermeneutical tools according to its different social, cultural, sexual, economic, and theological keys.

As God becomes like us, the incarnation has to do with the materiality of our world as Jesus's life was marked by concrete things that affected deeply his body, mind, and soul. Jesus belonged to the class of peasants; his father was a woodcrafter from Nazareth. He was born as a poor immigrant whose parents had to run away to protect his life. Jesus's birth attests to his incarnation, and to a life committed to the poor. He had nothing and was born in very uncomfortable circumstances. Why do we make it sound rich and comfortable? Can't we stand the poor elements of Jesus's birth? Why don't we remember the poor in our nativity scenes or worship services? As Eugene Peterson translated in The Message, "The Word was made flesh and blood and moved into the neighborhood."[2]

Jesus experienced the world from a particular place—as a male Jew in an occupied land. Jesus's life was a challenge to the ways people lived. He challenged understandings about the law, women, children, religion, community, and so on. His friendships, for instance with Mary Magdalene or his beloved John, were queer since they went beyond the limits of the social expectations of his time. Jesus embraces full humanity and full divinity. Leonardo Boff, a theologian from Brazil says, "A human being such as Jesus of Nazareth was in his life, death and resurrection can only be God himself."[3]

Mission to the World: The Liturgical Calendar and Globalization

Epiphany offers a new way of understanding the world:

First, it is about language—an increasingly strange language that alters the common language of the world. While we see eagerness to talk about

1. Caputo, *The Insistence of God.*
2. John 1:14 MSG.
3. Boff, *Jesus Christ Liberator*, 156.

money, social position, and to establish the fullness of life around things and possessions, Christians talk about the coming of God as poor to the poor. While life is measured by social accomplishments, Christians see worth in each person's value for who they are. While capitalism says it needs progress and development for societies to grow, Christians who have a commitment to the pace of the earth say there is no need for development. We can reinstate an order of things that does not need this form of economic development. Hope, peace, joy, and love are not only inner feelings to be felt during this season but public resources to be proclaimed, lived, and engaged in our relations, our work and on the streets. A public voice is constantly issuing a word of repentance to the world! Change your ways before the coming of Christ, says the eschatological voices of the gospel!

Second, this season is about a rhythm—a time frame that is contrary to the rapid pace of our time. While the world runs so fast and we learn to run faster every day, without any patience, any attention, or mindfulness, the liturgical calendar makes us slow down, it makes us wait carefully, expect God mindfully, ponder things consciously. The alteration of time is a strike against the structure of time used in our globalized world. While agribusiness exploits beyond limits and makes the earth overwork with two or three harvests per year, the Bible reminds us of Sabbath and the needed rest of the earth. The slow coming of Jesus to our world teaches us patience and perseverance, contrary to the fast results and intolerance in our workplaces and relationships. During this season we are taught to pray again without ceasing, contemplating the coming of Jesus and living up to his arrival in our midst. During Christmas, while everyone is still rushing with their lives to get to places and buy gifts, we are reminded to walk slowly. The arrival of a baby demands us to go slow. As Genesis 33:14 says, "Let my lord pass on ahead of his servant, and I will lead on slowly, according to the pace of the cattle that are before me and according to the pace of the children, until I come to my lord in Seir."

Third, it is about a new message—a message that is theological and lived liturgically. While the world is talking about war, we are talking about peace brought by the Prince of Peace. While the world is talking about the rise in food prices and millions of people going to bed hungry every night, we announce that in Jesus we have enough bread to feed the world and no one will go hungry in God's reign. No one! While the world says we should trust in our money, the gospel says that our trust is in God who created heaven and earth. While the world makes us anxious about the future, we announce that in Christ, justice will roll down like a river and our daily needs are met. While the daily news scares us and makes us sad and tense, we hold on to joy, hope, peace, and love, filling our lungs and shouting out loud, "Joy to the world!"

Nayeli, "Mis amigos y mi iglesia (My friends and my church)"

Nayeli is ten years old, from Guatemala. In this picture, she drew her journey experience. She traveled with her sister, mother, and five-month-year-old baby brother. When a volunteer asked what she will remember from home, she proceeced to draw her bilingual school and local church (Assembly of God).

Fourth, it is about life lived together. This gospel is communitarian but also cosmopolitan, local but also a transnational gathering of people. The Christian faith is a gathering of foreign peoples. This manger brings peoples from around the world to celebrate God's love together. The strangeness of this message is to make us, who are strangers to each other, become brothers and sisters even if we didn't know each other or never met before. Different places and rural areas in Mexico enact a powerful tradition that celebrates Advent. It is called *Posadas* and it is the enactment of the pilgrimage of Joseph and Mary nine days before December 24. From the 16th until the 24th, *Los Peregrinos, San José y la Virgen María,* in the form of two small statues, will be taken around the neighborhood by local people asking for a *posada*, a place to stay. Every home will have a Nativity scene. The hosts of the home are the innkeepers, and the neighborhood children and adults are *Los Peregrinos*, who have to request lodging. There will be candles and singing around a procession. Three different houses are asked to host them but only the third house will offer them a place to stay. The *posadas* reenact our human condition, namely, wanderers around the world, immigrants in this world waiting to find our home in God. *Posadas* also reenact the material need for a home, showing the displacement of people around the world, people without a place to stay, as we carry our children who are pregnant with dreams and hopes for a new life. The new wave of massive numbers of refugees is a desperate concern for those who are marked by the life together brought by the coming of Jesus in the Advent.

Lastly, Advent is about waiting for and living into the realm of God, a new world order. It reveals the disasters of our world today, it directs us to consider the root causes of poverty and oppression and anywhere life is threatened. As Epiphany is the coming of the Prince of Peace, we must pause and look at cultures of violence, where the arrival of peace is always endangered. Hope, peace, love, and joy are indeed about a new world, a world that is not only possible but terribly necessary! A world where we find a place to stay and are welcomed without having to show documents or be from a particular ethnic group; a new world where land is shared equally and food is available for all. A new world where social responsibilities—mutual care engaged with deep spirituality, righteousness married to love, justice kissing peace, caring for each other—go hand in hand with the sharing of our resources and the construction of the common good. It is a communal conspiracy, a revolutionary message that is supposed to change the world and turn it upside down. Do you believe it? Do you pray for it? Do you, "go tell it on the mountain, over the hills and everywhere," as the song says?

Interpreting Advent for Our Time

Advent holds time in its fullness: The past and the future arrive in the present. The past and the future tense of our lives are met in the full present mode of our collective faith.

How can we interpret the Advent Season for the beginning of the twenty-first century? There is a striking similarity between the conditions of the first century and the conditions of our life in the twenty-first century: roughly speaking, we live under the empire of the United States while Jesus lived under Herod, the client king of Judea working for the Roman Empire. Both power structures kept/keep alternating power with the same historical owners of the wealth of the country as the empire continued/continues to colonize its own peoples and countries around the globe.

In order to interpret our times from the season of Advent, we need to reinterpret the Gospel of Saint Matthew, chapter 2. Below are interpretations from two different perspectives:

Latin Perspective Interpretation

In the time of newly elected, build-the-wall Emperador Trump, after Jesús was born on the US side of the border with Mexico, some Catholic humanitarian agencies came from the East, asking, "Where is this niño Jesús? Where is the child who has been born as the disgrace and cause of all problems of this country? For we heard the salsa dance going on and we came to pay him homage." When the Rey-Emperador heard this, he was frightened, and all the United States with him; and calling together all of the pastors, priests, and rabbis, along with the judges and rulers of the country, intellectuals and theologians from the left and the right and all of the armed forces, they enquired of them where Jesús was born. And they told the Rey-Emperador: In Juárez o Nogales, on the US side of the border, for so it has been written by the prophet:

> And you, Juárez and Nogales, land stolen from Mexico, are by no means least among the new stolen territories of US; for from you shall come el Niño who is to transform, bless and challenge the people of the United States.

Then the Rey-Emperador called the secret services and the immigration offices and the military and promised to expose all of their acts publicly if they were not to say exactly where and when they saw the Niño. "Go and search diligently for the child; and when you have found him, bring me word so that I may also go and bring him a Coke, hamburger, and fries." When they had heard the Rey-Emperador, they set out; and there, ahead of them, went the sound of salsa dancing that they had heard at its beginning, until the stomp stopped and they knew the place where the child was.

When they heard that the sound had stopped, they were overwhelmed with joy. Cumbia, reggae, reggaeton, bomba, salsa, bachata, merengue and samba could be heard as well. On entering the house, they saw the child with Mary his mother; and they knelt down and paid him homage. Then, opening their treasure chests, they offered him gifts of a soccer ball, a soccer jersey from Corinthians, tamales, and *orchata*. And having been warned in a dream not to return to the Rey-Emperador, they left for their own country by another road.

Now after they had left, just like magic realism, an angel of the Lord appeared to José in a dream and said, "Get up, take the child and his mother, you are an undocumented family, refugees in your own land, you have left the country and now you cannot go back for you are from a country filled with terrorists. Wait until the people of good will go to the streets and put pressure on this evil act and things start to change; for the Rey-Emperador is about to search for the child in every single refugee camp, immigrant community, and people of other faith, to deport him and all his family. Then José got up, took the child and his mother by night, and looked for help, and they remained with people who are not crazy until either the death the Emperador or his removal from office by impeachment or the completion of his term. And they continued being undocumented immigrants, refugees in someone else's land. This was to fulfill what had been spoken by the Lord through the prophet, "Out of those whom you despise, I have called my son."

When the Rey-Emperador saw that he had been tricked by his own people who were resisting his stupidity and abuse of power, he was infuriated, for he could not deal with anything that went against his will and implemented laws to make it difficult for immigrants to stay, or to return, spending billions of dollars building walls along the borders, and deporting immigrants by the thousands. This was to fulfill what had been spoken through the prophet Jeremiah:

> A voice was heard in Ramallah,
> neighborhoods like the ones in Palestine, or in Spanish Harlem,
> wailing and loud lamentation,
> Umayya, and Doña Anita weeping for their children;
> They refused to be consoled, because they are no more.

Black Perspective Translation

At the rise of White-Orange Emperor, the one who said about a protester, "In the old days, he'd be carried out on a stretcher,"[4] like it was done by white people to black people during the Civil War, after Kwanzaa Jesus was born in a black hood in Chicago, some black folks came from the South asking, "Where is the black baby Jesus? Where is the child who will drop out of school when he grows up and will, most likely, be placed in jail when he is a young adult? For we heard the rappin' going on and we came to pay him homage." When the White Emperor heard this, he was frightened, and half

4. See Genova, "In the Old Days."

of the United States with him; and calling together all of the white pastors, priests, and Rabbis he could gather, some blacks too, along with the judges and rulers of the country, intellectuals and theologians from the left and the right, all the private business people and all of the armed forces, he enquired of them where Jesus was born. And they told the Emperor: In the small town of Selma, for so it has been written by the prophet:

> And you, Selma, land of those who began the fight for freedom,
>
> are by no means least among the black hoods in the US;
>
> for from you shall come a black King
>
> who is to transform, bless and challenge the people of the United States.

Then the White Emperor called the black folks and asked exactly where and when they saw the boy, "Go and search diligently for the child; and when you have found him, bring me word so that I may also go and bring him some tea and skittles." When they had heard the Emperor, they set out; and there, ahead of them, went people rappin', "We are gonna be alright," a song they had heard at its beginning, until the beat stopped and they knew the place where the child was.

When they heard that the sound had stopped, they were overwhelmed with joy. There were African American songs, freedom songs, blues, jazz, gospel, R&B, Motown, hip-hop, and rap as well. On entering the house, they saw the child with Mary his mother; and they knelt down and paid him homage. Then, opening their treasure chests, they offered him gifts of a basketball, a sports jersey, fried chicken, mashed potatoes, and sweet tea. And having been warned in a dream not to return to the White Emperor, they left for their own country by another road.

Now after they had left, just like magic realism, an angel of the Lord appeared to Joseph in a dream and said, "Get up, take the child and his mother, and follow the wet trails, listen for people under the bushes and flee your own land, for you are a slave in your own land! Get a train to the North, and remain there working in whatever you can find until I tell you. Be careful because your son could drop out of school very soon and be put in jail quickly because there is a war against kids who have the skin color of your boy; and the Emperor is about to search for the child, to put him in jail." Then Joseph got up, took the child and his mother by night, and went to the North, and remained there until the White Emperor was impeached or run out of power. This was to fulfill what had been spoken by the Lord through the prophet: "Out of those people you despise, whom you have tried to kill for more than two hundred years, I have called my black son."

When the Emperor saw that he had been tricked by the black folks, he was infuriated, for he thought they had nothing to lose in supporting him, and he continued the policies and the laws that kept police killing people on the streets, destroying families by putting men and women in jail for minor drug offenses, destroying all the social structures for health care that assisted black people, and went on dismantling all of the social fabric that was in place for the poor. This was to fulfill what had been spoken through the prophet Jeremiah:

> A voice was heard in Harlem and in the west side of Chicago,
> wailing and loud lamentation,
> "Do I really want to be integrated into a burning house?"
> So many black mothers weeping for their children;
> they refused to be consoled, because they are no more.

Advent: The Fullness of Time

Advent begins with the anticipation of Jesus's coming. This anticipation is like waiting for the arrival of the Spirit to put our bones back together. Every time our lives are like the Valley of Dry Bones we read of in Ezekiel 37:1–14, the anticipation of the coming of Jesus to us is the awakening of all that was dead inside of us! Individuals and communities turned into dry bones due to the evil actions of humankind, people abused, exploited, beaten up, abused, ripped apart to their bones, they are the ones who are to receive the angel of God speaking water into their dry lives, anticipating the changes that are about to happen.

People of faith don't give up! We have a memory of the past and of the future that builds our identities as fighters of the present! We have a commitment to what has happened both in the past and in the future since we are building a present that will unfold a better life for the future. Christians have been to the past with the people of God and we also have been to the future with the cloud of witnesses and Jesus Christ who received them at his table. Thus, work today in anticipation of the *Parousia*, the coming of Jesus, the new earth and new heaven!

Christians must be good historians to interpret the past not as a dead event but as a living mode of being that can be fully engaged in our present so as to transform it in many ways. Walter Benjamin helps us look at history:

> To articulate the past historically does not mean to recognize
> it "the way it really was" (Ranke). It means to seize hold of a
> memory that flashes up at a moment of danger. . . . In every era

the attempt must be made anew to wrest tradition away from a
conformism that is about to empower it. The Messiah comes not
only as the redeemer; he comes as the subduer of Antichrist.[5]

Surely the Messiah that Jewish thinker Benjamin is talking about is not Jesus. However, from a Christian standpoint, this rings true as Jesus Christ
does come as the subduer of the Antichrist!

The memory of Jesus is filled with a potency that can seize the moment and hold it in danger as it can transform the situation we live in. No
conformism can take place at the heart of a Christian who is always waiting
for Christ to come! The Christian believer is by his/her "nature," a restless
soul, a revolutionary, the one who cannot stay put, be tamed or told that
the circumstances are what they are and cannot be transformed. Even if the
"enemy has not ceased to be victorious,"[6] the Christian believer continues to
believe and work towards a transformed present that comes from the future,
from God's realm of love and grace.

Theologian Johann Baptist Metz helps us articulate our sense of historical faith and our political spirituality. Moreover, Metz helps us go beyond the privatization of our spirituality and the domestication of our faith.
Influenced by Benjamin, Metz develops his sense of dangerous memory.
In his book *Faith in History and Society: Toward a Fundamental Practical
Theology*, Metz focuses on the passion of Christ as central to the living of
our faith. It is the "dangerous memory" of Jesus's death and resurrection that
can keep us alive in the struggle, having the memory of the past to burst into
the present with forces of transformation and into a future that has already
been transformed in God. He said,

> Christianity does not introduce God subsequently as a kind of
> stopgap into this conflict about the future; instead, it tries to
> keep alive the memory of the crucified Lord, this specific *me-
> moria passionis*, as a dangerous memory of freedom in the social
> systems of our technological civilization.[7]

Metz is not saying that it is necessary to suffer in order to raise us up
to freedom. However, it is through the memory of those who suffered, those
who have lived under the shackles of slavery and economic deprivation,
that we can learn about the dangerous memory of Christ. Because Christ's
memory is a living event that shows how an apparent defeated situation and

---

5. Benjamin, "Theses on the Philosophy of History," 257.

6. Benjamin, "Theses on the Philosophy of History," 257.

7. Metz, *Faith in History and Society,* 89.

the killing of Jesus can become a force of transformation and resurrection. It is this memory that forms the identity of the Christian.

The identity of the Christian is Christ himself, God with us, the one who carries the particularity, incommensurability, and the universalizing aspects of the irreducible forms of our very vast ways of being human. It is the ability to keep our memories wrestling with the negative in history, with the loss and tragedy of our past, with the painful killing of Jesus and our own people that we gain the ability to forge a new present and a new future! Jesus's memory is always dangerous because it points to the moment of rupture, of transformation, of the possible revolution! Our ability to become somebody else, to rise to the circumstances, to face the day, to create forms of resistance, and to hope against hope come from those who have been molded by the dangerous memory of Jesus Christ.

If we look at the massacre of the indigenous people or black people brought as slaves to this country, their memories were bombarded with whitewashed cognition: religion, symbols, songs, food, behavior, reversed self-esteem, uprootedness from their territories, detachment from historical memorial landmarks, destabilizing forms of living, and so on—all deliberate tactics to erase any possible "dangerous memory" that would make these people go to their sources of strength and hope. Nonetheless, the survival of these people tells us about the resilience of the dangerous memories and collective wisdom in order to continue to exist.

On the other hand, the people who have always denied the wounds of history, the shaming facts that create nation-states, they tend to deny their present as well. Since they cannot feel they can't find a good and secure way of living, they keep looking for a memory of certain good old days that often never existed or existed only in their own fake memories. Often the good old days are grounded in misconceptions of historical fallacies, a trail of illusions that tends to recoil at forms of conviviality that were made only for a certain group that lived forever happy.

However, it is this people—with their eternal return to their own selfishness, and the denial of history's disturbing facts—who will be tremendously susceptible to a narrow view of history, have little resilience, and lack compassion. They will easily fall into the traps of populist and fascist politicians who will prey on their hopes with easy promises that go unfulfilled. These people will be easily manipulated by anyone who is willing to use politics for personal purposes regardless of any ethics of the common good. These people will turn belief and God into something to be negotiated like goods in the marketplace where private tastes, fear of social decline and personal demands will create a combustive form of religion exploiting many and saving few.

Beyond that self-evolving realm of fear and delusions, we are to face our time with strength and hope! For we do have a "dangerous memory" of a Jesus that can subdue the Antichrist of our time! We are called into that memory, living dangerously!

However, the connection to the past also mirrors a connection to the future. If the dangerous memory of the past can help us interpret our present, the memory of the future can also be a tool to empower us and expand the potentialities of our resistance. Metz connects our past and our future theologically. The longing for the coming of Jesus is fundamental to our ways of living now. He says,

> Following Christ when understood radically, that is when grasped at the roots, is not livable "if the time be not shortened" or, to put it another way, "if the Lord does not come soon." Without the expectation of the speedy coming of the Lord, following Christ cannot be lived: and without the hope of a shortening of the time it cannot be endured. Following Christ and looking forward to the second coming belong together like the two sides of a coin. His call to follow him and our plea, "Come Lord Jesus," are inseparable. The Testament of the early church, which committed itself to the demands of the radical following of Christ, has a purpose in ending with the plea, "*Maranatha*, come, Lord Jesus."[8]

Theologian Bruce T. Morrill, from whom I learned most about Metz's theology, reminds us that Metz later translates "*Maranatha*, come, Lord Jesus" into "What is God waiting for?"[9]

The coming of God entails a vision of the future. Our future will be what our future will have told us, what we were able to work for, to dream and to imagine. The future as well as the past are fundamental parts to the reimagining of our present and to the conditions of transformation of our lives today. We will be able to believe if we are able to see and to hear both the past and the present. Opening ourselves to a certain future in God that is telling us of a life together in expansive ways in Jesus Christ, and a past also lived in God by the dangerous memory of Jesus Christ, we can become able, by the grace and power of God, to see our days not in desperation or frustration but rather as a present that can be transformed right now, by the memory of those ancient days, both present and future. Thus, empowered by a plurality of "presents" lived by many communities, with their eyes looking back and to the future, we can rearrange together our present!

8. Metz, *Faith in History and Society*, 75.

9. Metz, *A Passion for God*, 58, quoted in Morrill, *Anamnesis as Dangerous Memory*.

Advent, then, is the necessary use of history as a living tool to discern our present. If we hold on to the dangerous memory of Jesus, we can have a pulsing sense of the past, a faithful witness to the mighty things God has done in history before us, that can trouble the waters of our present and reshape our lives, bringing life to our valleys of dry bones.

Conclusion

The "Celebration for a People's Church," by the New York Young Lords, done in 1970, can help us see Advent today![10] The God who comes as a child becomes bread in the Eucharist. In this process a whole world is organized. The church moves away from its true meaning but people bring the meaning back. Now, the church of the baby Jesus is the church that lives on the streets, in the midst of occupied territory! The fullness of time only occurs when "The liberated zone is [lived] here."

> God is not dead.
> God is bread.
> The bread is rising!
> Bread means revolution.
> Organize for a new world.
> Make the church a people's church.
> Wash off your brother's blood.
> The streets belong to the people.
> And the church belongs to the streets.
> In the midst of occupied territory,
> The liberated zone is here.

10. Quoted in Wilson, *The First Spanish Methodist Church and the Young Lords,* 15.

5

At Pentecost

Introductory Note

The season of Pentecost is developed here through some liturgical lenses taken from a local imaginary congregation that is celebrating Pentecost Sunday. This congregation combines the influences of various traditions and tries to avoid the differentiation between traditional, contemporary, emergent, multicultural, and Pentecostal worship services.

Before We Go into the Sanctuary

At Pentecost I arrive early to church. I am way too excited to miss any part of it. We are going to celebrate the movement of God through the Holy Spirit as we celebrate once again the beginning of the church of Jesus Christ that has become my home, my family, my country, the place I belong. I will remember my ancestors and those who came before me and who prepared the way for my salvation and new life. How can I afford to miss that? I arrive early because I am afraid to miss the joyful singing of the choir outside of the building calling me to celebrate the coming of the Holy Spirit, the pouring of God's glory upon us all and the whole world.

On Pentecost, the whole building and my brothers and my sisters are dressed up in intense reds, and the sanctuary has huge pieces of colored cloth hanging from the ceiling. At the door, people are wearing masks celebrating the craziness of Pentecost, the foolishness of this gospel. As we arrive we are already singing from the top of our lungs, as if our tongues were on fire, excited about the manifestations of God's glory, witnessing to each other the miracles of God in our midst and around the world. Our bodies get in motion and we start dancing in joy to the Holy One!

> Gloria in Excelsis Deo, Gloria, Gloria, Alleluia, Alleluia
>
> Halle-, Halle-, Halle-lujah, Halle-, Halle-, Halle-lujah, Halle-, Halle-, Halle-lujah,
>
> Alleluia, Alleluia

Glorias and alleluias are sung outside with drums and tambourines and congas and from inside, guitars and the piano are continuing the melody. Our hands and hearts are lifted up to the skies giving God all the glory. We already know we must thank God for God's coming to our world through Jesus Christ and the sending of the Holy Spirit to empower us and transform the world.

At Pentecost there is always this (non)sense of wondering why, like the disciples then, we get this "drunk" at 10 o'clock in the morning. Fear and trembling is everywhere, for the Spirit is already hovering around us. We never know what the Holy Spirit is about to do once again and we hold this excitement and trembling expectation at the same time deep in our hearts and at the shivering of our skins.

We come into the sanctuary led by a group of dancers who are weaving long pieces of cloth in red, yellow, and orange, creating flames throughout the sanctuary and keeping us on fire. The pieces of cloth in the ceiling are moving as well!

The dancers continue to dance throughout the sanctuary and the choir continues singing with us as we move to our seats. The music starts to fade and somebody takes the microphone and says something like a Call to Worship.

Call to Worship

Somebody says, "Brothers and sisters tell me that the Spirit has never done anything in your life? Tell me that God has been silent throughout your life and has never spoken to you? Tell me you don't believe that God is about to do something new to us and to our world?"

And we all respond in different ways for there is no bulletin. "Alleluia," "thank you Jesus," and "God is good," are heard everywhere.

Somebody says, "Sisters and brothers, we have seen God doing wondrous things in our lives. Even the fact that we could be here today is a miracle! God has spoken to us in loud and soft voices through people and things throughout history."

We all respond in various ways; here are some of the responses:

One says, "God has made me live up to this day and I am thankful to God almighty!"

Another says, "I have come this far because the Holy Spirit has given me faith to believe and continue on."

One says, "The Holy Spirit discovered me when I was almost gone. He took me from a pile of dirt and made me shine. As Psalm 113:7 says, 'God raises the poor from the dust, and lifts the needy from the ash heap, to make them sit with princes, with the princes of his people.'"

Another says, "My son was a prisoner to drugs and God gave him a new beginning."

One says, "I ain't telling anybody what the Holy Spirit did to me but I assure you this: the Spirit operated powerful miracles in my life."

Another says, "What can I say of God's wondrous presence in my life? I was nobody and God made me somebody!"

One says, "I didn't exist until I got here! Now I am found!"

Another says, "I felt completely invisible to society but the church shed the light of God on me!"

One says, "Our community has seen the dwindling of state resources, resources that are ours but never come here, but instead go to the rich neighborhoods. And yet, we are hanging on by a thread through the power of the Holy Spirit."

Another says, "I don't know how but God is making a way out of no way. Glory be to God!"

Then somebody says, "We must remember our ancestors, those who came before us! Those who prepared the way for us, those who were persecuted, those who lived under the sharp edge of the sword, those who offered their lives for a different way of living the gospel, those who were deeply affected by the Christian message and were transformed by the power of the Spirit and opened new paths in Jesus Christ: from the Apostle Paul to Saint Francis to Mother Teresa; from the disciples on the Emmaus road to the Waldensians; from the Ethiopian eunuch to Lydia and to Óscar Romero; from Mary and Mary Magdalene to Julian of Norwich and Dorothee Soelle; from Martha and Mary to Priscilla to Rosa Parks, to las Madres de Plaza de Mayo and las Comadres de El Salvador to Rigoberta Menchú; from Martin Luther King Jr. to Black Lives Matter! Let us now name those who have come before you who were moved by the Spirit to prepare the way of God for you."

We all mention name after name, and a crowd of witnesses fills the sanctuary and our hearts.

Somebody says, "And God is about to do something new in our lives and in the world once again! Behold, God is about to do a new thing!"

We all respond with alleluias and "Glory be to God."

We Sing: "Hush, Somebody's Calling My Name"

The choir keeps singing, "Hush, Somebody's calling my name" and we can't sit down. Slowly, the song ends and a rush of bodies singing and moving are calmed down and we sit in the hush of silence.

We Confess

Somebody starts to pray, saying, "God of love and kindness, have mercy on us . . . for we forget that you live in us through your Spirit.

"Have mercy on us for we don't expect the moving of your Spirit in us.

"Have mercy on us for we even fear that you will change things in our midst and turn us to other directions.

"Have mercy on us for we have forgotten that we are witnesses of this power and that we have a responsibility to each other, to the church of Christ, and to the entire world.

"Have mercy on us for we have abandoned your creation.

"Have mercy on us for we are destroying your creation with our uncontrollable desire to have more things than we need.

"Have mercy on us because our waters are polluted, our desire for stuff is incontrollable, and we think that there are no limits to whatever we want.

"Have mercy on us for we have confused unlimited capitalism with your unconditional grace.

"Have mercy on us because we have forgotten to live a communal life and have trusted more in our own wisdom and our own spirit than in the wisdom and in the Spirit of God that lives in our brothers and sisters.

"Have mercy on us for we don't see your face in the face of the poor.

"Have mercy on us for we don't have sustainable sources to help us deal with our daily needs: we have no hospitals, have no clinics for those with mental illness, we have no care for battered women, we have no care for pregnant teenagers, and we have no money to send our kids to college.

"Have mercy on us for our confession of lack is the confession of the abundance of few and there lies our evil forms of sin against you! Against ourselves!

"Have mercy on us for trusting more in the invisible hand of capitalism than in your visible providence through the hands of our brothers and sisters.

"Have mercy on us, O God."

And we respond singing the Guarani Kyrie:

> Ore poriaju vereko nandejara
>
> Ore poriaju vereko Jesucristo

We Are Assured of God's Forgiveness

The dancers come from all places and pour water in the baptismal font while we sing.

We Receive a Visit

We sit down and on a big screen a group of children from a church in Rwanda are waiting to sing to us live via Skype. They say, "Hi," and introduce themselves to us and say, "The Spirit of God be with you all!" We respond, "And also with you." Then they sing "Vuma Vuma: Believe in the Lord and you will be saved."[1] They tell us stories of eating, dancing, living, and going to school. It is our turn to sing back to them. We don't know exactly what to sing until somebody starts, "Jesus loves you, Yes, Jesus loves you . . . the Bible tells me so." We say goodbye to them, "May the Spirit of Pentecost keep you and strengthen you and empower you." Somebody stands in front of the camera and shouts to them, "We are here with you! We are here with you!" We don't know how this is possible but the fear of being forgotten makes us all feel desperate to hold on to ties with those we don't know well. Someone shouts, "We must know them better! They are precious to us!"

We Confess Once Again

A sister then stands up and says, "Sisters and brothers I feel we need to keep on confessing our sins. Let us pray please!" She kneels and starts praying, "God of mercy, we confess that we keep mostly with people like ourselves and have not welcomed the stranger into our midst. We confess we have forgotten our brothers and sisters around the world. We confess that we have not allowed into our sanctuary the immigrant community who worships

---

1. http://www.youtube.com/watch?v=93pec2585xQ.

God in this building on Sunday afternoons. We confess that we have locked the nursery room and put away the toy boxes so that their children will not mess up our spaces and our things. We can't quite figure out how we can still be loved by you, O God, but today, moved by your Holy Spirit, we can see our sins and turn back to you. On this Pentecost day, make us a new church! Fall afresh on us and make us a new church . . ."

As she prays the choir starts singing, "Spirit of the living God fall afresh on us . . ."

After the prayer she says, "Let us all talk to our elders and the pastor and let us invite this community to worship with us using both languages. Let them use this place as their own." And everybody says, "Amen!"

We Sing

The choir starts singing "The Summons," by John Bell, and we join in:

> Will you come and follow me if I but call your name?
> Will you go where you don't know and never be the same?
> Will you let my love be shown? Will you let my name be known?
> will you let my life be grown in you and you in me?

> Will you leave yourself behind if I but call your name?
> Will you care for cruel and kind and never be the same?
> Will you risk the hostile stare should your life attract or scare?
> Will you let me answer prayer in you and you in me?

> Will you let the blinded see if I but call your name?
> Will you set the prisoners free and never be the same?
> Will you kiss the leper clean and do such as this unseen,
> and admit to what I mean in you and you in me?

> Will you love the "you" you hide if I but call your name?
> Will you quell the fear inside and never be the same?
> Will you use the faith you've found to reshape the world around,
> through my sight and touch and sound in you and you in me?

> Lord your summons echoes true when you but call my name.
> Let me turn and follow you and never be the same.
> In Your company I'll go where Your love and footsteps show.
> Thus I'll move and live and grow in you and you in me.

We Pass the Peace of Christ

The music continues and we are ready to pass the peace of Christ to one another. Painters start painting a huge canvas on the chancel brushing colorful tones in circles, a whirlwind of movements. Dancing people surround the congregation with red scarves. As we receive the scarf with a holy kiss we hear the words, "The Spirit of God is in and around and through us dear brother. The Spirit of God is in and around and through us dear sister."

We Read the Scriptures

The choir stops singing and there is silence. The sound of wind can be heard everywhere in the sanctuary. A Bible enters the sanctuary carried by a child and goes to the middle of the central aisle. The Pentecost story in Acts 2:1–21 is read. In the midst of the reading, drums, clashing cymbals, and trumpets embody the readings as sounds and words fill the sanctuary. The reading ends:

> The word of God for the people of God.
> Thanks be to God.

The Sermon

The pastor starts her sermon by saying that Jesus has promised us the Kingdom of God and all we could do was build a church. People laugh. She continues, "However, Pentecost was not only the beginning of the church. Pentecost, or *Shavuot*, was a festival among the Jews also called the Feast of Weeks, the Latter First Fruits or Feast of Harvest. It was celebrated fifty days after Passover and was a joyful time of thanksgiving for the harvesting of the fruits of the earth. At Pentecost our hearts should be on high for the gift of *Patchamama*,[2] for the bountiful and gracious offerings of the fruits and all the food and everything we have that the earth continuously offers to us all. Thus, Pentecost is a mix of thanksgiving, of celebration of the fruits of the earth and the coming of the Holy Spirit and the beginning of the church. It is when those who don't count start to become important. That being said, we can now talk about the coming of the Holy Spirit.

At Pentecost people heard tongues of fire and were transformed. Three thousand people on that day. What the Spirit says turns people and things

---

2. That is what Native American people in Central and Latin America call the earth.

around. What we hear from God makes us who we are, and the hearing of God continuously makes us who we are constantly becoming. Thus, our autobiography relies heavily on our *otobiography*[3] and the words of others as well as the word of God! Tongues of fire continue to shape who we are to God and to our neighbors. What I mean by otobiography here is the hearing that defines our lives and shapes our biographies. The languages you hear, the stories you ponder, the testimonies you listen to carefully, the theologies you wonder about, all of these things heard effect your biography. For your biography is a result of many tongues in your ear. . . . Whose tongues of fire are you listening to?

At Pentecost, we remember that which cannot be remembered. At Pentecost we witness that which cannot be witnessed properly. We witness something beyond ourselves but fully part of ourselves! Fully divine, fully human! Beyond us, intimately ours! How can we keep from singing this absence, this full presence, in our lives?

At Pentecost we receive a revelation that transforms us in such a way that there is no going back, ever. We are visited by that which we cannot name, but we can't stop saying its name!

Pentecost prepares a time to go after the Holy Spirit in both grammatical ways: I mean, going after as searching for the Spirit to come, and also going afterwards, figuring out how the Holy Spirit has touched us.

Pentecost loosens up our theologies, for it is a time to wrestle once again with that which has no boundaries or contours, that which we can never nail down. Pentecost helps us realize that the Holy Spirit breaks down our arguments, undoes our finest theological assumptions, messes with our statements of faith and plays tricks on our serious disputes. The Spirit is free and comes and goes and moves and changes and appears whenever and wherever the Spirit wants. However, we can and must try to figure it out and work very hard to make our assertions and hopes and guesses in the best way possible, among people and communities in order to understand a little of how the Holy Spirit works in our midst.

The Holy Spirit is the wind who came down to the disciples and they were taken over by this force, by this presence that turned them around and made them go and tell the good news of Jesus Christ in other languages. I remember I was in a meeting with a Pentecostal group when I was a teenager and I was desperate to receive the gift of tongues. To my immense frustration, nothing happened to me. However, a friend of mine from another Presbyterian church was in the same meeting praying for the Holy Spirit to come, and all of sudden she stood up in the midst of us all and started

---

3. Derrida, *The Ear of the Other.*

to speak in Italian, a language she had never used or learned before: "Dio quanto ti amo, come io ti adoro, ogni onore e gloria a te, oggi e sempre" ("God, how much I love you, how much I adore you, honor and glory be given to you today and forever"). I was stunned by it and couldn't make any sense of it.

Nicson, "Felicidad (Happiness)"

Nicson is fifteen years old and traveled from Guatemala. In this picture he drew his home, family, and pet, "Hueso," with great care and a pondering disposition.

The Holy Spirit sets the imprisoned free. When I was a teenager, I used to see the Holy Spirit moving in various ways. Healing, transforming, and liberating people from their shackles, spiritual and social ones alike. I remember one day a woman came to my mother's house. She was going through a tough time and when I was praying for her a deep, scary voice came out of her mouth. "Don't touch me, let me go," this voice said. At the same time her body was thrown towards the wall and her face contorted. I was very scared but somehow could muster the strength to hold her arms and say, "In Jesus's name, the Holy Spirit will set you free, in Jesus's name, the Holy Spirit will set you free." In a few minutes her body was violently shaken and she was able to hear me and my mother again. We prayed for, her and she left our home in peace. I know this is a very strange story for many of you but what I can say is that since that day, I live in wonder and awe.

A community of people got together and started a movement to re-claim unused land for poor people in Brazil and to bring about agrarian reform. Every time they were able to gain a piece of land they first knelt down and prayed the Lord's Prayer and thanked God for the new life that was about to begin! The Holy Spirit moves in wonderful and strange ways, brothers and sisters!

At Pentecost we learn that there is no distinction between body, rea-son, and Spirit. Leonardo Boff once said, "The realization of one's life is not the work of reason that goes from here to there but of the gathering of the Spirit who harvests the richness of each situation. Spirit is not something at the side of the body or the highest form of reason. Spirit is the mode of our being which searches for the meaning of each thing. . . . It is the ability to be full in everything we do. This is the Spirit. Spirituality thus is to be able to live like this, God in each thing. Spirit is not science or technique but a way of living."[4] How is the Spirit shaping your way of living?

When I think about Pentecost, I think about *fire, ashes, and desires.*

Fire. Who set the fire of the Holy Spirit on that day? What kind of fire was that? Was this fire extinguished at a certain point? Is the fire still burn-ing today? Is there something related to the burning bush today?

Ashes. If there was a fire, were there ashes from that fire? If so, where were the ashes of the fire of the Holy Spirit on that day? Where did they go? But if we have ashes, does it mean that what was alive has died? Aren't ashes the sign of that which was alive and is now dead? If the fire is still burning and we celebrate it at Pentecost, where are the ashes? How do we connect the fire of Pentecost with the ashes of Ash Wednesday?

Desires. I am set on fire at Pentecost and I wonder what my desires are at Pentecost? What are the desires that come to my heart, mind, and body when Pentecost approaches? How do I feel Pentecost in my skin? How does my skin, burning with these desires, help me identify myself, my neighbor, and my God?

The Spirit lives between orality and writing, between my ears and the *otobiography* of the people of God, between the testimonies and archives of our communities, forming a constantly evolving multiaxial ethnography of our identities. The Spirit makes me African, Asian, Hispanic, Latino, Indig-enous, Middle Eastern, and so on. By the power of the Spirit, my identity is in between my brother, my sister, myself, and God!

The Spirit does not work much through the individual alone as we of-ten see in the United States, but rather through communitarian movements. José Comblin says that God delivers people "by means of communion and

4. Boff, *Seleção de textos espirituais*, 27.

solidarity of living communities and by means of the enthusiasm of multitudes that these communities and prophets succeed in arousing."[5] Communities go from passivity to consciousness, of becoming aware of their role
in history, of the exploration of their lives and land and fight for freedom
and justice. In this process, the Spirit empowers people by the mutuality
and presence and cooperation of neighbors, brothers, and sisters. The Spirit
works in and through communities! The charisma given by the Spirit is
indeed on individuals and on communities. However, the charisma of the
individual only has power if offered, lived, and worked in and through a
community.

Then the pastor comes down from the pulpit and asks, "What happens
at Pentecost for you?" And walking around the church she waits for people
to respond. She asks again, "What happens at Pentecost for you?" Then, one
by one, people start to make their connections to this precious day:

"I wonder if we've made Pentecost a day only in our liturgical calendar
rather than a season so that we don't need to deal with this burning power
of the Spirit in our lives for a long time. We celebrate it in one day so that we
can go on into the ordinary/regular time of our faith/life."[6]

"At Pentecost, I get afraid sometimes because there is loss and there
is hope, there is desire and there is the desperation for the coming of the
Spirit. However, the coming of the Spirit will disarrange my life completely.
I know that much!"

"At Pentecost, I am also afraid because the Spirit in worship will make
me see that what I am in relation to my brothers and sisters has to do with
my money and what I do with it. I am responsible for them as they are for
me."

"I am afraid at Pentecost, because the Spirit will make me pray without
ceasing, will make me say 'Gloria' and 'Alleluia' a thousand times, will make
me stay with people that I do not necessarily like for a little longer, will make
me forgive and offer second chances."

"At Pentecost I will hear again that without strangers around me, without offering a place and hospitality to foreigners, I will have no way to find
myself, much less God."

"At Pentecost, the Spirit makes us drunk with love, and we can't stop
our prayer of thanksgiving. Nobody understands us and people are eager
to see us get back to a 'proper way' of believing. There is some stupidity in
following this Spirit, in listening to its strange voice. There is also a certain
brokenness that is part of being taken by the Spirit, a broken body, a broken

---

5. Comblin, "Holy Spirit," 146–47.

6. This idea comes from a conversation with the Reverend Ann Deibert.

Spirit in us hoping to be mended, blessed, redone, revived, resurrected. Living with the Spirit of God is like wrestling with the Angel of God in the Jabbok Valley. We cannot lose the angel from our sight and we will go all the way in our battle to receive God's blessings. This holy battle entails a mark of God in our bodies and we may end up limping. However, we can know this much: we'd rather limp because of God's touch on us than walk straight without God's presence. Pentecost is to be marked by God forever."

"Pentecost is the time when we remember that to know God now is to know God forever."

"At Pentecost I lose all of my words and have to learn how to pray all over again."

"Pentecost is about talking about Jesus and all the time asking people, 'Have you heard of this Jesus Christ? I don't know what happened to me but I know I was transformed by this Jesus Christ and I must follow him now. Do you want to join me?'"

"Pentecost reminds us that church is the people of God and not endowments or market profits. As a matter of fact, Pentecost is about never having any savings or money in the market or in any bank account until all people are able to eat at least three meals a day."

"Pentecost is about equality of pastors' salaries: from those who deal with presidents of countries to those who 'only' baptize children in a far-away community. Ministry is about a call and not about a salary package! Every pastor should be cared for with decency and honor! *Everyone!*"

"Pentecost is about nobody receiving more than anybody else!"

"Pentecost is about a light shed on the shadows of society, illuminating those societies placed in invisible places!"

"Pentecost is about the healing of ourselves, the healing of our queer families, the healing of our communities, and the healing of the nations."

"Pentecost is about caring for God's creation."

"Pentecost is more; it is about restoring honor and respect to the earth and putting limits on ourselves!"

After the people have spoken, the pastor then says, "Pentecost is about remembering the least of these and all of the communities that are being destroyed by national and international capitalist companies. Pentecost is about God's deep care for the least of these, for subjugated and exploited people. Pentecost is about seeing life coming out of those we don't consider. Pentecost is about people gaining strength to not only survive but stand in the midst of all of the agents of death. Indigenous people, gypsies, non-documented and forgotten communities, and all of the poor communities kept excluded. At Pentecost, we renew our trust that all of them will gain new strength when the Spirit is poured out over them. Monseñor Leonidas

Proaño exemplifies this when he talks about the native people: 'We native people started to open our eyes and see, we started to loosen up and articulate our tongues, we started to recuperate our word, we started to speak with courage, we started to put ourselves on our feet, we started to walk, we started to organize ourselves, and start actions that could be transformed into actions of transcendental importance to us.'"[7]

And the people continue to respond:

"Pentecost is about learning new songs and new prayers and new liturgical practices."

"Pentecost is about being able to go beyond our one-hour worship services. As a matter of fact, Pentecost is about not being slaves of time."

"Pentecost is about eating the Eucharist every single day and consequently every Sunday!"

"Pentecost is about washing our mouths in the morning before we say the name of God. Pentecost is about washing our faces in the morning and thanking God for the miracle of life."

"Pentecost is about never ever taking this life for granted."

"Pentecost is about asking for God's mercies endlessly. *Kyrie eleison* every day!"

"Pentecost is about always looking after the poor."

The pastor says again, "Yes! Pentecost is about praying and fighting for a new world. Leonardo Boff says, 'The Holy Spirit was poured over everybody. The Spirit lives in the hearts of people, giving them enthusiasm, courage and determination. The Spirit consoles the afflicted, keeps utopias alive in human minds and in the social imagination, a utopia of a humanity completely redeemed, and gives strength to anticipate them using revolutions within history.'"[8]

An older woman responds, "Pentecost teaches us to end the day asking not, 'How did I do today?' but rather 'How did I bless somebody today?' or 'To whom was I a blessing today?'"

And her husband responds, "Pentecost teaches us to end our worship services not asking, 'Was I blessed today?' but rather 'Were any of my brothers and sisters blessed today?'"

And the people continue to respond:

"Pentecost is about living with our 'enemies,' even when they want to build a temple for their God near us."

"Pentecost is about bending our back and becoming humble."

"Pentecost is about weakness and not power."

---

7. As quoted in Hernandez, "Deus, tradições indígenas and globalization," 305.

8. Boff, *Seleção de textos espirituais*, 29.

"Pentecost is about fire, a burning fire."

"Pentecost is giving and accepting forgiveness."

"Pentecost is about believing that God is finding a way out of no way in our lives."

"Pentecost is a time when God makes nobody into somebody."

"Pentecost is about a father asking a son, 'How can we mend this relationship?' Or a mother who sees her son going to war and who, even though she does not support the war, prays ceaselessly for his well-being."

"Pentecost is about two lovers finding a way to love each other."

"Pentecost is not necessarily what we expect, what we believe, what we hope, and definitely not what we can do, but what it is that God can do in and through us."

"Pentecost is about shouting, 'The racist incarceration system that destroys our communities will go down!'"

"Pentecost is about shouting, 'We ain't gonna be evicted from our homes! All of us have the right to shelter!'"

There is silence in the congregation.

The pastor then walks toward the Eucharistic table and we are all pondering these powerful connections, not agreeing with everything that was said but wondering about what this powerful feast of Pentecost means in our lives today. We all feel we are ready to partake in the feast of Jesus Christ!

We Respond with a Global Prayer

Brothers and sisters from different nationalities affirm the presence of the Holy Spirit throughout the world in their own languages. A cacophony of voices and languages fills the air and stretches our minds to think about Mexico, Palestine, India, Pakistan, Bolivia, Mozambique, Nigeria, Honduras, and Mexico and back to our very neighborhoods where people from all over the world live.

We Pray the Prayer of Thanksgiving

It is at Pentecost, around the baptismal font and this global Eucharistic table, that we gain perspective on how God has manifested God's glory and love deeply in the world's history and in our own history promising time after time that life is stronger than death. This is the table of God for the entire world. Here at this table, we always celebrate Pentecost. Every Sunday! For at this table we always have present the Holy Spirit, the presence of the earth in its food, and the thanksgiving of our hearts.

One says, "God be with you."
Many say, "And also with you."
One says, "Lift up your hearts."
Many say, "We lift them up to God."
One says, "Let us give thanks to God our Creator."
Many say, "It is right to give God thanks and praise."

Let us now gather around the table and say how this table has shaped the way we understand the work and the movement of the Holy Spirit in each one of us, in our families, in churches, and around the world. Let us try to connect what we said during the collective sermon and these three things: earth, thanksgiving, and the Holy Spirit.

We all talk in small groups, and the mixture of voices and laughter takes over the sanctuary. After a while the pastor gathers us back together again and says, "Sisters and brothers, it is the Holy Spirit who helps us proclaim our faith and hope."

Christ has died, Christ is risen, Christ will come again.

We are then invited to pray for each other and for the world.

One says, "Friends, when we pray for each other we reassure each other that we are not alone, that God lives with us through the Spirit and we are God's presence to one another. Let us pray for those people and situations that are in need of an extra portion of the Holy Spirit today." We all raise our prayers and pray for each other. Then somebody starts the Lord's Prayer.

The dancers start to dance around the table and with the sound of music they dance and pray for the Holy Spirit to bless the food, and each one of us, and the world. After each phrase they repeat, "Come Holy Spirit, come and renew all your creation."

The words of institution are repeated in many languages and the bread is broken and the wine poured into the cup. There is plenty for all. And more food around the table that makes the oldest woman in the church announce, "Here nobody goes hungry!"

We are all invited:

Come, all of you, for the gifts of the Holy Spirit for you are ready.
The gifts of God for the people of God!

Dance and music resume and we start to share food over a huge table that has several breads, and wine, and juice, and fruits, humus, salsa, cheese, crackers, and cookies, and flowers, honey, and milk. There is food for all reminding us that this table is truly a feast, the feast of God, and the Spirit always provides for all when we share and give our lives to God and to others.

After the feast, we pray,

> We thank you, O God, for at this table you console us and confront our ways of living. At this table you challenge us to shift our paradigms and find new understandings and practices. At this table you teach us to turn and be turned, to move and be moved, to transform and be transformed, to lose and be lost, to find and be found. God of our lives, at this table you teach us to unlearn what keeps us away from each other and learn hard lessons of where to go to find our neighbor. At this table, you release us from our fears of sharing, and undo our feelings of the scarcity of goodness and mercy, and help us to offer instead hearts filled with generosity to our neighbors. May your Holy Spirit continue to work on us until you come back to us again. Amen.

We go to our seats and now we are challenged to give our money. We are reminded that to give is better than to receive and that to give is essential to our faith. We are reminded that by our offering the mission of the church of Jesus Christ can continue and many people in our community, as well as abroad, benefit from our offering of faith.

The choir sings "I'll Fly Away" and the dancers dance with the offering plates. After the money is collected the money is prayed over and the choir continues to sing.

We Are Sent Forth by the Power of the Spirit

As the choir hums "I'll Fly Away," the pastor sends us forth, saying, "Brothers and sisters, the Spirit is here, has always been here, will always be here! Inside us and around us and through us and all over the world. We are all filled with the Spirit to live better and fully! To care for the poor! We are empowered to forgive, to revisit our history, to critically think about our present and dream dreams for a future of peace, justice, and goodness. Go to the world and witness to the power and glory of Jesus Christ. Share what you have, care for the earth, welcome the stranger, love all those who cross your path and love your God with all your heart, mind, and body. For God is about to get us all drunk, get prepared! In the name of God who came, comes, and will come again, God the mother, father, sibling, God the creator, the redeemer, the consoler, God the earth, air, fire and wind! Amen!"

After the benediction, the choir continues to hum and a girl leads the church outside the doors carrying a white dove. As she gets to the door, she lets the dove fly and the whole church sings:

> I'll fly away, O Glory
> I'll fly away;
> When I die, Hallelujah, by and by,
> I'll fly away.

Part II: Liturgy of the Neighbor

6

Praying with Black People for Darker Times

Almost always, the creative dedicated minority has made the world better.
—MARTIN LUTHER KING JR.

It always seems impossible until it's done.
—NELSON MANDELA

Theology starts where it hurts.
—JAMES CONE

Break any of these rules sooner than say anything outright barbarous.
—GEORGE ORWELL

The thief comes only to steal and kill and destroy. I came that they may have life, and have it abundantly.
—JOHN 10:10

Introduction

In the Americas:

For more than 500 years, indigenous people have had their lands stolen, their culture appropriated, their people marginalized, oppressed, exploited, put in jail, and killed.

For almost 400 years, black people have had their origins uprooted, their culture appropriated, their people kidnapped, oppressed, pushed to the margins of society, exploited, put in jail, killed.

For more than 180 years, Mexican people have had their lands stolen, and with Latinx people, they have had their culture appropriated, their people abused, pushed to the margins of society, oppressed, exploited, put in jail, killed.

For all of its history, the stranger, the nonwhite, has been demoted, thrown away, defaced, abused, ripped apart, made a source for the building of a nation.

For all these years, there has been a whitening of the continent. The project of whitening the continent has been made possible by de-negrating,[1] blackening, making a Negro of everybody who was not white. The blackening of people was a way to clarify and organize nonwhites into a lower cast of a human kind by defacing their bodily features, sources of religion, culture, and forms of being human. Notions of white normalcy, control, order and so on, shaped through light and darkness was at the heart of this process.[2] The creation of race was thus necessary for the creation of whiteness as an uncontested form of superiority and power control. Over against blackness, Mbembe talks about the necessary appearance of whiteness. He says,

> The strength of race derives precisely from the fact that, within the racist consciousness, the appearance of things looks to be the true reality of things. In other words, the appearance is not unlike the "reality."[3]

---

1. Denigrate: "If you 'denigrate' someone, you attempt to blacken their reputation. It makes sense, therefore, that 'denigrate' can be traced back to the Latin verb *denigrare*, meaning 'to blacken.' When 'denigrate' was first used in English in the 16th century, it meant to cast aspersions on someone's character or reputation. Eventually, it developed a second sense of 'to make black' ('factory smoke denigrated the sky'), but this sense is somewhat rare in modern usage. Nowadays, of course, 'denigrate' can also refer to belittling the worth or importance of someone or something." https://www.merriam-webster.com/dictionary/denigrate.

2. Allen, *The Invention of the White Race* (2 vols.), and Heng, "The Invention of Race in the European Middle Ages I," 315–31.

3. Mbembe, *Crítica da razão negra*, 194.

Thus, the reality of things and also the appearance of reality forged racist ideas that grounded the very foundation of this nation and built a society with legislative and democratic views that wouldn't be able to distinguish whiteness from moral virtues and blackness from any sort of deviation, malfunction and misplaced origins. In other words, this historical racial process has been organized by white reasoning, that is, the whitening of sources, forms of thinking, living, praying, worshiping, believing and how to be human.

This whitening of the Americas has surely been accompanied by the stealing of the richness of this land. Europe and the US empire still live off of the riches stolen from the Americas and blackened people.[4] Since the beginning of colonization, and for all these years, powers have been in the hands of white families, while blackened/colored people have had to face all forces of death and struggle to survive. It has been the inner work of resistance and resilience, strategies and wisdom, strength and faith of all the blackened people that have kept these people and all of their wisdom and sources alive thus far.

During all these years, Christianity has also been a part of the creation of racial ideas and a fundamental part of the whitening of the American continent. The sources, contours, and content of the Christian faith have been built on white sources. This means that theology has mainly been a white project. Worship has been a white project over the bodies of people, in order to teach them to pray in white performative and content-heavy ways. Historically, white churches have learned to discern faith and life in white terms. In other words, to sense with the fullness of the body perceptions, the whole world and God through white religious glasses.

During all these years, only a few people have fought against the defacement of the indigenous, black peoples, Latinx people, as well as Asian people and all who fit the category of the stranger, who were thrown into the same exclusionary bus. Very few people prayed for people of color, with colored people, or concerning colored people and their histories!

For more than 500 years, this mighty project in the Americas also convinced us colored people that white people have always been the best thing that happened to this land. And to us! Civilization, progress, culture, manners, organization, order, sexual standards, and so on, where all forms of proper humanity are wrapped up in religious language. The civil religion was mixed with religious beliefs, conflating obedience to slave masters as obedience to God. Good and evil were established by the colors of religious ownership. The demonizing of forms of black(ened) bodies was

4. Galeano, *Open Veins of Latin America.*

fundamental to the conquest. In a play of values around what was to be considered human, what was worth honoring and what was to be condemned, there was a need for demonic[5] actions of white slave owners that created racial-social-theological constructions to turn black people (blackened bodies) into natural creations, social expressions, and cultural manifestations of the demonic. From there, the whole reasoning of racial demonizing was set. Disobedience/insubmission by blackened bodies was a sign of being taken by the devil and obedience/submission, proper (white) manners, no resistance, acceptance to God's will, and so on, were signs of those closest to God and obedient to the Bible. The formation of a white civilization came by the denial of those not white (blackened people). Its forms of colonization used liturgical sources such as prayer, hymns, orders of worship, and liturgical moral/gestural codes, all wrapped up in white religious reasoning. However, even if Africans and blackened people would embrace Christianity, the Christian faith didn't serve to give them worth or full humanity. Gayraud S. Wilmore writes,

> The British rationalized the enslavement of both Africans and Indians because they were different in appearance to themselves and because they were heathens. When it became evident that blacks were becoming believers despite widespread neglect by official church bodies, Virginia was the first of the colonies to make short shrift of the matter by declaring in 1667 that "the conferring of baptisme doth not alter the condition of the person as to his bondage of freedom."[6]

These forms of colonization, its inward and outward brutality, its ugly and kind forms of appearance, its angry faces and smiles, and its passive-aggressive moral conduct, have brought forth racist ideas that have shaped our societies, designed our common richness for only a few white people, and told us how and where we should live, how we should think, and they have molded our own feelings and established what is normal in our society. Five hundred years of education by the oppressor, pretending to speak from an apolitical, colorblind, and nonideological stance, has served to make all people, even people of color, unaware of the extent of racism in our society. Additionally, we are told we don't need to revisit the sins of the past because they no longer exist. This ongoing reminder is always quick to point out that minorities nowadays have a good living, good jobs, and some are even rich,

---

5. Throughout this chapter the use of the word *demonic* has to do with breaking and ripping apart, with destruction and death. The intent here is not to demonize any person but to name the powers and forces of destruction as evil structures of death.

6. Wilmore, "Historical Perspective," 21.

even to the point that minorities in America have their place: the United States had a black president, Brazil had a president who came from the lower class, and Bolivia an indigenous president. All of this shows that what is at stake is not the color of the skin anymore but rather the individual commitment and desire of someone to work and achieve greatness. The devil in our societies is not there any longer. He has gone fishing!

The Declaration of Independence, the US sense of exceptionalism[7] and Manifest Destiny, created a necessary mass of critical symbolic and concrete materiality that was both potent enough to establish a forceful white ideology of conquering and and expansive enough to secure its racist underpinnings. Grounded in an undeniable but also an idolatrous faith, turning into God was what not God—that is, sanctifying civic actions into God's promises—this country was chosen to be great from its very beginning and apart from everybody else. The theological and civic privilege, or better said, duty, to expand and conquer was given by God and protected by God. The moral superiority that is so prevalent today has always fed the formation of an Empire of demonic forces of destruction of blackened people. At the heart of these events, there were white people thinking, believing, acting, leading, and using power. This white dominion was guarded in demonic power that had indigenous, blacks, and Latinxs either killed or put into slavery so the conquering could be established. This power had to create laws that under the sacred cow of "democracy" allowed conquest to move on to the "wastelands" and use denigrated/blackened bodies in whatever way it was deemed necessary to build the empire. In this way, the demonic (that which breaks and rips apart, steals and kills) national and transnational business privatized what were God's land and natural resources and used the free labor of black people to promulgate the savage system of capitalism that now rules this country.[8]

This demonic power is still at work today, structuring life and our very forms of thinking and being. The ongoing killing and disenfranchising of blacks, indigenous, Latinxs, immigrants, with the control of the economic market by the white private sector, and the necessary US engagement with endless wars across the globe in order to maintain the structure of the US economy, and to protect/expand/fulfill the call to continue to be the American Empire.

7. Brown, *Stand Your Ground*.

8. Leiman, *The Political Economy of Racism*.

Same Power Structure, New Forms of Defacement

From the beginning of colonization until now, if we are to claim the gospel to witness to this process, we can call on the words of Jesus in the Gospel of John: "The thief comes only to steal and kill and destroy."[9]

The thieves that came more than 500 years ago continue to lie, steal, destroy, and kill. Our politicians lie, our economic structures continue to destroy the poor, the very few benefits the people have are taken away, and the few white owners of this country continue to get rich through their colonizing and empire-building project, while killing our people daily.

The symptoms of this ongoing demonic structure have surfaced with the killings of black people by the police across the United States. The recent awareness of the death of black people (Trayvon Martin, John Crawford III, Amadou Diallo, Manuel Loggins Jr., Ronald Madison, Kendra James, Sean Bell, Eric Garner, Michael Brown, Alton Sterling, and so many others) only exposed the pattern of the police that has existed since the beginning of slavery in America.[10] In the United Sates, "young black men were nine times more likely than other Americans to be killed by police officers in 2015."[11] These killings are fully associated with a demonic structure of living that was planned, organized, and enforced through a system that continues the whitening of the country by ways of defacing all that is not white. "The thief comes only to steal and kill and destroy."

The only reason we know about these killings is because of the power of phone cameras and social media used by common people on the streets that made these videos go viral. The historical lack of information about police reports has now surfaced, and police departments, often led by white people, had to start publicizing reports.[12] Moreover, the creation of alternative facts, the ongoing violence against black people in the media (often owned by white people), the heavy support of states that invest in jails rather than schools, the growing cuts to social support for blackened and poor white communities (often supported by white multimillionaire political representatives), and the racist policies that replaced Jim Crow[13] are all but a part of the same supporting structure of a white system of control of power and richness. Public policies are like thieves, killing systems sanctioned

9. John 10:10 NRSV.

10. In Brazil, a black person is killed every twenty-three minutes. See http://www.bbc.com/portuguese/brasil-36461295.

11. See Swaine, Laughland, Lartey, and McCarthy, "Young black men killed by US police at highest rate in year of 1,134 deaths."

12. Lowery, *They Can't Kill Us All*.

13. Alexander, *The New Jim Crow*.

by demonic laws that continue this control locally and nationally, and not many people know about it.[14] The thieves are in the highest places stealing from some and giving to others. Let me give one example: from 1934 to 1962 the US government backed 120 billion dollars of home loans that were given only to white people. The results of what is called *redlining* created a ripple effect in which white people were assisted in the acquisition of appreciating assets while black people had to continue in poverty with no help, living in "the ghetto" without state investments and consequently lacking good schools, jobs opportunities, and social expansion.

The thieves are everywhere! Along with public policies, the whole bashing of black people for being lazy, taking from the government in welfare but not paying taxes into the coffers, not wanting to work, are all lies deeply seated in people's consciousness, spread out as truth and affecting the feelings and worldviews of both white and black people, though in very different ways. The psychological effect of 500 years of colonization and the daily manifestation of racist ideas, gestures, relations, power dynamics, and so on have immense reverberations in the ways black people live their lives.

The thieves are deeply invested in the institutions of this country. Neither political party has ever fully served the minorities of this country. The best they have done was to mend parts of the system in order to keep the whole structure of exclusion running. These are just some symptoms of the larger disease of racism that plagues this country and has kept black people as second class citizens for its entire history, again, away from the wealth of the country and its social sources of sustenance.

Same Power Structure and the White Christian Churches

The thieves have stolen Christianity. They have stolen the revolutionary kernel of the Christian faith, destroyed its promises of equality and justice, and killed the central idea of God's preferential option for the poor. In a game of appearances and platitudes, the thieves and all its demons made a failed Christianity look like it was alive by performing perfunctory religious rituals.

This entire system has created in white Christian churches a strong oral performance of a gospel of unconditioned love and hospitality that in fact serves to hide the markers of racism and the exclusion of minorities and poorer classes. If we look at the structures of the white Christian churches, their theological and liturgical resources are often created by white people

---

14. Barber and Zelter, *Forward Together.*

for white people of a certain class.[15] This has immediate consequences on our prayers and how we pray. If prayer is the grammar of our faith, and the white church has never created a deep religious language to engage with black people, or indigenous people, or Latinx, or other immigrant communities, that means that the content of the Christian faith has never had a grammar where prayers could be spoken as a means to enter into solidarity with nonwhite communities. The results are that faith continues to have a totally white vocabulary that gives the scripts/scriptures of life a specific format. When dealing with nonwhite people, the response is often muted for there is no vocabulary to help address some situations. I have seen white people who are willing to engage in solidarity with black people but lacking the vocabulary to do so, and they get totally lost. This is especially true in tense or disordered situations where they are afraid of making a mistake or saying something wrong. When they can't communicate or deal with the tension of the struggle for peace, their inadequacy is often manifest in passivity or passive-aggressive modes of behavior.

The larger result in the public arena is that white churches end up supporting white Christians or white people in most political places. In the last election for President, 8 in 10 white Evangelical Protestants voted for Trump, and the majority of white Roman Catholics and Mainline Protestants also supported a candidate who has publicly shown his racist views against black people and other minorities. This number shows not only the inadequacy in engaging nonwhite people but a visceral rejection of "blackened" people, a rejection mixed with fear, anger, and resentment. In this vein, Donald Trump becomes the white man who gets it, the one who will correct the wrongs of the government who have put blackened people ahead of white people with social help, against white people who are suffering and did not receive the help of the government. Trump will get rid of the blackened people and bring the country back to a mythical and imaginary place where this country was once great.

This is only possible because white churches have always had pastors and theologians who have never engaged blackened people, their ways of living, their sufferings and their resources. There has never been a grammar for the prayer to move us all towards blackened people. Surely there hasn't been prayer in worship books against blackened people. However,

---

15. See my critique on the creation of liturgical sources in the Presbyterian Church: Cláudio Carvalhaes, "White Reasoning and What is Common in our Common Worship? A Methodological Critique to the Process of Renewal of the Book of Common Worship–Presbyterian Church U.S.A." in *Call to Worship: Liturgy, Music, Preaching, and the Arts.*

there hasn't been any in favor of them or created with them, or raising their concerns.

Thus the rest of this chapter intends to help Christians to pray with black/blackened people for the dismantling of the racist structures in place in this country. Perhaps it is wishful thinking, but I do believe prayers can offer seeds of change. Prayers can shift our feelings, move our ideas, transform our behaviors, invent new ecclesiologies and concrete forms of mission, create new practices and bring about forms of concrete love for people we never knew we could love or even had to love in a real way. Prayers enthuse us to engage in forms of life that really matter for the sake of restoring humanity to the lives of minorities. Providing a new vocabulary for our faith, prayers can shift a whole way of thinking, open a new kind of anthropology, one that is beyond the concepts we presently have that whites are above people of color and so should receive things first, and further that humans are above animals and creatures and that we have the earth to exploit for our own desires.

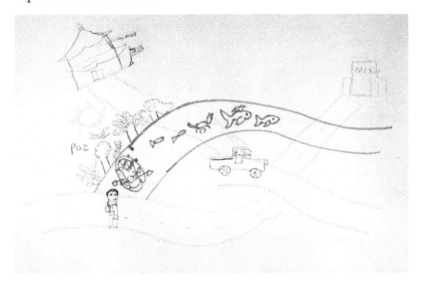

Praying with Dr. Martin Luther King Jr.

Thinking about that, I propose prayers for people, regardless of their color, to pray along with Martin Luther King Jr. To do so, in this section I am using several sources. I quote from two of King's works: "A Tough Mind and a Tender Heart," the first sermon in King's book *Strength to Love*,[16]

16. King, *Strength to Love.*

and the well-known "Letter from Birmingham Jail," written in 1963.[17] (The first three quotations are from "A Tough Mind and a Tender Heart," and the remaining quotations that follow are from his "Letter.") I also have in mind the work of artist Daniel Rarela, who "designed a series of memes to stop the late civil right leader from getting whitewashed."[18]

Professor James Cone explains the importance of King's "Letter":

> King's "Letter" was an eloquent and now classic statement of his theological and political views. It contained nothing new, nothing that he had not said in other sermons, addresses, and essays to white America, but when he restated what he had been saying for nearly eight years, it acquired a moral power that shook the conscience of the members of the white churches in America, especially northern liberals. King stated that nothing was more tragic for the church and the American dream than the continued existence of segregation. He saw segregation as a double contradiction: of America's democratic faith and of its religious heritage. Of the two contradictions, according to King, the religious one was the worst. He was severely critical of white ministers who tolerated segregation in their churches and remained silent about its practice in the society.[19]

Liturgically, the church cannot be silent either! It has to pray and sing and confess its ideological silences, its uncomfortable feelings, its theological "forgetting," and its liturgical absence. In a word: its vicious sins. For this reason, we are using King's words to help us pray a full and just faith. My hope is that the reader will read the whole letter as well as the sermon several times and see Rarela's images online. Here is, perhaps, a beginner's guide for engaging the world, the church, and our neighbors liturgically.

"A Tough Mind and a Tender Heart"

> Let us consider the need for a tough mind, characterized by incisive thinking, realistic appraisal, and decisive judgment. The tough mind is sharp and penetrating, breaking through the crust of legends and myths and sifting the true from the false. . . . This prevalent tendency toward soft mindedness is found in man's unbelievable gullibility. . . . This undue gullibility is also seen in the tendency of many readers to accept the printed

17. King, "Letter from Birmingham Jail."

18. See *Mic*, "Artist Creates 'Letter from a Birmingham Jail' Memes."

19. Cone, *Martin & Malcolm & America*, 140.

word of the press as final truth. Few people realize that even our authentic channels of information—the press, the platform, and in many instances the pulpit—do not give us objective and unbiased truth. Few people have the toughness of mind to judge critically and to discern the true from the false, the fact from the fiction. Our minds are constantly being invaded by legions of half-truths, prejudices, and false facts. One of the great needs of mankind is to be lifted above the morass of false propaganda. . . . Soft-minded persons have revised the Beatitudes to read, "Blessed are the pure in ignorance: for they shall see God" . . . There is little hope for us until we become tough minded enough to break loose from the shackles of prejudice, half-truths, and downright ignorance.

Prayer

God of our thinking,
give us a tough mind,
incisive thinking,
realistic appraisal,
decisive judgment.
For our weary times are filled with half-truths.
We know people are paid to misrepresented truths
so we can't find a way to oppose and resist.
We continue to be confused
so we pray for wisdom!
To know the sources of news,
the better forms of knowledge.
For we know where there is wisdom there is happiness.
Help us see the difference between truths and half-truths
and deliver us from ignorance and sadness.
God of wisdom,
more than anything we need wisdom
and the desire to learn,
to read,
to engage,
to listen to those suffering,
so we can have our minds changed.
So we can be transformed.
In Christ the truth, we pray. Amen!

"A Tough Mind and a Tender Heart"

> But we must not stop with the cultivation of a tough mind. The gospel also demands a tender heart. Tough mindedness without tenderheartedness is cold and detached, leaving one's life in a perpetual winter devoid of the warmth of spring and the gentle heat of summer. What is more tragic than to see a person who has risen to the disciplined heights of tough mindedness but has at the same time sunk to the passionless depths of hardheartedness?

Prayer

God who sees us all,
we pray for these two gifts: a tough mind and tender heart.
May we gain a tough mind
so we can go about the world without being surprised all the time.
May we gain a tender heart
so we can trust that goodness and love will remain.
Teach us to be disciplined in this search and discernment
so we can develop these gifts.
Help us know how to live with these two gifts together,
like a bird that needs two wings to fly.
In your mercy!

"A Tough Mind and a Tender Heart"

> I am thankful that we worship a God who is both toughminded and tenderhearted. If God were only toughminded, he would be a cold, passionless despot sitting in some far-off heaven "contemplating all," as Tennyson puts it in "The Palace of Art." He would be Aristotle's "unmoved mover," self-knowing but not other-loving. But if God were only tenderhearted, he would be too soft and sentimental to function when things go wrong and incapable of controlling what he has made.

Prayer

We praise you, O God,
because from your tough mind and tender heart
you have looked upon us equally.
But we have made your love look more favorable to some white people.
We who have everything
have not looked at those who don't have.
We even think that the have-nots are where they are because it is their fault!
We love to contemplate you and you alone
without contemplating those who have been wronged by history.
We pray that in our worship together
you help us see how some have benefited from a certain sense of your love
while others have not.
Discipline us to see racial structures of love and hate everywhere,
to see that our society is only made for some to live
while others are sentenced to jail or death.
But we praise you for also being tenderhearted towards us,
taking away our fears to approach blackened brothers and sisters.
May your tough mind and soft heart help us engage the color lines but also
go beyond them.
Help us find courage to hear what we need to hear and engage with one
another without being shackled to politics of difference.
We praise and worship you!
In your blackened name we pray!

"Letter from Birmingham Jail"

> You deplore the demonstrations taking place. . . . But your state-
> ment fails to express a similar concern for the condition that
> brought about the demonstrations. I am sure that none of you
> would want to rest content with the superficial kind of social
> analysis that deals merely with the effects and does not grapple
> with the underlying causes.

Prayer

We confess
that we are afraid of street demonstrations and protestors.

We confess

that we are angry that they don't follow proper order and the law that we follow to make change.

We confess

it has to be our way or no way because we understand the more democratic ways to do things properly.

We confess

that we feel we built this country and they came later.

We confess

that we do not see the perspective of the marginalized and are content to believe major news reporting.

We confess

that we tried to settle the case of black people as quickly as possible, blaming them for violence without looking at the violence of our racialized systems of oppression.

We confess

that we blamed black people for their own violence against themselves without understanding that it is the lack of basic conditions of life that creates violence and dysfunction.

We confess

that we cannot understand this situation because we have no clue what it is like to be a black person in this country.

In your mercy!

"Letter from Birmingham Jail"

> You may well ask, "Why direct action?" Why sit-ins, marches and so forth? Isn't negotiating a better path? You are quite right in calling for negotiation. Indeed, this is the very purpose of direct action. Nonviolent direct action seeks to create such a crisis and foster such a tension that a community which has constantly refused to negotiate is forced to confront the issue.

Prayer

God of our abysses,

we do indeed ask why we need direct action, sit-ins, marches, and so forth. We cannot understand why they can't talk, calmly, in the order that makes us comfortable.

Why can't they kindly ask for change?
We think we have always wanted to negotiate,
but now they invade public and private places and demand things.
Why, oh my soul, do I think that way?
What is it in me that I cannot grasp the fact
that their need is bigger than my fear?
That their time is not my time?
That my fulfilled needs allow me to wait through longer transformation?
That my entitlement cannot process the immediacy of their complaints?
Help me, God, to rid my soul from the thinking that only my life is important.
With your help, I will understand that we have refused to wrestle with the difficult issues related to black people.
With your help, I will be able to see that blacks or indigenous or Latinxs or immigrants are no less than our children.
In your mercy!

"Letter from Birmingham Jail"

> We have not made a single gain in civil rights without determined . . . nonviolent pressure. It is an historical fact that privileged groups seldom give up their privileges voluntarily. We know through painful experience that freedom is never voluntarily given by the oppressor; it must be demanded by the oppressed.

Prayer

God who can change us,
help us go through conversion.
May your Spirit create in us a true change, conversion, *metanoia*
for we cannot see we have privileges
We have instead seen what we have as blessings
that you bestowed upon us!
The place we have now was given to us by our fathers and fathers' fathers
who worked hard for it!
And we now work hard to keep it.
Why now do we have to give anything?
God of change,
we cannot really see this.

We cannot change.
But we pray.
Help us change
and see that power is not voluntarily shared.
Help us see that!
In your mercy!

"Letter from Birmingham Jail"

Justice too long delayed is justice denied.

Prayer

Oh God,
why do we see this sense of justice only when it has to do with us and our needs?
Why do I believe in long democratic processes for the justice of others when I am inpatient for justice when I am hurting?
Why don't I go out to the streets and demand justice for black people right now?
Help us, O God, to join the fight! May we learn the justice and injustice of our country!
May we go to the streets with Black Lives Matter! And listen to them, and see what is needed to support them in love, care, and sustenance.
Help us go to the streets where minority communities, now my people, are fighting for justice!
Help us O God!

"Letter from Birmingham Jail"

When you have seen hate filled policemen curse, kick and even kill your black brothers and sisters; . . . when you have to concoct an answer for a five year old son who is asking: "Daddy, why do white people treat colored people so mean?" . . . then you will understand why we find it difficult to wait.

Prayer

Merciful God,
When a child asks, we often listen.
But when our children ask about race or black people, we deny that racism
exists in us and in our country.
Yes we have mistreated black people, yes we have enslaved them, yes we
have put them in terrible places.
Help us, O God, to be honest with our kids.
Even when they don't ask,
help us to be honest
with you,
with our children,
and with blackened people,
so we can be attuned to your own voice!
In your mercy!

"Letter from Birmingham Jail"

> One has a moral responsibility to disobey unjust laws. I would
> agree with St. Augustine that "an unjust law is no law at all" . . .
> Any law that uplifts human personality is just. Any law that de-
> grades human personality is unjust.

Prayer

God of truthful laws,
We are learning with our brothers and sisters that law is not sacred, that laws
are a human creation and not sanctified by you. Give us strength to fight the
laws that privilege some people and dismiss others. Give us strength to fight
the state when it creates laws that support the lives of a few people and put
many others in jail. Help us go after the local policies of our communities
and see how racism is so fully present here. Help us dismantle the unjust
system of laws, so we can create legislative equality for all.
    In your mercy!

"Letter from Birmingham Jail"

> I have been gravely disappointed with the white moderate. . . .
> The Negro's great stumbling block in his stride toward freedom
> is not . . . the Ku Klux Klanner, but the white moderate, who is
> more devoted to "order" than to justice; who prefers a negative
> peace which is the absence of tension to a positive peace which
> is the presence of justice; who constantly says: "I agree with
> you in the goal you seek, but I cannot agree with your methods
> of direct action"; who paternalistically believes he can set the
> timetable for another man's freedom. . . . Shallow understand-
> ing from people of good will is more frustrating than absolute
> misunderstanding from people of ill will.

Prayer

We confess
that all we've attempted to be is moderate,
to uphold the order,
to find a common ground,
to foster positive peace,
so we wouldn't need to change anything, much less ourselves.
Help us move away from that place, where order and decency is a façade for
the protection of white people.
Give us courage, for we are weak and slow in making up our minds.
May we finally see that we are not free unless our brothers and sisters are
free.
Our churches have not necessarily associated themselves with the KKK, but
we have been silent, we have not spoken up.
So we pray that you might give us voices and words to speak,
to you, to each other, to our congregations, and to those in power.
Help us sit with and listen to those who are suffering.
Help us change, O God, help us change!
In your mercy!

"Letter from Birmingham Jail"

> One who breaks an unjust law must do so openly, lovingly,
> and with a willingness to accept the penalty. I submit that an

individual who breaks a law that conscience tells him is unjust, and who willingly accepts the penalty of imprisonment in order to arouse the conscience of the community over its injustice, is in reality expressing the highest respect for the law.

Prayer

God of love,
In your name we will go to the streets. We will disobey the human laws that trap the poor so we can obey you! From you, we have learned that when we are fighting for those suffering, we discover where Jesus actually is. Help us always commit to stand alongside the poor. Help us see that your love is given to all, but preferentially to the poor and those who are on the margins of history, of our communities.

In your mercy!

"Letter from Birmingham Jail"

We who engage in nonviolent direct action are not the creators of tension. We merely bring to the surface the hidden tension that is already alive. Injustice must be exposed, with all the tension its exposure creates, to the light of human conscience at the air of national opinion before it can be cured.

Prayer

God of solidarity,
we will join our colored brothers and sisters.
We will go where they are.
We will ask for a common meal.
We will ask what it is to live the lives they live.
We will listen and try to find common ground.
Our communities have people who are sick.
Help us visit each other.
Our communities have families who have beloved ones in jail.
Help us visit each other,
and fight against the incarceration of blackened people.
Help us find places, organizations and people so we can fight together!

May our community cry out loud, "Black lives matter!"
May our local churches be chapters of justice, making a grassroots revolution.
In your mercy!

"Letter from Birmingham Jail"

> I should have realized that few members of the oppressor race
> can understand the deep groans and passionate yearnings of the
> oppressed race, and fewer still have the vision to see that injus-
> tice must be rooted out by strong, persistent, and determined
> action.

Prayer

May we be those who can understand the deep groans and passionate yearn-
ings of the oppressed race. May we see, hear, and sense the anxiety, fears,
and all the challenges of growing up as a black and colored people in this
country! May we engage in deep listening! Now and for the days to come!
   In your mercy!

"Letter from Birmingham Jail"

> We have to repent in this generation, not merely for the hateful
> words and actions of bad people but for the appalling silence of
> good people. Human progress never rolls in on the wheels of
> inevitability; it comes through the tireless efforts of men willing
> to be coworkers with God, and without this hard work, time
> itself becomes an ally in the forces of social stagnation.

Prayer

We repent, O God.
   For we have run this race without paying attention to those who run
with much more weight on their bodies. May we have our minds and our
hearts transformed. Help us see that we have also created and supported
systems of injustice. Help us create innovative structures of peace, the redis-
tribution of money, the sharing of resources, health care for all, free college

tuitions, and an egalitarian education system. Remind us that we are each other's keepers. May we fight all of the forces of social stagnation, including the ones inside of us! Now and forever! We pray that by your grace and mercy, our world will grow darker by the blessed presence of colored people! May we see the gift of darkness against the illusion of a self-made light! In your mercy! Amen.

Conclusion

Professor Stephen Ray reminded me once that while the blackening was meant as evil, as with all things, God has brought good out of it. So many of us found freedom in the Christian faith! Christ has become our liberator! Now, we can have a church that is taking over its historical failures and moving towards justice and the true love of God by dismantling the work of the thieves. If Jesus says in the first part of John 10:10, "The thief comes only to steal and kill and destroy," in the second part Jesus says, "I came that they may have life, and have it abundantly." Together, whites and all blackened people, by the grace of God in Jesus Christ, will turn lies into truth, restore what was stolen from oppressed people, bring life where there was death, and rebuild what was destroyed! Together, we will show this abundant life we live in Jesus by building and defending together the beloved community, which has people of all colors! "The Beloved Community" is a term developed and popularized by Dr. Martin Luther King Jr. and Howard Thurman. King wanted to use this metaphor as a springboard, a symbol and also a concrete point of arrival for our society, a place where love, peace, and justice could live together. Dr. King's hopes for this beloved community were grounded in nonviolence, with the belief that through our common *agape* love we could make it happen—knowing all the while that it was a place with generative conflicts, where justice should be a constant struggle.

We can also build, defend, and expand the beloved community through its liturgical structures, orders, and rituals of transformation. For liturgy is always a call to conversion! The "liturgy's danger," says liturgical theologian Nathan D. Mitchell, "is to resist or ignore its call to conversion."[20]

To pray with a blackened faith in a darker context begs us to consider the relationship between the *lex orandi, lex credendi, lex vivendi*, and *lex agendi*, that is: the intertwining of the *rule of prayer*, the *rule of belief*, the *rule of life*, and the *rule of action*. This is because when we pray, all vulnerable life is at stake, especially black lives! When we pray, our very breathing, our hunger, our limitations, our desires, our social systems, everything enters

20. Mitchell, *Meeting Mystery*, 42.

into a movement of circulation of feelings, energies, and thinking. When we pray, our own breathing reminds us that we are made of the air, the sun, the soil, the birds, and all God's creation. When we utter words in prayer we are disclosing our hearts to God, and so even our biases are exposed, our racist upbringing becomes clear. When we give our offerings in prayer we are also showing the systems to which we are connected, where we live, what kind of health insurance we have, what culture we are part of, and what and with whom we have our deepest commitments. Thus, prayer is always prayed in some deep context, which includes the race and ecological systems we are immersed in and many times help to sustain.

Thus, to pray is to weave together the liturgy of the church, the liturgy of the world, and the liturgy of the neighbor against forms of racism and exclusion. To pray is to make an option for the poor! To pray is to turn our hearts into a darker faith, because we are now unequivocally inhabited by all people of color. With faith, also hope is turned black! And love is turned black! For to pray is to enter the darker side of all those disfranchised, of all colored people, which surely includes "darkened" whites, where the number of disposable people across the globe grow every day. Darker ethics and darker creeds, darker social actions and darker prayers, all shaping desires, giving contours to hurts, establishing ways of living, creating economic mechanisms of control, forming joys, elaborating concerns, relating us to the earth, defining pain, making us sing some songs, and throwing us into living in certain ways with our local communities and our plural world. All of these things together compose every prayer we pray.

With this chapter I tried to follow what Willie James Jennings said in his book *The Christian Imagination: Theology and the Origins of Race*: "I yearn for a vision of Christian intellectual identity that is compelling and attractive, embodying not simply the cunning of reason but the power of love that gestures toward joining, toward the desire to hear, to know, and to embrace."[21] I also tried to follow Emilie Townes and her call for justice and peace and via Howard Thurman, head and heart, prayer and belief, *lex orandi* and *lex credendi*. Townes says, "Our world needs a new (or perhaps ancient) vision molded by justice and peace rather than winning and losing if we are to unhinge the cultural production of evil. Doing so is to respond to the call by the Black mystic and theologian Howard Thurman who joined others in encouraging us to blend head and heart."[22]

Our Christian intellectual identity calls us into new and constant *metanoias*, change of ways of thinking, shifting our views of the world,

21. Jennings, *Christian Imagination*, 8.
22. Townes, *Womanist Ethics*, 164.

embodying individual and communal prayers of justice so we can create a praxis of solidarity and transformation with the poor and the earth. And we can only do that if we engage our prayers into the breaking of the potencies of racism! In order to do that we must embody Christ as our full prayer.

6

"Speak Louder Please, I Can't Hear You"

Voices, Spiritualties, and Minorities[1]

There is no such thing as silence.

—JOHN CAGE

Sometimes you have to scream to be heard.

—AVITAL RONELL

The calling to speak is often a vocation of agony.

—MARTIN LUTHER KING JR.

In 2006 the American Waldensian Society celebrated one hundred years of existence, a short span of time compared to the history of the movement since its beginning with Waldo of Lyon. It is a time to speak out loud, rejoice with our sisters and brothers and renew our resistance and resilience against

1. This text was written in honor of Prof. Daisy Machado. Her soft and yet intense voice speaks in my ears ever since the day she gave a speech at Union Theological Seminary (New York City) in 2003. I don't remember much of what she said but the tone of her voice was unforgettable; it was loud, intense, trembling, as if she was screaming even though she wasn't. Since that day, her voice speaks somehow in and through me.

intolerance. The survival of the Waldensians is a great testimony to the survival of many minorities across the globe.

Reading some of the documents of the Waldensian Church, I was struck by one of its oaths. It says,

> Waldensians by these oaths,
> Heaven blessed our fathers,
> And in these days is still ready to bless us.
> Joining our brother's hands, let us loudly proclaim:
> At the altars of my God,
> So, I want to live and to die.

This is a powerful statement of faith, a radical shout that clearly places life on the edge ("to live and to die"), which understands both faith and life as one event, an event that is always at risk. This profession of faith was a second step, a response from a community who knew well what faith in *praxis* meant. For this short paper, I would like to reflect on just one word from this oath, namely, *loudly*.

The oath says, "let us *loudly* proclaim." That word caught my attention. Why this need for volume? Why not say "let us proclaim" or even "let us boldly proclaim"? Why is it not enough to proclaim, declare, or confess? I might be wrong but it seems that this oath refers not so much to *what* you say as to *how* you say it, which, I guess, is very Italian, or Brazilian . . . Loud! The oath seems to be more preoccupied with the levels of energy, trying to instill a mixture of awe, fierceness, and urgency, and intending to fill the believer with a necessary intensity that she or he will need in order to live the challenges and perils of this faith, perhaps to the last consequences. Thus, the *how of the confession* might have to do more with the liturgical ways the believer attaches her/himself to the belief than to the theological aspect of the belief. In order to believe, one cannot only proclaim what one believes, one has to do it in an intense and loud way.

This oath claims a faith that combines words and sounds, making every affirmation sound like an exclamation, a shout, a scream, a creed confessed with a loud voice. Moreover, you cannot understand this faith if it does not come with the gestures of the body moving closer to the altar and the movements of the hands searching for somebody else. "Joining our brother's hands . . . At the altars of my God." What we see here is the connection between liturgical gestures of companionship, bodies closer and hands together with the assurance of a God who belongs to them (my God).

"Let us *loudly* proclaim . . ." Again, the volume of one's voice radically affects the way one believes, and consequently determines the ways in which one understands, negotiates, lives, and performs one's spirituality.

What does "voice" have to do with our faith and to the ways we develop our spiritualties and worship God? If we pay attention to the voices that speak our theologies or create the hymnody of our congregations, what voices are they and whose voices do they represent? The voices of our theologians and liturgists, and their ways of talking about God, bring the voices that they carry with them, representing a certain point of view. The problem with these particular and local voices is when they become or want to become a universal voice that has to be listened to by everybody else. In Latin America, for instance, for far too long we listened to the voices of European and North American theologians and only later realized that we also had a voice, that we could speak and, more interestingly, that we could speak about God, too.

In the midst of foreign voices, we had to learn to find our own. We then realized that the processes of gaining a theological and liturgical voice are so difficult. It is a matter of trust and confidence that God has given us a voice as well to speak. But how to speak if no one is listening?

What is at stake among liberation theologies, for instance, is the search for difference, alterity, i.e., other ways of speaking, listening, understanding, believing, and experiencing life. Differences that were denied, avoided, and erased in the construction of Western theological thought. In this process, the task of hearing the voice of the voiceless has been a major and complicated one. Among many questions, we should ask: can we hear and move beyond the pleasurable tone of our voices and hear the voice of the other? If so, how can we hear the voices of those who have been silenced for so long, the poor and the oppressed, whose voices have been smashed down and whose mouths have been brutally shut up? How can we hear if they don't speak? Why don't they speak?

The voices of minorities have been historically dismissed and forbidden. The construction of an official voice in history, determining what existed and what did not, was made by those who, imposing a sort of pre-Babel world, decided to speak for all the others and establish a *lingua franca* that provided straight and proper measures of how life should be heard, spoken, and understood. Within theology, there was always an attempt to establish an unambiguous voice that would tell us what to believe and what to do regarding God's will. In this process, this exclusionary voice was so loud that it made mute many other voices, the voices of women, the voices of Black people, the voices of the southern hemisphere, the voices of religious difference, and the voices of nature. A voice so loud that it ended up deafening many of those who were trying to say something, an uninterrupted noise that intended to continuously strike at the ears of the others until all agreed, like the movie *1984*.[2] If any voice goes on without being challenged and interrupted, within no time this voice will become the truth and the measure of life for those who are listening.

However, within the spaces of the words pronounced by major voices, there were those who resisted and decided not to conform or to obey. These voices of marginal people ended up writing history in different shades, modulations, and tonalities. These voices, hidden under the colonizer's voices, were sounds and vocabularies of different understandings of God and the world. These voices of dissent gave us different histories filled with examples of resistance and possibilities to perceive, experience, and live our "common" faith differently in the world. Waldo of Lyon and the Waldensians are some of these voices.

Waldo's strange voice shaped an *other* spirituality that challenged proper and acceptable measures of faith at his time, creating other theological and spiritual possibilities for the believer to live life and faith beyond the stream of the official discourses. He *shouted* as if in a desert, voicing *other* ways for the coming of God. The sound of his voice echoes within us today and it is mixed with the screams and shouts of those who decided to listen to strange voices. As we pay attention to Waldo's voice, we must continue to listen to the voices of those who lived and died on the margins, and those who are still living and dying in the mute gutters of our world: Are they saying anything? What are they saying and what we can learn about about God with them?

In a continuous exercise, we must ask ourselves whose voices are speaking in and through us, since our voice is never a single voice. Our voices depend on the economic structures and cultural settings in which we are confined. My voice, for instance, depends on the opportunities, on the education I had, and the network of possibilities in which I am integrated; it also depends on the voices I have heard and the choices I have made; the voices I didn't hear, the things nobody ever told me; it depends on my history, the limits of my world and the multiplicity of voices that I allow to speak for and with me.

Our voices are necessary tools to determine who and what we are always becoming. Our voices determine the ways in which we develop our communal spiritualties. Is it possible to develop a sense of spirituality if we cannot talk? How can our voices, and more specifically the *volume* of our voices, give contours to our faith and a place of dignity in the world?

2. Based on George Orwell's novel *Nineteen Eighty-Four*.

Ana, "Dejando la casa (Leaving my house)"

Ana is a nine-year-old girl from Guatemala. In this picture she drew her father and her leaving the home that they love. They are in search of new work, as there are few opportunities in their homeland.

Frantz Fanon, in "This Is the Voice of Algeria," says that the Algerian people were only able to incorporate a larger sense of "the struggle of an assembled people"[3] when they were able to buy a radio and listen to the *Voice of Fighting Algeria*, which was "an official voice, the voice of the combatants, [to] explain the combat to him, tell him the story of the Liberation on the March, and incorporate it into the nation's new life." But due to the highly trained French services, they detected the "sound-wave warfare" and the programs "were then systematically jammed, and the *Voice of Fighting Algeria* soon became inaudible."[4]

The *occupier* of foreign territories intended a people that would become gradually mute and without voice to lose its grasp on its memory, capacities and promises. By dismantling the voices of colonized people, the colonizer wants to prevent the colonized from discovering the power of their voices and the concatenation of their thoughts, and from establishing any movement of resistance. Fanon says, "Imperfectly heard, obscured by an incessant jamming, forced to change wave lengths two or three times in

3. Fanon, "This Is the Voice of Algeria," 84.
4. Fanon, "This Is the Voice of Algeria," 85.

the course of a broadcast, the *Voice of Fighting Algeria* could hardly ever be heard from beginning to end. It was a choppy, broken voice."[5]

Voice matters and the processes of colonization, then and now, tries to obliterate the voices of the other, cracking its codes and shattering its nuances, rendering other voices imperceptible, unpleasant, unimportant, a mere distraction. When only one voice speaks, the silence of the other voices amplifies the volume of the one spoken. Moreover, unheard voices usually sound strange when rarely spoken and they end up being used as reverberations of the negative side of a spoken one. The relations between silence, voice, amplification and reverberation perform an acute role in the Waldensian service where silence constitutes an important aspect of the service. Silence then is not the absence of a voice but rather the condition of the possibility of their sounding voices. For in silence, we are able to hear our own voice, and articulate it in various ways.

Fanon was in favor of adding new sounds into the univocal sound of the colonizer. I believe that theologies, liturgies, ecclesiologies and spiritualties must be populated by many voices. The voice of the other is that constant challenge to my certainties and a continuous sign that shows that my voice is not absolute in any theological, liturgical, or faithful matter.

By adding different voices and sounds, even the "sound" of silence, to our spiritualties, the connections between voice and word can help undo the *logos* of any dominant voice into, perhaps, a more plural and Pentecostal voice of God. Fanon says that "the French language, the language of the occupier, was given the role of *logos*, with ontological implications within Algerian society."[6] Our task is to break the "ontological implications," i.e., the will to sovereignty of any dominant theology, and turn the one logo-centric voice of any theologian/occupier of "God's understandings," into a Babel/Pentecostal epiphanic moment, where God visits and transforms us in unimaginable ways. Between Babel and Pentecost, we might be able to find a fairer place where the monolithic voice of the occupier gets distracted and transgressed by the multiplicity of voices of the Spirit, which comes from those who were not used to speaking but only to listening. Then, we might even be able to hear the *logos* of God through these unheard voices.

Therefore, by listening to different voices that speak a "foreign" theological language to our unaccustomed ears, we might become able to listen to an unpredictable singing of strange songs in strange lands. The ability to listen to somebody else's voice is the opening of the Spirit within us to "see" God's movements in unexpected people and places. The voice of an other

5. Fanon, "This Is the Voice of Algeria," 86.
6. Fanon, "This Is the Voice of Algeria," 91.

has the power to signal to our ears the creation of liberating processes that the Spirit operates in and through people who we might have never imagined before. Moreover, by adding strange voices and sounds to our foreign/ mother tongue, we can learn how to re-create and reinvent ourselves as we enhance, change, or add new possibilities for our spiritualties in praise of a God who always speaks in many tongues. The voice of the other within my voice, and my language within the language of my neighbor might take us to what Edmond Jabès once said, "My mother tongue is a foreign language."[7]

When I think about my voice, I realize that my voice is never my own voice, as it never comes alone. Instead, it is always marked by the mute screams of those who came before me, those who were enslaved, exploited, and forgotten. My voice is a historical horizon of sounds, utterances, mumblings, words, and speeches that dispute a place and a right in my mind, in my heart, and in my throat. One thing is certain: I can only speak through the timbers and sounds of those who colonized me, those who taught me how to speak and how loud I could be. It is with and against this voice that I try to engage and unravel my own history. Let me tell you a story.

It was July 2004. I was in Bahia, a vibrant state in Brazil with 80 percent of its population composed of Afro-Brazilians. I went to visit *Mercado Modelo*, the "Model Market," where people negotiated for and sold slaves in the eighteenth century. Under the main floor, there was a large basement where people who came from Africa were thrown after arriving in Brazil, and kept until they were negotiated for and sold to slave owners. Women and men of all ages were kept under the market with water covering their bodies up to their waist. On the walls, there were holes with images of Christian saints, trying to teach them a proper and civilized faith. This place was opened for visit only a few years ago by the local government after the complaints of various Afro-descendent movements who wanted to show a very important part of the history of Brazil. It was there, in that basement, that I had a conversion moment. All of a sudden I heard a myriad of voices indecipherably speaking and shouting out loud to the point of almost making me deaf. Words and sounds that I had never heard took my mind and my heart. There were sounds of weeping mothers and fathers away from their daughters and sons, shouts of utter despair from people who were taken away from their homes to a strange place, desolation and unredeemable cries of free people all of sudden turned into slaves. Nonetheless, among these sounds and voices, there were also screams of resistance, words of command not to give up, and prayers to all the Orixás for deliverance.

---

7. Jabès, quoted in Waldrop, *Lavish Absence*, 155.

As I heard those voices, I realized that I have never lent my ears to this part of the history of my country and my people. Why did it take me so long to be able to hear those voices that formed who I am? Why has nobody ever told me about them, and why have they never told me they were part of myself and my history?

That day I realized that when I speak with my own voice, my voice is a blur of silenced and loud voices that speak inside of me. Voices that are unknown to me, voices that are telling me things that I am not able to understand, voices that are screaming inside of me and I cannot not hear them, voices of others that are trying to find their way into the volume of my voice. And yet, they make me what I am trying to be, they subvert my thoughts, they challenge me every time I try to speak just for myself and not for my community, the community of those who lived before me and those who are yet to come.

These voices in the *Mercado Modelo* taught me that I cannot develop my spirituality without those voices, black voices, disrupting and undoing my theological frames of reference and indexes, and giving me life. I learned that my theological grounds and the spirituality that is shaped from these grounds must be this place between Babel and Pentecost, where indiscriminate sounds and incomprehensible voices abound, voices that I can hear and understand, and voices that are both unspeakable and untranslatable, near and afar. In order to stand on sound theological ground, I must learn to pay attention to the voices that went unheard and were lost in the loud archives and monotone records of the official history of the Western world.

Thus, if we are an archive of silenced voices, how should we proceed to listen to them? The way we answer this question is the way we construct our theologies and spiritualties and the way we worship God. My guess is that we must keep listening, or trying to listen, digging into our history and the history of our countries, listening to these faded and mute voices, seeing erased traces, looking for the obscured remains of a people that we both know and know nothing about. Moreover, we must listen not only to the voices of the past but also to the silenced voices that are present today around our lives and communities. I must listen to those who live on the streets and on the borders, near and afar, "loudly proclaiming" what I cannot or do not want to hear. I must make an oath to them saying, "With you I want to live and die." My faith can only make sense if I listen to those who are on the margins of this world, a world, like God, made mine, not "theirs." It is in the middle of the cacophony of these voices that I must linger with my theologies and spiritualties knowing that there is no such a thing as me and them. In this Babel/Pentecost world, I must take on my faith and "loudly proclaim" *with* someone else, always with someone *else*, different from me, strangely and absurdly different from me, the many ways and the many voices of God in this world, trying to find the contours of my faith and the possibilities of my God with the God of my neighbor.

Stretching the possibilities of our sounding theologies, let us assume, for now, that our spiritualties are closely related to the ways in which we speak, and to the *volume* and tonalities of our voices. If that is so, how can we measure, understand, or relate to the spirituality of minorities? The Waldensian spirituality had to find ways to develop itself in hidden places, dangerous situations, always using a lower voice, negotiating its place in the world with a quiet voice. A louder voice would mean death. What kind of spirituality and theology could be developed under such circumstances?

Nowadays, we see the same situation happening to undocumented immigrants throughout the world. Even though their presence is well known by the authorities, their presence must be made invisible, silent. The watchword within these communities is "don't draw the attention of the police, they want you here to do the worst jobs and receive lower salaries, but be quiet in everything you do, do your job and don't call attention to yourself." This invisibility entails the lowering of their voices. They cannot speak out loud, they cannot fight for rights, they cannot complain about sexual and other abuses and exploitation, they cannot scream their sorrows and hopes for, if they do, they are put in prison and sent back to their countries. In order to survive, they learn to pay a high price for their nonexistence and learn that their voice can be a weapon against themselves. They learn to turn an exterior voice into an inner voice, a voice that says, "Don't speak; your voice can kill you."

Without a voice we cannot speak our language and without language there is no God, there is no creation, there is no world.[8] Without a voice, without a language, one lives in the shadows, as if one has disappeared without a trace. As Gloria Anzaldúa says, "I am my language."[9] And Ray Gwyn Smith says, "Who is to say that robbing a people of its language is less violent than war?"[10] And Irena Klepfisz writes,

> And our tongues have become
> dry the wilderness has
> dried out our tongues and
> we have forgotten speech.[11]

8. "In the beginning was the Word, and the Word was with God, and the Word was God" (John 1:1 NRSV).

9. Anzaldúa, *Borderlands/La Frontera*, 59.

10. Smith, *Moorland is Cold Country* (unpublished manuscript), quoted in Anzaldúa, *Borderlands/La Frontera*, 53.

11. Klepfisz, "Di Rayze abeym/The Journey Home," in *The Tribe of Dina: A Jewish Women's Anthology*, 49. Quoted in Anzaldúa, *Borderlands/La Frontera*, 54.

Churches usually are, or have the potential to be, the space where un-documented immigrants choose to develop their spirituality, a ghetto where they can at least check their existence and be certain they are not fake indi-viduals. In spite of walking "undercover," they have a real name, even if they cannot say it out loud. In the whispering sanctuaries of usually storefront churches, an undocumented immigrant searches for:[12]

- A place where one hopes to find a measure of sanity and safety and where one can be *with* somebody else in order to find solace over and against rampant fears that have the power to disrupt and disarticulate one's subjectivity and to destroy hopes, desires, and resistances.

- A place where one becomes a citizen for a while, without worrying about getting caught.

- A place where colliding worlds try to make sense out of a communal life, a place between places to call home. Worlds trying to be con-nected together through the liturgical practices that develop a certain spirituality that allows them to breathe for a while.

- A place of recovery when the experience of utter and indescribable violence plagues the individual and the community. A place to speak when silence seems to fill one's heart with fear, anger and sorrow.

- A place where one learns *with* others, is changed by others, and ex-pands one's ways of seeing and experiencing God and life. The sharing of our roots and our faith is always an impediment to a single group or community to attest they got it right. Mixed roots spread as *rhizomes*, always unfold within transnational communities.

- A place to use one's own language to do practical, "illiterate" theology, giving measurement to oneself, God, and the world. A place where language marks off space, locates time, and tries to control both the known and the unknown world.

- A place where broken spiritualties reflect broken lives made of so many stories of pain, abuse, and oblivion; a place where a displaced spirituality mirrors an exilic faith and fosters a theology of diaspora by trying ceaselessly to find rest in an insecure land, *terra incognita*, *terra infirma*. A place where halfway spiritualties reflect a land without maps, a theology without clear references, encapsulating life in a des-ert of scattered dreams and increasingly fewer possibilities.

12. The generalizations of these assertions are based on my experience as a pastor for undocumented immigrants in Massachusetts, USA, and have the sole intention of provoking our thoughts to a more particular and nuanced engagement with these very diverse communities on undocumented immigrants.

- A place where the transcendence and sovereignty of God must be a reality in order to help the wandering immigrant to get through the hardships of life, where hopes are cherished and horizons are stretched.

- A place for social connections, shelter, healing, and consolation where the body cries its brokenness and hopes to be somewhat joined together, mended by the Spirit. A place to contrast, to counteract, to challenge, to prophesy against the "open wound"[13] of many unfair borders.

- A place to re-member, i.e., to be reminded of God's love in Christ and to be constantly reconnected with one's dignity. A place where resistance is always reinvented, where identities, theologies, and struggles are constantly rewritten, redone. A gathered community that develops courage as strangers, immigrants, foreigners, and excluded people, through the fresh and insisting moving of the Spirit.

- A place where voices find faces that make ethical demands. There, we look at each other's faces without putting our heads down, as brothers and sisters having to decide how to live life together in spite of injustices and difficulties. In these liturgical spaces, we are called to listen and to speak, to love, and to be challenged to find the "Face of the Voice."[14]

- A place where an incarnated spirituality is always pressing our faith in Christ.

The spiritualties of undocumented immigrants are unmapped terrains, with fading and hidden marks, broken landscapes, moveable sights, and unclaimed territories. Borders are written all over their bodies. This way of living engenders a spirituality that is always under negotiation. The substratum, the source of their spiritualties is made of contingent material supports that are always under suspicion. They cannot talk out loud for too long outside of the church, and are always relying on fake ID cards, or expired driver's licenses, without a permanent address. It is a life made of impermanence that ends up fostering cracked, moveable spiritualties and where theologies are always on the go, as we live, as we learn to live with one another in a foreign land.

The task for us Christians is to invite these immigrants to embark into our faith journey as we join their journey as well. In this process of listening to the voices of the other, we must be aware that there might be a constant

---

13. See Anzaldúa, *Borderlands/La Frontera*, 2.

14. Dworkin, *Reading the Illegible*, 32.

vanishing point within our faith that can spur hatred and xenophobia. As we try to live together, we must hold tight to the Holy Spirit in order to learn, again and again, how to welcome the other in our midst. To do that, we must acknowledge that we are a people who are always on the move to a better theology, better liturgical practice, and a better sense of our faith. Our spiritualties must be touched by the presence of the other, by the voice of the other, as we incarnate the gospel of Christ within our communities of faith. The incarnation of our faith will entail the sharing of our sacred spaces and also of our belongings. We must learn to lose as we negotiate our liturgical actions and our faithful decisions. How do we give an account of our faith if we never hear about forgotten communities of poor people around the world and invite them to worship with us? What would it take from us to develop our spiritualties in the midst of a variety of strange people turned brothers and sisters? How can we find our own voice if we cannot hear the other who is silenced? How can we experience the Pentecost if we do not go through the Babel of our faith?

Strangers and voices have a strong relation to our beliefs, spiritualties, and theologies. Like the Waldensians, how do we get to the altars of God? By ourselves? How much do our theological "musts" set apart the other who cannot fit into our beliefs? At the Eucharistic table, for example, are we the hosts or the hostages of God's sacrament? Should we raise our voices and speak out loud our own stories in the midst of God's story until we don't know any more whose story belongs to whom? Or are we only to regurgitate "properly" the words of institution as if a miracle were to happen? Saint Augustine's famous line says, "be what you can see and receive what you are."[15] Who is the body of Christ around the table? How many languages does this body speak? Where are the borders of our spiritualties, of our Eucharistic tables, of our countries?

In this endless web of questions, undocumented people everywhere have to learn to talk out loud, speak up and loudly proclaim whatever they believe, think, and imagine. They are living in the shadow of our Eucharistic tables. The hope is that, by developing a Christian spirituality *with* the other, the stranger, the immigrant around the altars of God, listening to their voices and paying attention to what and how they say and sing and how they move, we will be able to engage in a negotiation of our faith that will help us to move from Babel and Pentecost.

In this process, our ears are very important. Our ears are key elements for any theology and liturgy. To talk about God is to talk about us, in disfigured words, in unspeakable words, in words yet to be said. Thus, we need to

---

15. Fitzgerald et al., *Augustine Through the Ages*, 88.

hear, hear the other. Our ears are connected to our mouths, and our mouths can only make sense when our ears listen to the words we speak. There are words, wounded words that we cannot speak, words tainted by the horrific and impossible to our ears to grasp. As Jacques Derrida says,

> The ear is uncanny. Uncanny is what it is; double is what it can become; large or small is what it can make or let happen (as in *laissez-faire*), since the ear is the most tendered and most open organ, the one that, as Freud reminds us, the infant cannot close; large or small as well the manner in which one may offer or lend an ear.[16]

Speaking and listening, being able to talk and to hear, mouth to ear and ear to mouth, might be one way for us to develop our spiritualties, to make our organic theologies grow. Grow until we get to the point where speaking and listening become the same thing, your tongue in my ear, my ear in your mouth, always negotiating our sacred spaces, our becomings, our spiritualties, re-writing our stories, translating each other and expanding what we know and what we wish we knew about ourselves.

The Waldensians can teach us how to get from imposed silence to loud proclamation. Every time they were persecuted, destroyed, and killed, this community was able to resurrect and continue its journey. Through various tonalities of voices and uneven heartbeats and bodily gestures, they were able to come together, hold hands and loudly proclaim what they believed. They learned how to voice their faith, their spiritualties, and their lives.

We can also learn that when an oath is *loudly* professed. In the case of the Waldensians, it tells us something about the conditions of this community. When you proclaim out loud whatever you believe, you are willing not only to be heard, but also to tell your peers that you can, that you are capable of something, that you cannot and must not stop.

An oath professed from the top of our longs, as a scream that sounds like a liberating deliverance. Perhaps, we could add to our directories of worship that everyone who wants to profess their faith in Christ must affirm their faith out loud as they hold hands with the rest of the congregation! Thus, speaking our faith out loud with one another, we learn that trust is in God, but also within each other's hands. This is how we should begin to profess our faith and the first step to follow Jesus. For when we do that we are saying, "Yes, we are here! We exist as a community, as a body! And more, we have something to say. Loudly!"

The voices of the Waldensians are now stretched to the voices of my African ancestors in Brazil along with the voices made mute, the unknown,

16. Derrida, *Ear of the Other*, 33.

the uncared for, the improper and *unlanded*[17] marginalized voices from all over the world. By now, our voices must have become a matter of life and death as well, as the Waldensian oath teaches us. So, as one and multiple communities, with different faces, colors, voices, bodies, classes, ears and tongues, springing a variety of spiritualties and experiences with God, it is our task to create a hospitable community that is marked by diversity. We live under the guidance of the Spirit and the many tongues of the Pentecost. The voice of God is plural, received, and spoken not by one major voice but by many voices. It is among our differences, voices, and languages that we can loudly say,

> Joining our hands,
> Let us LOUDLY proclaim,
> At the altars of my God,
> So I want to live and to die!

---

17. "It refers to the condition of dispossession and displacement that occurs during war and to zones of the world that have been effectively abandoned, where life has become absolutely intolerable." Doris Salcedo, in Siobhán Garrigan, "Worship Audible Only in the Mouth, So Far." Not yet published.

7

"Gimme de Kneebone Bent"

Liturgics, Dance, Resistance, and a Hermeneutics of the Knees

To Nancy Cardoso Pereira

When my knee and your knee fall together in affliction and quietness, and the nest of the bed becomes the comfort and grace that will not want anything else but a hug, I will repeat with Teresa (de Avila) the question of the flight, entangled in your leg: God with us!

—NANCY CARDOSO PEREIRA

Introduction

Shall we all dance to the *Lord*? But what Lord? Whose Lord shall we bend our knees in prayer, honor, dance, and praise to? Can our knees be naked? Can we open our legs? How much skin can we show without apologizing? Are we allowed to get the sensuous fever while dancing a tango, a salsa, or a samba? How should our knees behave in the *House of the Lord*? And whose house is God's house? Is there a proper way to dance in a worship service? What parts of our bodies can we move without distressing the proper liturgical order rooted in respect, faith, rationality, tradition, and good manners?

Our knees connect liturgy with ecclesiology, our sweat with theology, colonization with dance and bodies. I wonder how our bodies can move beyond the "please stand" and "you may be seated" parts of the service. While worshiping, we usually don't need more than our eyes to see the altar/table and the priest/pastor, our hands to hold the bulletin, to have awkward handshakes during the peace, and to hold hymn books. We need our mouths to sing and pray but mostly, we need ears to listen. Endlessly.

My contention in this article is that the problem with our dancing has to do with theological problems with our knees. The knees have always been a dangerous element in the Christian faith. God's revelation had the *knees* of Jesus as a privileged place for God's mission. Jesus moved and danced and rejoiced and moved freely. However, the Christian body in general has remained a frightened place where things can easily get out of control. The Christian faith saw the knees holding possibilities for pleasure, desire, and resistance, these fervent enemies of reason and control, and decided to have it denied and/or to stay under the surveillance of a proper spiritual faith. Rubem Alves, a Brazilian thinker and poet, says,

> We thought of finding God where the body ends: and we made the body suffer and we turn it into a heavy load, an obedient entity, a machine of work, into an enemy to be silenced, and that way we persecuted the body to the point of praising death as the way to God, as if God preferred the smell of sepulchers to the delights of the paradise. And we became cruel, violent, allowing exploration and war. For, if God can only be found beyond the body, then everything can be done to the body.[1]

Our evangelization in Latin America, both from Roman Catholicism and Protestantism, taught us to be careful, suspicious, and even hateful of our bodies. We learned that there was a proper (read civilized) way of moving, believing, acting, singing, looking, gesturing, and touching within the worshiping space and in the world. Silently, the Christian evangelization targeted first of all our knees. They were taken from our own control and educated by priests and pastors to behave accordingly. Put another way, through a powerful and continuous catechesis, we were/are taught that we were/are to learn three main things: to control our knees, to internalize a proper code of behavior, and to be happy with it.

This education began when Latin America became the host of (well-intended) guests and missionaries. But in no time we suddenly became the guests of our once guests, now our hosts. Soon we began appealing to be accepted in our own land, to learn how to be worthy, and to become citizens

---

1. Alves, *Creio na ressurreição do corpo*, 7.

of our own countries. Our hosts became so violent, and they pressured our knees so intensely that one day we could not hold our knees together anymore. In 1985, when Pope John Paul II visited Peru, he received a Bible from an indigenous leader in Cusco—once the heart of the Inca empire—and heard that the Bible had taken most of what he had, systematically disrespecting the knees and the dignity of the indigenous people since 1492.

This long, complicated, and yet simple educational process made us become something else, that which we never knew we were or could have been. Now we try to know that which we can only imagine we might have been, and do that imagining through colonized eyes and a colonized imagination.[2] We became estranged from our bodies, and the shadow of shame and punishment still hovers around our bodies. As we lament all that was taken from us, we are not ungrateful for what Christianity has given to us. However, for many, our knees have become completely stiff, without memory of movement, freedom, and joy. We don't even know we can dance. So much so that we don't even ask for permission. We just can't. To move is to stir things up, and perhaps get too much "in" control rather that "out of" control. There is a way in which the battle between body and spirit is a way of never being able to own our own bodies, and be responsible for them. It is the church and the state that must own the desires, dealing with bodily liquids, and sexualities, and gender in ways that are not strange/queer to anyone. It is better if God and the church control our bodies, movements and sexualities.

In this article I will investigate the ways in which our liturgical grid/order/proper faith provided/allowed patterns for us to move accordingly within very specific limits. Second, I will analyze ways in which the liturgical proper eliminated differences and turned all of us into the same hosts-once-guests. Finally, inspired by Nancy Pereira Cardoso, one of our most creative and fascinating biblical scholars and theologians in Brazil, I will engage with what she calls a de-evangelization of our knees and propose a feminist hermeneutics of the knees as a way to help us move and, hopefully, to dance.

The Liturgical Proper

Let me start with a story. It was a Saturday morning in 2001 and I was seated quietly in an empty pew of Corpus Christi Church in New York City. An old woman came in and went straight to the first painting of the Stations of the Cross, rather than sitting in the pews or making any sign of reverence to

2. Gruzinski, *A colonização do imaginário*.

the altar. There, standing alone, with her plastic shopping bags down on the floor, she slowly started to touch the first painting with her right hand, her eyes looking deeply into the painting and her lips moving quickly and indefinably. After that she moved to the following station and repeated her gestures, successively, until the last station. Then, she left the church. This long religious scene made me think about the ways in which we ritualize our religious contours, contents, and formats. Questions immediately came to my mind: What was she doing? Was it her way of thanking God for something? Or was it a lament, a longing, a cry for a lost child, or even a supplicant's way of begging God's favor? Did it have anything to do with faith? Did it have anything to do with an unknown desire? Was it a liturgical movement? Or instead, should it be considered *merely* a theatrical performance? If so, what could differentiate it from a liturgical action? This religious scene made me think about the structural frames that constrain the contents, sources, and *representations* of the Christian faith, as well as the porosities and uncertainties of such frames that separate format and content, as it questions inclusion, exclusion, legitimacy, and proper ways to perform/*liturgize*.

The historical array of liturgical possibilities within Christian churches, in general, have always been determined by historical procedures and definitions, which have been turned into official documents that control the tradition. These not only presuppose certain conditions and possibilities, but also ordain behaviors, establish ethical demands, and a proper faith, including a prescribed assortment of beliefs and practices. The range of these sets of liturgical possibilities, i.e., *lex orandi* and *lex credendi*, practices and beliefs, have historically been developed out of official canons based on theologically chosen and approved sources, all of them defined, limited, and established over time according to a determined power control, namely, tradition.

These liturgical Christian possibilities have always gravitated toward or drawn upon the same structure that one might call a *liturgical proper*.[3] This *liturgical proper* entails a universal *logic or code* that surrounds the liturgical and the theological with a fixed, unmoved structure that, by the very condition of its fixed and immobile essence, makes it possible for liturgical thought or practice to always be reasonable, meaningful, and intelligible according to a proper acceptable theological ground.

3. The proper is the *essentialization* of a term, the belief that words and things can be properly related in a meaningful way, through the understanding of clean/clear and literal meaning(s). The proper is the essentialization of a thing, the internalization of the meaning, the capacity to apprehend whatever is happening in the moment. It is the understanding of the logos as that which carries specific meanings and a final purpose. The proper is the universal array of categories and references to being.

This ground is specified by *onto-theo-logical* underpinnings or *metaphysical* understandings that define the ways in which the Christian religious meanings are conceived of and consequently practiced.

The *liturgical proper* demarcates the worship patterns of the Christian *ordo* (from the Latin meaning order, structure, shape, pattern), and by determining the *ordo* it determines the movements of the body: kneeling, proximities, the precise distance from the altar, the ways of the body in the pulpit, the necessary lack of extravagant expressions of passion, the proper covering of the body. All due to the necessary respect for God who can be easily disturbed by an unexpected movement of the body, a different gesture, or a disturbing sound. I remember "Cuica," a homeless person who would come to church and during the hymns would make a sound with his mouth like the sound of the Brazilian instrument called *cuica*. He was totally inappropriate, even disrespectful of the solemnity of the worship. Sometimes he would even start to sing in parts of the liturgy that had no singing. At the beginning there were some people telling me this was not acceptable and others saying, but he is here, let's go with it. For two months, the church was divided since this was intruding, breaking the solemnity and order of the church. Besides, Cuica would come drunk and would dance a little and imitate *cuica* loudly with his mouth at every hymn. After this time Cuica disappeared, and the next service without him was empty. Cuica's sounds and free body made a mark on that church. Should have we changed to add him to our services?

That we could not let Cuica stay with us showed that we have clear presuppositions as to how the sacred should be conducted and how bodies should behave. His body didn't understand the shape of the liturgy, his singing didn't follow the presuppositions of the ritual, his presence didn't fit into the onto-liturgical-theological present structures of the meaning of the Christian service. Cuica was not part of the meaning of worship for he was apart from the structure of the worship. Either he had to juxtapose himself to the very order of the worship or he had to move away from it so as not to disturb the meaning God intended for the worship.

Gordon Lathrop defines *precisely* the liturgically unmovable structure where Cuica has to either acquiesce or leave. The metaphysical and onto-theological underpinnings of what I am calling here the *liturgical proper* Lathrop demarcates as the worship patterns of the Christian *ordo*:

> The pattern of the Bible in Christian worship is the pattern of the *ordo*, that ritual ordering and "shape of liturgy" that has united Christians throughout the ages. Ordo here will not mean simply the written directions about what service to schedule at what

time or what specific rite, scripture readings, or prayers to use, although that is one primary meaning of the word in the West, but the presuppositions active behind such scheduling. If we wish to inquire about the meaning of the assembly, we may find help in books of scheduling and reports of ordering and in the patterns they presume. To inquire into the structure of the *ordo* is to inquire about the way meaning occurs in Christian worship. The thesis operative here is this: Meaning occurs through structure, by one thing set next to another. The scheduling of the *ordo*, the setting of one liturgical thing next to another in the shape of liturgy, evokes and replicates the deep structure of biblical language, the use of the old to say the new by means of juxtaposition.[4]

The wide spectrum of liturgical possibilities, with its own specificities defined according to each Christian denomination, and each of them established by its own liturgical procedures and theological account regarding their own tradition, rely on a metaphysical structure, on this *onto-theological* pattern that regulates the relation of being (us) and Being (God) through an unchangeable order of worship. This pattern cuts across liturgical studies through its presuppositions, ordering, scheduling, meaning, structure, shape and juxtaposition, or in one word, a logical and excluding kind of reasoning. For God might not be able to figure out something that goes beyond the proper presuppositions and already expected meanings in worship.

Mark A. Wrathall writes about the metaphysical, onto-theo-logical structure:

> Since Plato, philosophers in the West have proposed various conceptions of a supreme God that was the ground of the existence and intelligibility of all that is. In the works of St. Augustine (and perhaps before) this metaphysical God became identified with the Judeo-Christian creator God . . . According to Heidegger, all metaphysical philosophy was essentially oblivious to being, because all metaphysics took the form of "onto-theology." This means that metaphysics tried to understand the being of everything that is through a simultaneous determination of its essence or most universal trait (the "onto" in "onto-theology"), and a determination of the ground or source of the totality of beings in some highest or divine entity (the "theo" in onto-"theology").[5]

4. Lathrop, *Holy Things*, 33.
5. Wrathall, "Introduction," 1–2.

The Christian liturgical logic understands *being* under the overarching realm of Being. In other words, this code relies entirely on a metaphysical structure that works from and within a given presence, an *a priori* idea of God as the origin of everything that *is*, a totalizing presence that encompasses past, present, and future and cannot be denied. Since this idea of God is a given, originating from its own origin, it becomes what it already is, i.e., self-referential and self-determined. Thus, the liturgical endeavor is a way of *re-presenting* that which has always been *there* through a constant and irrefutable metaphysical presence that makes itself present even in/and through absence and proper and confirming juxtapositions. Thus, this self-enclosed God does not have a body, much less knees, and cannot move or be moved, but instead, God moves everything through revelatory patterns, meaningful categorization, proper theological concepts, and liturgical actions. It can neither be corrupted nor transgressed by human language or sexual accidents but can only be reached through proper re-presentations of its self-revelation. Within this structure, the consequence is that theologians and liturgists become the gatekeepers of the proper.

However, what this proper does and offers is directly related to what it cannot offer and cannot do, or rather, to its improper parts. In other words, the understanding of God can only be possible because of what it excludes. For instance, the approved liturgical/theological documents in any denomination only exist at the expense of what it avoids, represses, and/or denies. The oblivion that structures the ground of God and its liturgical assets has to do with that which conditions the remembrance of what God actually is or might be. In other words, the condition of the possibility of the existence of God and consequently its theological and liturgical developments depend on that which is *other*, strange, unfamiliar, and impossible to *God's self*. Or, one can only talk about the knee because it has never been part of the confession of the Christian faith.

Liturgy and Alterity[6]

Let me start by giving one definition of alterity:

> Etymologically alterity is the condition of otherness . . . many modernists pursued alterity for its disruptive potential, but it never had a fixed location. In the wake of feminist theory and postcolonial discourse, the term has taken on a renewed valence, wherein alterity is privileged as a position of radical critique of

6. A version of this part was developed in my book *Eucharist and Globalization*, 167–72.

the dominant culture—of what it cannot think or address or permit at all—more than as a place of romantic escape from it.[7]

How should liturgy deal with *alterity*, that which has to do with *difference*, that which alters its order, confuses its scripts, transgress its postulates, and does not resemble the very idea of the same, but rather can only be related to something akin to an intrusion, a foreigner matter, a deviant behavior, an iconoclast move, an improper performance? In other words, how should liturgy host a parasite, that which undoes the condition of its possibility and scatters the very element of its structure? Or, more succinctly, what has this liturgical code forgotten, denied, repressed, and negated?

To answer this question, it is necessary to explore the shadowed rational and not often paradoxical consequences of the logic of the modern liturgical code that is based on hierarchical dichotomies: body and soul, knee and mind, good and bad, God and Evil, safe and condemned, us and them, black and white, clean and dirty, true (proper) and false (improper), men and women, etc. These binary structures have set aside and denied that which they cannot sense, whose appearance cannot be identified or accepted, since it disrupts and disfigures the figural status of its rationality. Nonetheless, as said before, that which the liturgical logic denies is what gives possibility to the structure of its rationality. In other words, the very identity of the Christian liturgical code can only be defined by that which it cannot identify, that is, its own *alterity*, that which is different, unknown. Mark C. Taylor states,

> The history of society and culture is, in large measure, a history of the struggle with the endlessly complex problems of difference and otherness . . . A [twentieth] century that opened with the publication of *The Interpretation of Dreams* should have learned by now that the repressed never goes away but always returns— sometimes violently . . . The problem of the other, however, is not only political; it is also an issue of considerable artistic, philosophical, psychological, and theological importance. The search for irreducible difference and radical otherness obsesses many of our most imaginative and creative artists.[8]

Historically, one result of this dualism and repression within the field of liturgical studies has been the absence of women in liturgical rites and the imposition of white, patriarchal, and heterosexual religious frameworks that settle the universal mode for liturgical gestures. The women, along with

7. Foster et al., *Art since 1900*, 681.
8. Taylor, *Altarity*, xxi.

queer, black, and colonized people, represented the other in the liturgical structures. As a consequence, these colonialist liturgical movements still deny, dismiss, and/or bracket the presence of the *other* in the proper religious spaces where power control is always at stake. The *other* has knees, and they should be evangelized in order to behave accordingly to the proper Christian faith. The colonizer spreads and forces its familiar rationality within the colonized as a way to move the *other* into sameness, turning the *other* into the colonizer's self-realization. Thus, the unknown becomes knowable, safe, and open to deal with and to control. This makes Barbara Brown Taylor, a prominent and wonderful Anglican thinker and preacher, feel *at home* in the worshipful service in a "small, tin-roofed (Anglican) church in Western Kenya." She said,

> I did not understand a word of the service, but *I understood perfectly what we were doing* that morning. I had learned it halfway around the world in another language, including the part that begins: "We believe in one God . . ." *Essentially mysterious but entirely accessible, the sacraments are pure genius for teaching us what we need to know about our relationship with God.*[9]

This *pure genius* of the sacraments teaches and establishes the limits of the familiar, the figurable, the representable, the controllable, and the attainable. This *genius* turns the other and its unfamiliar, threatening assets into a mirror, changing the unfamiliar, what does not resemble *us*, into familiar, recognizable terms, elements, postures, rationality, behavior, practices, gestures, and so on. The universal liturgical code, based on universal understandings of being (us) in relation to Being (God), serves as a movement between us (the proper, the colonizer) and them (the improper, the colonized). This movement turns the other into itself, providing connection by establishing a safe distance through binaries (us and them), clearing up differences, edges, and oppositions, and firming the ground of the *unmoved mover*, i.e., God/colonizer, as the only ground for comprehension, perception, and rationality.

This strange familiarity came to Barbara Brown Taylor with the fact that the *liturgical code* was pulsing at that small church the same way it pulses at her own denomination in the United States, giving frame, meaning, rhythm, authenticity, and thus security to that moment. The *otherness* of the Kenyans was shadowed by the light shone through the structures of the inherent liturgical and theological logic that made Taylor say, "*I understood perfectly,*" and felt it "*entirely accessible.*" In the proper performance of the sacraments, she *knew* everything she needed to know about her relationship

9. Taylor, *Preaching Life*, 66. Italics are mine.

with God, so much so that the people of Kenya, the *other*, became a joyous surplus, since they were not actually needed once the liturgical frame and theological words were already given. This surplus could come then as a native dance or an offering by Kenyans in colored clothes, which obscures the idea that it was a colonized, universal logic that framed, structured, and imposed the whole reasoning of religion over *the other*. Moreover, in her experience, *the other* was turned into her sameness and she didn't have to deal with any scary element of a strange faith.

This overarching control of modern and colonial rationality means that anybody from Europe to the United States, Latin America to Asia, the Azores Islands to Papua New Guinea, can sense some kind of familiarity with the logic of Christian liturgical representations. Outside these *meaningful ways* there are only shadows, the shadows of the *other*, of inconsistency, of moving knees, of unpresentability, and the absence of a proper knowledge.

As we try to move our knees, our task is to find that which is not proper within and outside of this exclusive horizon of meaning, so that the colonized, the subaltern, the *other*, might have a chance to become the owners of their knees and their own dancing relations around the world, rather than always continuing to be the same as its colonizer.

In order to do that, one must *liturgize* that which might have been left unthought, *unliturgized*, that which does not fit into an acceptable rationality and waits to spur the imagination. In other words, one tries to capture what cannot be captured, to hear the noises of the *other*, its absurdities, and how it made us deaf and blind. According to Mark C. Taylor, to think the unthinkable is to *think not*. To think not is the attempt to escape these dualisms by trying to overcome them through the impossibility of a synthesis of a dialectic term. He says that things should be related to the negative, including religion:

> To think not is to linger with a negative, which is not merely negative. The not is something like a non-negative negative that is not positive. It is virtually impossible to articulate this strange notion in terms that do not seem utterly paradoxical. (Unlike the structuralists who taught us to think in dualistic terms.) Thinking not explores territory that is not only unmapped but it is unmappable. The not does not exist; nor does the not not exist; neither something nor nothing, the not falls between being and nonbeing.[10]

10. Taylor, "Retracings," 271.

The unmapped/unmappable territory of religion invites us to linger a little longer with the negative, i.e., that which cannot be named because it is so scandalous, improper, unethical, outrageous, unbalanced, and scary. In this lost territory, where *the labor of the negative* happens, liturgical performances become similar to what Taussig calls *writing*. He says,

> So our writing, becomes an exercise in life itself, at one with life and within life as lived in social affairs, not transcendent or even a means to such, but contiguous with action and reaction in the great chain of storytelling telling the one always before the last. Yet, how can you be contiguous with the not merely empty, but negative, space?[11]

By moving into the negative space, into the shadowed spaces rejected by the traditional proper, we can add to our liturgies some of the things we never thought we could. We should not only play but perform, sing, protest, dance, and enact the negative that goes on in the world, those disastrous aspects of life. Not only the death of Jesus on the cross, but also the unspeakable pain of people in Asia after the tsunami, or the complete abandonment by the government of African-Americans in New Orleans, or the monstrous gap between the rich and poor in Brazil. To move into the negative space is to linger with questions that are not so easy to console or find answers. It is to think our liturgies as *liturgical performances*, as moveable, fluid, and changeable performative orders with different set ups of spaces, renewed wording of prayers and songs, as ways to break down the merciless imposition of the *immediacies* within our society that narrow us down into the known and approved; immediacies that shrink our lives to a handful of binary oppositions, our bodies to fossilized identities, and our imaginations to economic wants.

However, moving into the shadows does not necessarily mean shedding light any more than establishing newness. There is no rush into the new but rather, to complicate the already intricate relationship between shadow and light, and work from the opacities of many shades of perspective and perception, old and new. We have a huge tradition to follow and we are responsible for it and for the work of our ancestors. However, there are shades within this tradition, and within these shades we might approximate knee movements and thoughts (sexualized incarnation), remembrance of past and future (*anamnesis*), presence and absence (sacraments), reality and illusions (political faith), revisiting the constant coming of what might have never been (the possibility of God).

---

11. Taussig, *Defacement*.

Again, I do not intend to deny or dismiss the official definitions and designations of liturgy since these definitions are not going away anytime soon, but rather to think about ways to open up the field of liturgy to wrestle with unimagined movements of our knees, of our bodies, of our feelings, sensations, and perceptions, wondering about and between the (ir)rationalities of God, our faith, and its (im)possible representations. Heidegger said,

> Perhaps, there is a thinking outside of the distinction of rational and irrational, more somber-minded still than scientific technology, more somber-minded and hence removed, without effect, yet having its own necessity.[12]

The movement of our knees might be what Heidegger calls a "clearing."[13] It provides a *thinking* that does not entail only our heads but also our bodies. It may begin with our knees and the ways we might think, move, touch, kiss, and praise God. It does not serve as a way out of metaphysics but offers a way of thinking our faith and liturgical space through our knees.

A Feminist Latin American Hermeneutics of the Knees[14]

Liberation theology forgot to pay attention to our knees as well. They didn't see that it was our knees that were tied up by injustice and stiffened by death. We were taught to stay put and that they would bring redemption to our lives. Especially for women, the knees were targeted in an effort to silence them and control their acts of resistance. In order to become subjects of one's own history, one has to move and take over their own knees. Perhaps we never heard about our knees because liberation theology had its own bodily and sexual stiffness.[15]

Our knees are placed between the proper of the other and the otherness of our own subjectivities, between that which we were turned into and that which we were/might have been/might be. Our knees perform our lost identities. Between the streets of carnival and the road to church lies the ability of women to dance, and also to survive between poverty, violence, and resistance. In the midst of the abuse and abandonment of men and government, poor women hold their lives and the lives of their children

12. Taussig, *Defacement*, 449.

13. Heidegger, "The End of Philosophy and the Task of Thinking."

14. This part is a conversation with Nancy Cardoso Pereira, who wrote a fascinating article titled "De-evangelization of the Knees," 119–24.

15. See Althaus-Reid, *Indecent Theology*.

right at the bending part of their legs. But they are not bending their knees to accept somebody else's impositions anymore. In spite of all the catechesis and attempted rigidity, it is between the femur, the tibia, the muscles, and the patella that they carry their strength and know how to hold and bend life, the world, and the word of God.

The knee is not only a place to hold weight but also a place to think. Rodin's famous sculpture *The Thinker* shows that the left elbow of the thinker is placed on the right leg right at the knee. This is a very unusual position for thinking. It is both uncomfortable and painful. Perhaps Rodin wanted to tell us the obvious, that to think is a painful action. However, perhaps Rodin suggests that the exercise of thinking happens at the knees.

Nancy Cardoso Pereira is a third-world theologian working with poor people in Brazil and Latin America today. Working with poor women she realized that the knees are a powerful theological-erotic-biblical-bodily-political-hermeneutical exercise to empower women. With them, she discovered how women's knees have been domesticated, obscured, and exploited, and that for one to have freedom, one has to be in charge of one's own knees. Pereira says,

> The interior part of our knees is also the bending of our morality, and of our shame. The construction of bodies and the metabolisms of knowledge production, the domestication of objective and subjective bending of men and women. Knees are educated and evangelized in distinctive ways, with different dislocations, vertices and openings. Knees learn to control and are controlled.[16]

The movements of our knees are intrinsically related to the ways we think, create, and live our worlds. Our knees, along with our bodies, learn what to accept and to reject, and are aware of control and subjection. Our knees know what touches are allowed, what movements they are supposed to do—so much so that she says,

> Ah! The necessary caresses of a secularly domesticated knee! Ah! The basic work! What I had to redo myself in the circular shape of my own knee. To pull the layers of terror and genuflections of all my female ancestors and slide my hand between the spaces of my knees, and find at the end my hair and my hand without feeling vulgar, paralyzed, or an orphan.[17]

16. Pereira, "De-evangelization of the Knees," 121.
17. Pereira, "De-evangelization of the Knees," 122.

Melany, "Una flor (A flower)"

Melany is six years old, from El Salvador. In this picture she drew a flower. During her time at the bus station [in McAllen, Texas], she drew a series of flower pictures.

The coming-to-know of her own body, without shame or apologies, the grasping for the fact that she came to discover that some *erased* parts of her body were actually there, and that what was deliberately denied, terrorized, and made null could be felt as joy, pulsation, movement, pleasure, and whatever she wanted it to be. And that was all because she started to touch her knee.

And men, having to read/see/listen to her without thinking about vulgarity, exactly how Pereira says she would have felt, would also have felt that way if it was not for her own affirmation and pride of her body. Pereira's hand gets to not only her naked knee but to ourselves as well. We see them and have to come to terms with what we have made of ourselves, what we have lost, and how rigid we are.

Pereira says,

> It is because we always had ill-evangelized knees . . . bent liturgically in the shape of Fear, Feast and Death. The gesturing of the Christian final conquest in the Latin American continent was marked by the long stretch of inquisition (end of the sixteenth century in Brazil) and ended up educating our knees with a disproportion between the gesture and belief.[18]

Our liturgical gesturings are usually schizophrenic. Our bodies are often disconnected from much of what happens in the worship services. It is as if our bodies must be shut down while the mouths of the preachers speak endlessly, and the ears of the people listen eternally. The knees are made to

18. Pereira, "De-evangelization of the Knees," 120.

be quiet, to carry the body in appropriateness. The equation of belief and rigidity is the correlation between silence and death, and our bodies are caught up in this entanglement. Our knees are made to believe and not to move, to stand together and never, ever open the legs. Pereira powerfully establishes the following connections:

> The bodies learned to obey first the weight of violence and of the punishment that were accompanied by the catechesis and the homily. Nobody was invited to be convinced. The knees were co-opted to bend and then belief was invented.[19]

At first, the Christian message of love came to our hearts through the bending of our knees. Once our knees were bent appropriately, we were evangelized, converted. And we believed in this love. The symbols were so beautiful. Kneeling to God, what better expression of surrender? But then, when we tried to stand up and walk and dance, we were told that we could not do that anymore. Along the way, we forgot that we had knees and that there was dance. We were left only believing in our liturgies. Pereira continues to relate liturgy and the domestication of our knees:

> To be on our knees for the *Angelus* means a lot: first, this prayer represents the acceptance of the major beliefs regarding Mary: Divine Incarnation, maintenance of Virginity, Annunciation; second, the ringing of the bells mark the prayers of the *Angelus*, regulate the hours of the day and emphasize the dominium of the church over time. To the first ring, we begin to work, then the second ring and it is time to eat and finally the last ring and we must go back home. Thus, kneeling at the ringing of the bell at the *Angelus* is to accept the Church as owner of time and the sacred history as the fountain of order.[20]

None of our gestures in our liturgies are done without a purpose, a sense, a history, an intention and, unfortunately, they are not done only out of piety. The religious structures of power take over our hearts, minds, and bodies and place us under a power that suppresses and controls our bodies according to the rules made by man. God might not have much to do with it. And everything is done there, at the liturgical space, a space that is never neutral, never untouched by politics, power or control.

> Seated: legs crossed. The repeated aspects of learning by generations of women: the gap within the legs avoided. The gap between the legs and its cartography . . . All the effort placed

19. Pereira, "De-evangelization of the Knees."
20. Pereira, "De-evangelization of the Knees."

on the knees with the learning of yes! And the no! The knees as collective knowledge, deposited in the joint and its capacity to bend. To transit between allowed positions and through the vortices of abused movements, absorbing what centuries of culture and biology had developed for the female knees: obedience, seclusion, grace.[21]

To undo this abusive control over the cartography of the female knees and legs is to undo the metaphysics of patriarchalism, heterosexualism, and centuries of learning the proper that men have imposed and learned to gladly approve. Women must discover their knees again and then be able to dance and move their knees in our worship services without fear, anxiety, grace, or obedience. Pereira says,

> Connected: femur, tibia, patella, cartilage and ligaments. These are my knees. I got here alone. I am not going to tremble from fear, shame, coldness or indecision. This is the best lost night of all nights. Besides, from now on, I am the owner of my knees and nobody else.[22]

Who controls our knees? This is a key question. What has the church done to our knees? Were our knees shadowed by the proper? At church, our knees had to bend in a sign of obedience and had to follow the places that we were told. The knees could never jump up and down, could never be shown, could never misbehave. Knees became the location in our bodies where we are put to shame. To bend our knees is never a sign of resistance but a sign of giving up, of surrender. With our knees bent we cannot go anywhere, cannot escape, cannot run, cannot affront. The bending of our knees is the controlling of our movements and finally, the usurpation of our own lives, in the name of the proper, for the sake of sameness and safety.

What would happen to our liturgies if women started to open their legs and loosen the rigidity of their knees in this sacred space? Would we *allow* them to dance that way? To let the knee dance is to open up the possibility to entertain the unknown, which could be a parasite and disturb our safe, proper, and respectful ways of worshiping God. Thus, all this boils down to this one question: Who holds the control of our knees?

21. Pereira, "De-evangelization of the Knees," 121.

22. Pereira, "De-evangelization of the Knees," 119–22.

Conclusion

The title of this article makes a clear reference to an expression found in a song sung by African slaves in United States, "gimme de kneebone bent." Jacqui Malone writes about its origins:

> Africans brought to North America were no doubt affirming their ancestral values when they sang a slave song that urged dancers to "gimme de kneebone bent." To many western and central Africans, flexed joints represented life and energy, while straightened hips, elbows, and knees epitomized rigidity and death. The bent kneebone symbolized the ability to "get down."[23]

The ability to get down does not mean surrender or subservience, but rather an assurance that the body had strength to move, to twist, to shake, to hold an energy that was like a belief. If the body was alive, they were alive. The knee bent was a certainty that final death was not close by, and that even the rigidity of the social system demonstrated through exploitation, violence, and death could not hold back the aliveness of those bending knees. Moreover, it was these bending joints, these fighting knees that, along with the movements of hands, arms, hips, torso, head, and foot that would bring about changes in culture and would write and change history.

We must develop a new hermeneutics of our knees for our theological-liturgical practices and thinking. They are signs of resistance, of political struggles, of sexual battles. Those who are in charge of their knees are perhaps more aware of their sexual lives. Against the fixation of the phallic, erected, fetishized discourse of a Christian message that makes our bodies stiff, we should shout with our bending knees and challenge the metaphysical arrogance of heterosexuality.

Liturgical performances that invoke "Gimme de kneebone bent" and evoke a hermeneutic of the knees can, even if awkwardly, loosen up the structures of stiffened truth and develop the power of women, making uncomfortable that which seems to be safe. The metaphysics of the proper and the denial of difference have an immense influence in the controlling of our knees and respectively our ability and desire to dance. Once we are able to find and practice ways to unlock the codes that keep alterity away and the theological and the liturgical proper that keep women's knees stiffened, controlled, exploited, secluded, and obedient, we will be able to dance with God and create liturgical performances that will not do away with the order

23. Malone, *Steppin' on the Blues*, 12.

of our liturgies, but will expand the possibilities of its liturgical gestures and movements.

"Gimme de kneebone bent" and we will blur the borders of the liturgical spaces with the borders of the economic, the sexual, and the political, and we will create hospitality for other possibilities of life and other possibilities of God.

Then, and perhaps only then, will we understand, and dance what Shakira says in "Hips Don't Lie":

> I never really knew that she could dance like this
> She makes a man want to speak Spanish,
> Como se llama, bonita, mi casa, su casa
> Shakira, Shakira
> And I'm on tonight
> You know my hips don't lie
> And I'm starting to feel it's right
> All the attraction, the tension
> Don't you see baby, this is perfection
> *Baila en la calle de noche*
> *Baila en la calle de día*
> She's so sexy every man's fantasy
> a refugee like me back with the Fugees
> from a third-world country
> I go back like when Pac carried crates
> For Humpty Humpty
> We need a whole club dizzy
> Why the CIA wanna watch us?
> Colombians and Haitians
> I ain't guilty, it's a musical transaction
> No more we do snatch ropes
> Refugees run the seas 'cause we own our own boats
> Oh, you know I'm on tonight and my hips don't lie.[24]

A feminist approach to the knees is just the first stop on this road of hermeneutics of the body, an approach that should always be corrected by other knee movements and thoughts. Then we should take on Shakira's suggestions and de-construct the hips, then the hands, the feet, the hair, the belly, the eyes, the mouth, the vagina, the neck, the penis, the skin, and so

24. Mebarak, Alfanno, Jean Duplessis, Diaz, and Parker, "Hips Don't Lie."

on. Paraphrasing Derrida, I would say that the constancy of God in my life is called by other movements of the body. In order to finish, I will mention another quote from Nancy Cardoso Pereira, who taught me to be aware of my, her, and our knees. She said,

> One day, I hope nobody will listen, I will pray with my hands on my knees. I will open my skirts and show my knees before God as a living and holy sacrifice. These are my knees and their works! Blessed be them! Scratched and tired, and other paralyzed and ill. They are the ones who ordain history and time, not others. I learned to introduce myself to God with strong knees and a curious face. Now everything is urgency: I take everything by my hands. And this is going to be my de-evangelization. I de-catechized myself by revolving my knees and my obedience, its excessive contours. In my late years, I will not be afraid only of osteoporosis but the interrupted memory of my knees, the hindered possibilities and postponement of alternatives. From the knees up. From the belly button down . . . the interminable exercise of being alive as whole. Mystery.[25]

With our kneebones bent and our hips telling the truth, we will be able to dance to God as we never did. In order to get there, we desperately need Nancys, Shakiras, Marcellas, Ivones, Janets, Marias, Mahalias, Deloreses, Daisys, Antonias, Beneditas, and so many other women's knees moving, in order to teach us how to move/live/love, to undo centuries of colonization, to help us discover our own naked knees and finally, to learn how to dance.

25. Pereira, "De-evangelization of the Knees," 122.

9

Praying with the World at Heart

Prayer is an invitation to God to intervene in our lives, to let God's will prevail in our affairs; it is the opening of a window to God in our will, an effort to make God the Sovereign of our soul. We submit our interests to God's concern, and seek to be allied with what is ultimately right. Our approach to the holy is not an intrusion, but an answer.

—Abraham Joshua Heschel

Where do we start when we pray? Where are the places that we go to pray? What sources do we use to pray? What do we pay attention to when we pray? What theologies, gestures, bodies, communities, and commitments inform our prayers? Where does our grammar for prayer come from? To talk about prayers is to talk about that which gives us life. Prayers have the power to create, transform, and hold our worlds together. Growing up, my mother would repeat a phrase that I think is from E. M. Bounds but was used by Billy Graham: "Much prayer, much power. Little prayer, little power. No prayer, no power." My mother has always been a woman of prayer, and if I know the power of prayer today, it is because of her own devotion to prayer. She prayed without ceasing.

My mother would never let me leave the house without a prayer and always reminded me to pray before going to bed. These habits are still within me. Lately, to pray has become both easier and more difficult at the same time. It became easier because I don't carry the anxiety I once had to see my prayers answered. I somewhat know, especially when I am not suffering, that God will do whatever God wants to do. On the other hand, it has become increasingly more difficult to pray because there are so many disasters piling up in our world today that I don't know what to pray for. Prayer holds together both an aspect of agency and powerlessness. In any case, we are called to pray. When I was in my early teenager years, my father gave me a globe with the map of the world. I used to pray holding the globe/world within my arms, next to my heart. I had learned that I always had to pray for the salvation of the world. To this day, I still pray with the world close to my heart. We pray not because God needs our prayers but because the world needs our prayers.

My prayer life has been marked by both the brutality and gentleness of our daily lives, by the un/bearable, un/framed materiality of our glorious/disastrous reality, by the heaviness/lightness of our bodies, a dizzying search for answers and what I should pay attention to when I pray. Below you will see an array of prayer sources that create, perhaps, an unrecognized theological discourse embedded in a heart filled with vast blessings and emotions, and a mind tormented again and again by the disasters of the world and the life of the poor. The events of the world both shrink and expand a faith that longs for a new time, a healed world, where the poor find food and shelter, the economic powers come crumbling down, the afflicted find some solace and those that are laid back become disturbed by the burning events of our days. I always pray with my community with a broken heart, wrestling with my own faith or lack thereof. While I am still far from "be still my soul . . ." I am learning how to pray. Slowly.

People are dealing with life and death right now as we read/pray! We have always to pray more! Prayers do have the power to change things! For I believe that "much prayer, much power. Little prayer, little power. No prayer, no power."

In this chapter, we will hear stories and songs and poems that pertain to the realm of prayer, utterances of the soul searching, claiming, confronting, recognizing, connecting God in expansive ways.

Lost Grace

She was at the counter of a drugstore waiting for the medicine. In her arms, her daughter was sleeping. In her hands, a torn paper, the prescription given by a doctor. After a while, the pharmacist comes to her and says "I am sorry you don't have insurance, we cannot give you the medicine." She didn't understand and said, "Medicine for my daughter. Please." The man repeated, "I am sorry you don't have health insurance, can you pay?" "Yes, yes"

she said and the pharmacist replied, "It is $450.00." She opened
her purse and while holding her exhausted sleeping daughter,
she picked up twelve dollars and 37 cents. While she was putting
the money at the counter with some difficulty, the pharmacist
said, "Madam, I am sorry, this medicine is too expensive . . ."
She stretched out her arm showing the sign "wait" with her hand
while she was trying to find more money in the ends of her purse.
The pharmacist was embarrassed and the people on the line
were starting to lose their patience. She found a couple of nickels
and added them to the rest of the money she had placed on the
counter. The man said, "I am sorry, this is not enough." She said,
"Take it please." "Everything," she said. "Medicine please." "I am
sorry but this is not enough. Please step outside of the line. I
need to help the people in line." She said, "Medicine please, my
daughter sick, very sick." "Please step aside," said the now impa-
tient pharmacist. She didn't understand and her exhausted face
was filled with fear. She said, "Please doctor, please." A man in the
line took the money from the counter and tried to give it to her
but she refused, "No please take, medicine for my daughter, very
sick, very sick." The man opened her purse and threw the money
inside. "Please step aside," this other customer screamed. She
stepped aside saying, "Please medicine, my daughter very sick.
Please." The pharmacist and the people in the line started to act
as if she was not there and kept doing their business. She started
to scream, "Medicine please," while trying to get the money out
of her purse. The pharmacist said, "Madam, if you continue to
scream I will have to call security." The woman started to say,
"Sorry, sorry, medicine please, medicine please. My daughter
. . ." And while she was crying she went through the line asking people, "Money please, my daughter very sick, look," while
she showed them the prescription given by the doctor. People
started to complain saying she was bothering everyone and the
pharmacist called security. "No please" she said, "medicine only.
I go, please medicine my daughter very sick, I go, I go." Security
came and she started wailing so loud that she woke her daughter
up. Both were crying when the two security guards came to take
this five-foot, five-inch woman with her four-year-old daughter
in her arms. While security took her out she cried even louder,
"Señor Jesús ten piedad, ten piedad! Ten piedad Señor Jesús, mi
hija está tan enfermita, por favor les pido que me dé la medicina
que mi hija necesita. Por favor. Por favor Jesucristo . . ." And she
was taken out of the drugstore and placed on the street and the
two guards secured the door. She sat on the cold street. She and

her daughter were crying and she was praying, "Jesucristo ten
piedad." Jesus Christ, have mercy.

Her prayers were never answered. Surely God did not have mercy on
her. Surely her daughter went without medicine. Can we say that God had
mercy on her? How so? Who was to blame? God? The easy way out, "If she
wasn't here illegally," one could say, "she wouldn't have to go through this."
But she was a citizen of this country . . . We are the arms and legs, hands and
eyes, mouths and ears of God's answer. Her prayer will never be answered
if not through us. Thus, prayer is an exercise in becoming, in our bodies,
through our feelings, breathing, and thoughts, always available to the poor.
To pray to God is to become that which we pray for. To sing the *Kyrie* every week in Christian worship services is to become, by God's grace, God's
merciful flesh in the world for the lowly, for those who have no agency, no
access, no voice, no place in the world. To pray thus is an act of love, love for
God, love for my brothers and sisters, love for the world. To learn to pray is
to learn how to become Christ in the world. To learn how to pray is to walk
around in the world with our hearts outside of our bodies witnessing the
least of these being mercilessly crushed. To learn how to pray is to find ways
to change things and create conditions of an honored and blessed life for all.
Prayer is to make laws that change her situation! Prayer is the opposite way
of throwing her on the streets. It is a whole economic system that demands
dignified life for all! And nothing less than that! Politically, socially, cultur-
ally, to pray is to become God's love for the least of these. I will not learn
how to pray until I learn how to serve, how to commit with the less favored,
how to make sure that the poor are cared for and attended to by the mercy
of God in and through us.

Until this woman receives medicine for her daughter, I will never learn
how to pray. Every time a prayer like this woman uttered is unanswered, a
grace is lost. Sadly, we live amidst "lost graces,"[1] possibilities of God's tangible manifestation in our midst, offered to us in order to expand us, to help
us become more committed Christians and better humans. But we don't
pray, we often miss these opportunities. *Lost graces* are God's graces offered
to us, and yet we do not pay attention to them because we don't pay attention to the poor. We don't have eyes to see, the ears to hear, the hands to
touch, arms to embrace, or boldness to fight for the right causes with the
poor.

---

1. "Lost grace" is a term used by André Breton in *Mad Love*.

The Theological Weight of the Circumstances

Ivone Gebara, a Brazilian theologian, said in a recent article published in Brazil, "In general, theologians reflect very little of the poetic expression of the joys and pain of Christian communities. There is a distance between the work of those who analyze the contents of the religious tradition of our days and those who are responsible for the animation of the community, its feasts and weekly celebrations."[2]

She is right! Theologians reflect mostly on the high dogmatics of our theological systems, engage with the philosophical aspects of our beliefs, the historical and linguistic aspects of our creeds, the articles of our books of order, liturgies and confessions. However, we don't take much time to pay attention to the full exuberance of things that affect the daily lives of people: the price of the bus or daily bread, the violence on the streets, the symbols in their houses, their music, their love life, their joys and dreams. They do not wrestle with people's pains. Whether theologians pray or not, the daily life of people does not often find itself in our theological books or liturgical books.

Perhaps Gebara says this because her daily life is interrupted by the daily affairs of the people. She cannot become a recluse in a writing retreat. Instead, she always has to stop her writing/researching because a couple started a fight, a woman was raped, kids couldn't get food at school, and so on. In her theology, the relationality of people is what helps her understand who God might be and it is in the tapestry of life where God appears and acts in people's lives. Getting deeply involved in the daily life of people, theology must become the breathing of joys and pains of the people. God has no reason to be-come if not reasoned through the lives of the poor, where God is be-coming all the time. Becoming acquainted with people's daily lives helps us gain a new grammar of faith, thus a new grammar for our prayers.

Gebara says that, "The world of our circumstances is our life, with its grandeurs and personal and relational miseries. It is from this world that our prayers and our music, even the most sublime ones, are born."[3] The *lex orandi* (law of prayer) is born out of the law of life (*lex vivendi*), the daily life of the poor, as it gives shape to their joys, concerns, and beliefs (*lex credendi—law of belief*). The task for theologians is to attend to the *lex orandi-vivendi-credendi* of the poor, listening to their prayers and learning with them how to pray properly. It is there, rather than in our liturgical books, that we can find the most powerful and sublime prayers, hymns, and

2. Gebara, "Liturgia e Theologia," 60.
3. Gebara, "Liturgia e Theologia," 59.

affirmations of faith. There, in the midst of the struggle for justice with the poor we learn the ethics we need to judge, act, and live. These are some of the prayers people pray that Gebara mentions:[4]

> "I believe that the world will be better, when the smallest one who suffers believes in the small."

> "You are the God of the poor, a human and small God who sleeps on the streets, God of a torn face."

> "To receive Communion with this suffering people is to make an alliance with the oppressed people."

> "All of sudden, our eyes cleared out, cleared out, cleared out! And we discovered that the poor have value, have value, have value!"

> "The people of God marched to the promised land. Moses was walking ahead of them. Today we are Moses when we face the oppressor."

> "I have so many brothers I can't count, and a beautiful sister whose name is freedom."

These prayers, like daily actions, feed utopias, and transform the world.

Holding the World with Affection

For a Protestant boy, it was a surprise to discover a monastery of Protestant nuns in the midst of the mountains in Europe. I always thought that only Roman Catholics had monasteries. And I could never figure out why people would give their lives to be inside of a monastery. Spending a few days with those nuns transformed my vision. In one conversation I asked them, "Why do you stay here, what is the purpose of you giving your life to live here?" And one of the nuns said, "We are here to pray for the world every day. There are so many people going through pain, turmoil, and suffering, we must tend them, we must care for them, we must stand before God on their behalf. God does not need us to do it but these people might need us. We hold all of the suffering and the world in our prayers with affection."

---

4. Gebara, "Liturgia e Theologia," 62.

Gratitude and Forgiveness

To be grateful in life is a constant challenge. That is why I love to have communion every week because it forces me to see the ways that God is blessing my life and I must be thankful no matter what I am going through. At the Eucharistic table I must say, "God, thank you!" At the table I must learn with the early Christians who organized their prayers around gratitude and forgiveness. At the table I learn with my brothers and sisters that I have been blessed. If I can learn to wrap my days as well as my heart around prayers of gratitude and petitions of mercy, I will gain a kind of wisdom that will help me go through life better. Every day, at least three times a day, I must utter a prayer of gratitude and beg for forgiveness. Life is better lived if lived through *Eucharistia* and *Kyrie*, thanksgiving and mercy. God have mercy, thanks be to God!

Reconstructing Past, Present, and Future

Our prayers have the power to recreate the past, reshape the present, and invent a future where the Reign of God can happen. Time and time again, we must create prayers that take the conditions of the world, inform us of the tragedies of the world, and offer a new way of being, acting, hoping, learning, and believing. Bishop Pedro Casaldáliga, a prophet in Brazil, wrote a mass to celebrate the past-presence-future of the *Quilombolas*, heirs of African slaves in Brazil. In this prayer, past, present, and future are remembered, renamed, reframed, and reorganized. The whole mass begins with the following prayer:

> We are coming from the bottom of the Earth,
> coming from the womb of night,
> made into meat at the butcher,
> we have come to remember.
>
> We are coming from the death of the seas,
> coming from the dark and muddy basements,
> heirs of the *banzo*[5] we are,
> we have come to cry.

---

5. *Banzo* is the feeling of something lost, left behind, a longing for something one had but doesn't have anymore. The Africans, when brought to the American continent, used to mention this feeling of *Banzo* about their homeland, people, things, and life.

We are coming from the black rosaries,
coming from our *terreiros*,[6]
from the cursed saints we are,
we have come to pray.

We are coming from the shop floor,
coming from sounds and shapes,
of art denied, we are
we have come to create.

We are coming from the depths of fear,
coming from the deaf currents
a long lament we are,
we have come to praise.

A de Ó (Recited)

From the Exile of life,
the mines at night,
the meat sold,
the Law of the Scourge,
the *Banzo* of the seas . . .
to the new *Albores*![7]
we go to *Palmares*[8]
with all the drums!

We are coming from the rich stoves,
coming from the poor brothels,
of sold meat we are,
we have come to love.

We are coming from the old slave quarters,
Coming to the new slums,
of the margins of the world we are,
we have come to dance.

6. *Terreiros* are places in Brazil for some of the African religious worship services.

7. *Albores* here can be new mornings.

8. *Palmares* was a well-known, large free community made up of Africans who resisted slavery along with outcasts.

We are coming from the trains of the suburbs,
coming in crazy pendants,
with life between the teeth we arrive,
we have come to sing.

We are coming from the big stadiums,
coming from samba schools,
dancing the samba of rebellion we come,
we have come to sway.

We are coming from the womb of *Minas*
coming from the sad *mocambos*,[9]
of silent cries silent we are,
We have come to charge.

We are coming from the cross of the power mills,
We are bleeding the cross of Baptism,
tagged by iron we were,
We have come to scream.

We are coming from the top of the hills,
coming from the lower parts of the law,
from the unnamed graves we arrived
We have come to cry out loud.

We are coming from the ground of the *Quilombos*,[10]
coming from the sound of drums,
the new *Palmares* we are,
We have come to fight.[11]

These prayers said in unison shape not only people of African descent in Brazil but also all who live in Brazil. The whole prayer is structured around

9. *Mocambos* were villages formed by Africans who freed themselves from slavery.

10. *Quilombos* are like *mocambos*.

11 Casaldáliga and Tierra, "Missa dos Quilombos" (music by Nascimento). My translation.

"We have come from" and "We have come to," showing not only their diverse origins but also the places they are going now, opening up spaces of creation and life in the present. Naming who they are, they embrace their past of utter pain and struggle and prepare the way for a future of struggle empowered by their ancestors, organized by their songs, encapsulated by their gifts, strength, wisdom, and all of the movements of their souls and bodies. Such a prayer has the power to scare the white patriarchalism and racism still in place in Brazilian society and to create a new world of justice and hope, one that is already happening under their feet. Stepping on this new holy ground, their/our holy ground, all of us are affected by its power. By praying their prayers with them, I learn to honor them. I dance with them. I sing with them as I become one of them, loving them deeply and fighting now the same fight of justice and hope. That is why we must pray each other's prayers!

Psalms

My mother taught me the best way to contextualize the use of the Psalms for our days. Here is a story that my fifty-six-year-old brother Joe told me based on Psalm 121.

For almost four years Joe could not find a job, and his situation was getting worse and worse. He lost a very good job he had, then he lost his car, and his house had several payments late. His wife got sick, his daughter had to stop going to school, and in spite of it all he went to the streets of São Paulo every day looking for any job he could find. His shoes had holes in them. . . . One day, he went to my mother's house for lunch and there is a long corridor from the gate at the street to the door of her house. He rang the bell and entered. As he walked towards her, his head was down, his body tired. . . . My mother went to meet him and as soon as she saw him walking she screamed, "Son, look up! Look up right now! I ain't gonna let you look down this way . . ." He was absolutely exhausted, his soul and body beaten up, lonely, with no strength or hope to continue anymore. . . . She approached him, held his head up with her little but strong hands and said, "Look up, son! For your help will come from the Lord . . ." He started to cry and could barely stay standing. My eighty-year-old mother had to hold his body, and crying with him she said, "Look up and say with me, 'I lift up my eyes to the hills—from where will my help come? My help comes from the Lord, who made heaven and earth.'" He couldn't say a word but my mother said, "I am going to continue to say it until you say it with me. Come on . . . 'I lift up my eyes to the hills' . . . say it . . . 'I lift up my eyes to the hills—from where will my help come?' With me now, 'My help comes from the Lord, who made heaven and earth.'" In the midst of tears of exhaustion, with his head still held up by my mother's hands, he started to whisper some words with the salty taste of his tears: "I lift up my eyes . . . I lift up my eyes to the hills . . . I lift up my eyes to the hills." "Continue with me now, son: 'My help comes from the Lord, who made heaven and earth.'" And she continued the psalm for him that she knew by heart: "'He will not let your foot be moved; he who keeps you will not slumber. He who keeps Israel will neither slumber nor sleep. The Lord is your keeper; the Lord is your shade at your right hand. The sun shall not strike you by day, nor the moon by night. The Lord will keep you from all evil; he will keep your life. The Lord will keep your going out and your coming in from this time on and for evermore.'" They ended up saying the whole psalm on their knees. "Look up!"

From the use of Psalm 121 my mother was able to give my brother perspective, new hope, and empowerment. By re-positioning my brother's body, she helped him reposition his soul and his mind towards God. With his head up, he could see God's vastness beyond his immediate surroundings and was reminded of God's grace. He was able to add another possibility for his life, letting something new grow inside of him that didn't exist before, and brought a part of him back to life that was already killed by the adversities of life. My brother's life changed only a year after that day. Today my brother has a new job. He and his family are doing well! Psalm 121, recited by his almost illiterate mother saved his life.

Praying with Brothers and Sisters of Other Traditions

If my references and prayer life were confined to the Christian tradition, my life would be narrow and my God incredibly small. While we have a wealth of prayers from the many Christian churches throughout history, I believe we can gain more of life and of God if we learn to pray the prayers of sisters and brothers of other traditions. My work and my hope is that increasingly, we will be able to pray each other's prayers and sing each other's songs, blessing ourselves with each other's blessings.

So I learned to pray in silence with a Buddhist cylindrical prayer wheel from Tibet. A spindle made of metal, the prayer wheel has a piece of paper inside with a mantra. The way to pray is to spin the wheel. As we spin the wheel, it serves as the spoken prayers and spreads the prayers around the world. Indeed a beautiful silent way of praying! It was Leonardo Boff who said somewhere, "I prefer the silence of Buddha to the endless babbling of the theologians."[12]

I am challenged to learn to pray with Mahatma Gandhi who said, "Prayer is not asking. It is a longing of the soul. It is daily admission of one's weakness. It is better in prayer to have a heart without words than words without a heart." The admission of my weakness can be compared with the *Kyrie* in the Christian tradition. Gandhi reminds us that what is at stake in prayer is what our heart carries, not exactly what we say.

In Rumi, the thirteenth-century Persian poet, jurist, theologian, and Sufi mystic, I read, "I'm like a bird from another continent, sitting in this aviary. The day is coming when I will fly off, but who is it now in my ear who hears my voice? Who says words with my mouth?"[13] As a colonized foreigner, I never know whose voices I am speaking, who is whispering in my ear and who is speaking these words in my mouth. Rumi helps me pray and find a better way back to the multitude that I am.

With Lalla Ded, a fourteenth-century mystic of the Kashmiri Shaivite sect, I learn in countless ways the ways of scriptures, of the real, of my eyes, of my longing and my walking where I always meet myself again.

> To learn the scriptures is easy,
>
> to live them, hard.
>
> The search for the Real
>
> is no simple matter.
>
> Deep in my looking,

---

12. See http://gnt.globo.com/programas/viver-com-fe/videos/2306495.htm.

13. Rumi "Who Says Words with My Mouth?," in *The Essential Rumi*, 2.

the last words vanished.

Joyous and silent,

the waking that met me there.

Prayers to be prayed like mantras, like poetry, like *re-ligare*, hundreds and thousands of times. Our prayer life must learn to pray in another language, another religious tradition, another culture, and another heart. Endlessly. Until we finally learn how to pray.

Praying without Ceasing

My body is suffering

It is my great torpor

I'm languishing

I give you a thousand thanks, my Lord

My bones are shaken up

My shade becomes invisible

My soul is confused

Pierce me, my Lord

My God

Open to me the gates

Of eternal servitude

Throw me your cholera

In the Temple of Zion[14]

A friend has problems with drug addiction. He stole almost everything that had value from his parents' houses in order to buy drugs. He is still wandering around the streets of Brazil, but his parents don't even know if he is still alive. Another friend used to read the obituary section of the newspaper every morning to see if his son was still alive. Another friend had to visit her son in jail because addiction caused him to steal and he was imprisoned. Drugs are spreading throughout the world, consuming the lives of innumerable people. The war against drug cartels initiated by the Clinton administration was a big mistake, and it continues to have no results even with the millions of dollars spent. The drug cartels rule over so many places around the globe. Los Angeles is filled with drugs. Hong Kong lives under their rule. The streets of São Paulo are now filled with people dependent on crack. They live in a region called "crackolandia," in eternal servitude, living

14. Buarque and Lobo, "Salmo."

the cholera of life. The local state and other social and religious organizations are hopeless in their efforts to help them. The descent into drugs is a descent into hell and there are very few who make it back. How do we pray for and with them? How does our prayer create new ways to fight, to struggle, to find new life possibilities? How do we walk/pray with them?

It is not only drugs; more and more our societies are inhabited by people with some kind of disorder. We live in brutal times, where the pressure for distinction and high expectations for success are combined with high anxieties and no space for failure, or opportunity for gentleness. People live with addictions, disorders, and disabilities of so many kinds and face cruel hardships in life. People with mental illness are completely forgotten in Pennsylvania.[15] And there are those who receive the news of terminal illness; death with its open mouth while people are still living. Insults and violence, atrocities, death and no control, anger, and life at the edge of the abyss. So many people go without help and so many people who want to help do not know what to do. Moreover, threads in society run the risk of unraveling on a daily basis. People are trafficked and enslaved, children turned into soldiers, women are battered at every corner of the earth, and the news of disasters is relentless.

My mother is now eighty-two years old, and she still visits my cousin in a mental institution every week. She also goes every week to a nursing home to pray for the elderly and visits hospital rooms offering a prayer for the sick. In times of pain, prayer is fundamental! When we are in pain, creed does not really matter. What matters is the help, consolation and hope for healing that can come from any corner of the world, under whatever name, through whichever medium. Pain is an equalizer of religions and healing options. Whoever is in pain knows no boundaries in their search for healing. The presence of God through family, friends, and loved ones is an answer to a prayer people don't even know how to pray. God's answer to our prayers comes in unexpected ways. In our social life, economy, and culture, immediate relief of pain is always demanded and it is hard to wait on God. So we must be countercultural and pray and say like the psalmist, "Wait for the Lord; be strong, and let your heart take courage; wait for the Lord!"[16]

Along with all of the Psalms, we will continue to wait and pray for each other until God's healing fills the earth. Until then, we will embrace each other and all who are waiting for God, and pray for them ceaselessly.

Three more prayers we should pray daily, with or without faith, for us, for our family and friends, and for the world:

15. Flatow, "DOJ Finds Unconstitutional Solitary Confinement of Mentally Ill."
16. Ps 27:14 NRSV.

God, grant me the serenity to accept the things I cannot change,
Courage to change the things I can,
And wisdom to know the difference.[17]

All shall be well, and all shall be well, and all manner of thing
shall be well.[18]

Stay with us, because it is almost evening and the day is now
nearly over.[19]

"A Future Not Our Own": Prayers, Seeds, and Tears

On many Internet sites this prayer is attributed to Óscar Romero, but it
seems it was composed by Bishop Ken Untener of Saginaw, drafted for a
homily by Cardinal John Dearden in November 1979 for a celebration of
departed priests. As a reflection on the anniversary of the martyrdom of
Bishop Romero, Bishop Untener included in a reflection book a passage
titled "The mystery of the Romero Prayer."[20]

It helps, now and then, to step back and take a long view.
The Kingdom of God is not only beyond our efforts,
it is even beyond our vision.
We accomplish in our lifetime only a tiny fraction
of the magnificent enterprise that is God's work.
Nothing we do is complete, which is a way of saying
that the Kingdom always lies beyond us.
No statement says all that could be said.
No prayer fully expresses our faith.
No confession brings perfection.
No pastoral visit brings wholeness.
No program accomplishes the Church's mission.
No set of goals and objectives includes everything.

This is what we are about:

17. Reinhold Niebuhr, quoted in Smith, *The Serenity Prayer*, 175.

18. Julian of Norwich, *Revelations of Divine Love*, 34.

19. Luke 24:29 NRSV.

20. See http://www.journeywithjesus.net/PoemsAndPrayers/Ken_Untener_A_Fut
ure_Not_Our_Own.shtml.

We plant the seeds that one day will grow.
We water seeds already planted, knowing that they hold future promise.

We lay foundations that will need further development.
We provide yeast that produces effects far beyond our capabilities.

We cannot do everything,
and there is a sense of liberation in realizing that.
This enables us to do something, and to do it very well.
It may be incomplete, but it is a beginning, a step along the way,
an opportunity for the Lord's grace to enter and do the rest.
We may never see the end results,
but that is the difference between the master builder and the worker.

We are workers, not master builders; ministers, not messiahs.
We are prophets of a future not our own. Amen.

Ours is the task of *ora et labora*, praying and working for this world and a world not our own; a work of hope. Rubem Alves quotes Nietzsche and says that trees grow slow. He wants to plant trees knowing that he will never eat of their fruits. His happiness is in knowing that he is providing for a future, where these trees will offer shade and fruits for future generations.[21]

As Christians and human beings made in the image of God, we all have responsibility for this world and for all of its people. Ours is the social and theological work of spreading seeds of peace, health, healing, and love, seeds watered by the very tears of our eyes. Praying with tears and seeds in our hands, this is our *ora et labora* (prayer and work). However, this is not enough. To the *ora et labora* we must add *et saltare*, which is the Latin word for dance. Unless we learn to dance we won't be able to pray and work. By dancing, we learn to live the fullness of life, for there is no life or religion without dancing. We should follow very closely what Nietzsche said: "I should only believe in a God that would know how to dance."[22] To pray, work, and dance. And back again. To pray, work, and dance with our knees, our hands, and our hips, as well. Tears added to the sweat of our bodies. Thus, we pray in our flesh as much as in our hearts and souls. We are fully committed to God, to the well-being of our sisters and brothers, especially the poor, to the world, and to the joy of life.

21. Alves, "Sobre Política e Jardinagem," 26–30.
22. Nietzsche, *Thus Spake Zarathustra*, 24.

Decolonial Wound

The song says, "Come celebrate with me that everyday something has tried to kill me and has failed." Sisters' and brothers' prayers never disconnect suffering from celebration, all mixed up and connected. A promise of hope is enough for us to pray endlessly. Did somebody say hope? I'm praying. Did somebody say faith? I'm praying. Did somebody say love? I'm praying. Praying also when nothing is being said. Hope against hope! Faith against lack! Love against violence! Yes, we are praying! The prayers are the balm of Gilead, to heal the historical wound of oppression, the so present wound of invisibility, the undeniable wound of death. Prayer in hopelessness, in powerlessness, hope in celebration. Howling, wailing . . . nobody knows the troubles I've seen! Longing for a day of peace that I never knew, longing for what I never had, longing for a chance I refuse to see it so clearly. Stretched to my core I pray! For my prayers are seeds! Seeds that will produce trees from which my grandchildren will eat fruit. So I pray! For them to survive! For the trees to grow. Perhaps one day, the colonial wound will disappear.

The Lord's Prayer, by Rubem Alves

To end this essay, I finish with a version of the Lord's Prayer written by the Brazilian theologian, educator, and poet Rubem Alves. Shall we pray?

> Father, mother, with meek eyes
> I know that you are, invisibly, in all things
> May your name be sweet to me,
> The joy of my world.
> Bring me good things that delight you:
> Gardens
> Fountains
> Children
> Bread and wine
> Tender gestures
> Unarmed hands
> Bodies embracing
> I know that you desire to give me my deepest desire
> The desire that I have long forgotten
> But you never forget.
> Make manifest your desire, so that I can laugh.

May your desire be made manifest in our world
In the same way it pulsates within you.
Grant us contentment in the joys of today
Bread, water, sleep . . .
That we may be free of anxiety.
That our eyes would be as humble with others as your eyes
are with us, for if we are ferocious,
we will not be able to welcome your kindness.
Help us to not be deceived by evil desires, and free us from that which
burdens our eyes with death. Amen.[23]

May God teach us how to pray!

23. Alves, *Perguntaram-me se eu acredito em Deus.*

Part III: Liturgy of the World

10

Preaching in the Midst of the Liturgy of the Church, World, and Neighbor[1]

Whatever else the true preaching of the word would need to include, it at least would have to be a word that speaks from the perspective of those who have been crushed and marginalized in our society. It would need to be a word of solidarity, healing and love in situations of brokenness and despair and a disturbing and troubling word of justice to those who wish to protect their privilege by exclusion.[2]

—LETTY M. RUSSELL

Introduction

Preaching, like raising a child, takes a village! Preaching never comes alone but it is a part of a long past that has brought us this far. When we preach, we preach among other brothers and sisters, writers, artists, and a cloud of witnesses who sustain our words and our passion. Preaching begins at the crossroads between our life with Jesus and our history, along with those

1. This article was published in Brazil. "A Pregação na Liturgia da Igreja, na Liturgia do Mundo e na Liturgia do Próximo," in TEAR, Liturgia em Revista, Centro de Recursos Litúrgicos (CRL) e Grupo de Pesquisa Culto Cristão na América Latina, Programa de Pós-Graduação em Teologia da Escola Superior de Teologia, São Leopoldo, RS, 2012.

2. Russell, *Church in the Round*, 139.

with whom we are sharing life at that moment. But more than that, preaching is part of a liturgy, a larger liturgy that is always framing and changing and challenging us. Preaching is "just" a part of a liturgy where words and prayers and singing and eating and washing happen together. Preaching, as the word of God, is uttered, lived, proclaimed, and shapes the world on this privileged theater/worship stage. For this chapter, I will consider the movement of preaching as a key part of a complex work we must do in relation to the "liturgy of the church, the liturgy of the world and the liturgy of the neighbor," as Nathan Mitchel puts it.[3]

As we consider the art of preaching within this confluence—liturgy of the church, the liturgy of the world, and the liturgy of the neighbor—we must attend to the cultural background we are living in today. Preachers are cultural agents and we all must attend to the ways in which our culture works and sends signs of value and formation to all of us. As cultural agents, preachers must continuously check what ideological lenses we use to *see, hear, feel, touch, and taste* our social-economic-political-religious realities in our sermons. What are the theoretical/practical lenses that help us interpret the global designs, our culture at large and our communities in relation to the gospel of Jesus Christ? It is precisely this awareness of our own political, social, economic, cultural, and theological lenses that will help us define what, how, and where to preach. Preachers are called to challenge, dispute, denounce, and fight values, principles, and patterns of culture that go against the gospel. As cultural agents, anthropological researchers, artists in the making, local healers, social challengers, and environmental protectors, preachers are called to transform the world by helping communities see the many ways in which we can fully engage the gospel of Jesus with the lives of churches/communities.

As preachers, shaped around the word of God, we are called to denounce what is producing death in our culture and to protect and reinforce what brings life. In this task, we are called not to defend what is good for Christians but for all humankind, and especially the poor. As preachers, we must get reconnected with the earth and understand that we must be eco/ *oikos*-preachers, that is, preachers deeply drenched in the life of the ecosystems of which we are a part, limiting the abuse of the natural resources as the only way to create the *oikos*, the house of God in our midst.

Our task is fundamentally local, with our own communities, but as we get into our local missions, we see that the global economy renders our local practices of living deeply connected with the larger world. We become responsible for God's world, locally and globally. As the church of Jesus

3. Mitchell, *Meeting Mystery*, 44.

Christ, we are called to witness the gospel through an incarnated spiritual life, social-justice commitments, ecological consciousness, and proper use of the common goods for all in our local communities.

Deeply marked by our cultures, the way we look at our lives and the critical instruments we use to interpret them pretty much shape not only the content, the feelings, and the format of our preaching but also the content, the feelings, and the format of our local communities and cultures at large. So, every preacher is always making social, political, cultural, economic, and religious choices that affect the lives of our parishioners and consequently the culture of our societies.

What Do We See?

Our ministry will depend on our ability to see both the individual needs of our congregants and also the ways in which the world spins. When we look at this crossroads, what do we see? For instance, what are the things that we think are endangering the church of Jesus Christ? Who or what are our so-called enemies?

We must begin with eyes turned towards global war—in the words of Foucault it is *biopower* or bio-politics, and in the expansive use of this notion by Achille Mbembe, in *Necropolitics*. Biopower has to do with the ways in which the state controls life. Power, Foucault says, is always "working to incite, reinforce, control, monitor, optimize, and organize the forces under it: a power bent on generating forces, making them grow, and ordering them, rather than one dedicated to impeding them, making them submit, or destroying them."[4] Biopower "fosters life or disallows it to the point of death."[5] Achille Mbembe uses the term *necropolitics* to emphasize the ways in which the state employs its technologies of power to inflict violence and defines not only who is to live but also who is to die. Thus, the state subjugates its population to the power of death. For Mbembe, "To exercise sovereignty is to exercise control over mortality and to define life as the deployment and manifestation of power."[6] The center of power that enacts power and sovereignty has to do with "the generalized instrumentalization of human existence and the material destruction of human bodies and populations."[7]

4. Foucault, *History of Sexuality*, 1:136.
5. Foucault, *History of Sexuality*, 1:138.
6. Mbembe, "Necropolitics," 12.
7. Mbembe, "Necropolitics," 14.

This way of understanding power explains the necessity for wars under international policies, why deportation can be called a legal strategy for protection of internal walls, and why incarceration is explained as social security. All of these ideological systems are technologies of death orchestrated by the government under the sacred limits of the so-called law.

How do we preach life in a culture where life and death do not belong to us? How do we use reason when reason is not organized to think of life as common ground but as a result of people's ability to survive? How do we reason about the need for proper care of creation and about the limitation of desire and accumulation when the existent economic reason says that unless we develop, unless we buy, we are not going to survive, and that there is no reason to be alarmed about the destruction of the earth? How do we reason about the common good when the *extractivist* state exploits everyone and everything in order to hoard accumulations of wealth for some?

These larger issues have to do with our self-deception in believing that we humans are the measure of the world, which means among so many things: (a) the fact that we think that we are in a line of superiority and not equality with animals and that means that we must control, cage, kill, and use them for our own needs, or fun; (b) the lack of connectivity with a network of mutual dependence in which we depend on each other's lives; (c) because God created us we think that we reign over the infinite cosmic systems and we think that we individuals are the only thing God should care about.

All of this can be translated into a heightened sense of narcissism. Beyond the presence of immigrants of the Muslim religion, our major delusion is the sense that the United States is the greatest nation of the world and can do whatever with whomever, which includes the childish feeling that we are entitled to everything we want. This dream of stupidity confuses social freedom with personal desires and deeply affects our Christian faith. Why adore God if we prefer to adore ourselves?

This dream has symbolic and material contours. The cult of personalities and private needs rules individual entitlement: individual choices, individual decisions, individual needs, and individual desires are turning us increasingly more self-sufficient, with a heightened sense of the private, minding our own business and making it more difficult to live together with somebody else or in any community that challenges us. Is that why there is a one-hour time limit for our worship services? Personal freedom is valued more than mutual solidarity, the protection of private spaces more important than the common spaces of communities. Contrary to that, church only makes sense when we need each other.

Our culture fosters a life lived on one's own needs, where the individual is responsible only for him/herself. Consequently, the presence of an-other creates an opponent, a barrier to the happiness of oneself. Along with this rising narcissism, we are also becoming more cynical, dispassionate about the world, indifferent to the pain of others, searching for our own pleasures, and structuring our lives solely around our own likes, dislikes, and personal enjoyment. This way of being affects every aspect of our culture. All that matters is my privacy. Even worship services and pastors are falling prey to the culture of personal choices. How many pastors have heard that if they don't do what Mr. Joe wants in church or worship, his family will leave the church and with them their money? Last year I heard a good Christian saying that he decided not to go to church anymore because he had to protect his own bubble of sanity. Indeed, church can be maddening, but it is a place where we learn to live together and deal with our estrangement and madness. What I don't hear anymore is how we are our sisters and brother's keeper, how church is our refuge where God enables us to get through another week. Unfortunately, we, the church of Christ, a collective, a fundamentally social group, have also contributed to the development of our narcissistic society.

The economic market that drives the very core of our culture reinforces the cult of the individual. Gilles Lipovetsky, a social thinker from France, defines our times as "hypermodern," which is characterized by hyper-consumption and the hypermodern individual. "Hyper-consumption," he says, "is a consumption which absorbs and integrates more and more spheres of social life and which encourages individuals to consume for their own personal pleasure."[8]

In this process, *enjoyment* is a key word. More than ever, an individual experience is located not in communal processes of discovery and communal agency, but rather in the personal enjoyment of things. Our pleasure is made captive by the market that releases temporary joy through our capacity to buy things. Our satisfaction becomes a product and the market offers credit for us to fulfill our desires created by the same market. Since the church also lives under the logic of the market, some church leaders think that the church has to offer its message as a product to be consumed and to guarantee satisfaction to its members/consumers. The sermon is key in this process. If preachers do not offer a sermon that will guarantee satisfaction, our members/customers will shop for another church and a better preacher/sermon, often a sermon that does not challenge its listeners too much. By making us passive consumers, the market binds us into the empire of private

8. Lipovetsky, *Hypermodern Times.*

enjoyment and our identities end up being whatever the market allows us to construct by ways of our money, status, and class location.

Adorno and Horkheimer are right when they say that capitalism creates our needs and uses culture to induce us into sheer passivity.[9] Along with this cultural passivity, Brazilian thinker Maria Rita Kehl says that the cultural industry lives under the rubrics of the spectacle and includes us all in the same process of alienation that is the establishment of the distance between us and our capacity to become subjects of our own history.[10] This gap generates the desires created by the cultural industry that promises to fulfill it with the products it needs to sell. A track of unending, unfulfilling desire is created and we fall into this trap. Along with these promises, our culture makes us passive and fearful so we won't go to the streets to change anything.

As preachers, we should ask hard questions: What is it that fulfills this gap? How does the gospel of Jesus Christ help us to move away from this self-enclosed way of living, and respond to this never fulfilled sense of enjoyment promised by a culture of products and practices that rob us of our own selves and one another? What is it that makes us become subjects of our history?

The quest to become subjects of our own history continues to be a central question for liberation theology in Latin America and should be a fundamental question for us today in the United States. To "mind the gap" produced by the presence of the economic market in our culture is to engage understandings of identity and its multiplicities that can empower us to make choices, to learn to deal with our desires and the pulses of life and/or death present in every desire. Identity performs ways of being in the world that we individually and collectively create, expanding or limiting the ways in which we decide to live.

In this sense, the whole worship event can have a countercultural effect on this alienation. The worship space is a meeting place, where people with different cultures and multiple identities gather together and around Jesus, the many Jesuses of our faiths, and learn how to appreciate somebody else's ways of living. The love of Jesus affirms identities that carry both self-respect and respect for others. In worship, I learn that my identity, my ethnicity, my cultural ways of living are just one way along with the multiple cultural ways of worshiping of the churches of Jesus Christ. Also, my understanding of God and God's grace grow, are challenged and expanded by other ways of singing, praying, preaching, and listening to God's word. Moreover,

9. Horkheimer and Adorno, *Dialectic of Enlightenment*.

10. Kehl, *Sobre ética e psicanálise*, 24.

somebody else's desires can teach me to limit my desires. Our cultural alienation is called upon when we gather and the word of God proclaimed. This happens because multiple communities gather together and this community of interpreters of culture, gospel, and faith teach each other how to become subjects of our herstories/histories.

Through our sermons, sacraments, singing, praying, and orders of worship, through our honoring of God and one another, we can gain tools to respond to our social alienation, to this shallow world of pure enjoyment, to the delusions of our never fulfilled, unregulated desires, and expand understanding of ourselves based on the gospel of Jesus lived in community, in and through our multiplicities, many configurations, conflicts, and ways of living/believing.

How so? If our sermons are proclamations of the good news of God's love, our worship ways of honoring God, our prayers ways of connecting our hearts and emotions and bodies to God, our sacraments ways of experiencing God's presence, our singing ways of expressing our deepest gratitude to God, our liturgies then can and must be promises of models of just societies. Because the worship we offer to God must reflect our caring for one another and God's creation. The common work of the people of God, i.e., our *ora et labora* (prayer and work), in and out of the liturgical spaces, convey a mission, an interaction of practices, beliefs, and desires that organize and help us rehearse a society where the least of these are honored and we all live well.

The incarnation of the word of God in our world gains temporary frames of life through the materialities of our liturgies, gestures of mercy and compassion, dreams and hopes that spill over into communal forms of organized society, and that struggle to give power to people in a true democratic society. In other words, the word of God expands our imagination and becomes material support for our daily lives. The word of God must help us think, desire, and live in ways that offer life to one another. The preaching of the word of God teaches us to relate and coexist with God's creation, honoring the processes and rhythms of the earth. Within God's word, Jesus—actualized in word and practice, made known in and through and beyond ourselves, pulsing in possibilities—becomes the central stone where we build each other's lives and societies. The word of God we hear brings forth a message that says that our multiple identities are not to be erased and made into one identity, or one faith, but to be lived in its very differences. The oneness of God comes in a plurality of ways and this is the precious and fascinating aspect of being a disciple of Jesus. We walk in awe with this Jesus manifested in such radical differences.

In our culture, Jesus's life, death, and resurrection orient and empower our desires, connecting our fulfillment not with alienated self-created hopes but in serving and loving, sharing and enjoying each other and God's creation. Through the word of God, our desires connect, create, and expand our lives in each other's direction, making *sym-bolic* acts of re-membering. Without the word of God, our desires are turned into *dia-bolic* modes of living, dispersing, tearing apart, and weakening the very threads of our lives. We do not and will not engage the dia-bolic notion of social Darwinism, where the strongest win, but will work for those who cannot compete to have the same possibilities of life.

Marjorie Procter-Smith says that liturgy is a place of dialogue,[11] where we engage in expansive ways of learning, nurturing, blessing, and empowering each other. Our common-plural-diverse identity manifests itself in a variety of ways, in eating, believing, engaging, worshiping, and nowadays, in an expansive way within virtual communities. To relate to someone is to learn limits and possibilities and in a virtual community this is not different. A virtual community can also enhance, bless, transform, and expand our lives. There is possibility for a sacramental presence of God in our virtual communities the same way that there is a possibility for God's sacramental presence in our real communities. The virtual community has become an ally to our faith and many sources of blessings come from this common space. Thus, the word of God must travel across the real and the virtual realities to create dialogues and help us learn how to see our limits and possibilities. I will bless you from here and you bless me from there. The incarnational aspect of the Christian faith can indeed be "felt" in the virtual world. However, the aims of both communities should be for us to meet again and its task to bring us together. The virtual community is not enough. The virtual world is not enough and cannot be lived without the fullness of our bodies, flesh that becomes words, and words that are turned into looks, touch, smiles, and embraces. It is only together, in the materialities of our bodies, that we can fulfill our desires. We hold each other's hands and pray together, we kiss each other and share the peace of Christ, we praise and smile, sing and cry, preach, and rise up to the challenges of life.

More, in worship, our very sense of humanity should learn that there are other forms of being and thinking that are human, and only when we are able to stretch ourselves in a most vast sense to what to be human is will we be able to worship God fully.

Having this economic/cultural/liturgical/theological reading in our background, how can we shape/reshape, frame and reframe, figure and

11. Procter-Smith, *In Her Own Rite*, 49.

refigure the "art of preaching" in our world today? Let us go back to what I have suggested earlier, that is, that the art of preaching is embedded in our ability to work at the confluence of the "liturgy of the church, the liturgy of the world and the liturgy of the neighbor." What is that?

The Liturgy of the Church

We are all steeped in ecclesiastical and liturgical traditions. We all have received a complex history, a wealth of resources, wisdom, guidance, and ways to wrestle with life and faith. We must honor all of that. As we honor it, our task is to make these traditions come alive, and we do that by engaging the resources we have received with the resources we have in our hands, based on the social-historical locations in which we are entrenched. Each historical time has its own challenges and specificities that are translated into specific ways of preaching, praying, singing, and eating together.

So the challenge for the art of preaching as it relates to the liturgy of the church is to help the church experience the life of the communal body of Christ, which means to create a web of connections that will foster and facilitate the possibilities of a life together. This challenge has to face the many ways our culture says that we must protect our private space and that each of us must mind our own business. Our culture is growing so many private needs and individual choices that our communal life is eroding or at least taking new shapes. I remember the time when my entire family would have to listen to the same LP at home. We had no choice.

I am also from the time when we had only one TV at home and had to share it. We also had to listen to the same music in the car. Nowadays many people have access to so many electronic gadgets that are made personable in order to fulfill all personal desires. The empire of personal choices is also invading the church and we mirror those practices in our worship services.

One consequence is that we are losing patience with other people. We can't listen too long about peoples' concerns, we are losing the sense that our offering is also to provide care for somebody else, we cannot have people sitting too close to us in the pews, we can't share the peace of Christ by touching anybody, we can't sing songs we don't personally like, we can't listen to a sermon that is more than twelve minutes long, we get mad when our pastors "invent" something new, and we can't stand staying together more than an hour.

To accept this growing inability to be with others is to lose the possibility of creating a complexity of feelings that can engage differences and communal problems. Christianity is a powerful cultural experience in *communal* living and as preachers we must cherish that living within diversity and complexity.

What we do in our worship services, the prayers we pray, the rituals we perform, and the Word of God preached and received, should reflect the ways in which the world should live, an attempt to model life in the world for the world, rather than only reflecting the world's own distortions. At the liturgy of the church, we rehearse what life should be all about. It engages the "should" over against the "is" of the world. Thus, eating together should be a sign and a symbol that conveys the enormous depth of God's generosity.

Singing should be our way of learning each other's songs in order to press forward together, prayers should be our standing with one another no matter what, and preaching should be a way of getting us all moving, a way of helping us reinvent ourselves, a way of renewing our lives, a way of reminding us of the challenges of the gospel that God places in front of us every day. I wish we could all say what our African-American brothers and sisters say when they leave their worship services: "We had church today!"

Our preaching should help us get there. Preaching is God's breath to us, expanding the lungs of our faith and our ability to see new worlds, with new neighbors; a window into the ways we should look, feel, ponder, think, and act in the world and relate to our fellow brothers and sisters in forms of hospitality, friendship, and the arrival of a blessing. Preaching is as ongoing remaking of ourselves in God's hands within the liturgy of the church. Preaching in the liturgy of the church should evoke the mercy and love of God that provides the possibility of a new world for our communities, hope for the poor, and transformation of people and systems. The liturgy of the church is always at stake when we worship. People go to worship to hear God's voice and God goes to the worship service to see what we are doing there. It is in the worship service that we regain a sense of worthiness.

When the world is saying, "You are a loser," I go to church and hear my pastor preaching, "You are a beloved child of God!" When the world is saying, "You are nobody," I go to church and among my brothers and sisters I hear the preacher say, "Son, you are somebody very special in God's hands" and I shout, "Alleluia, praise be to God!" This is the countercultural and religious way of destroying the empire of personal choices and systems of value of our culture and a way to provide a tapestry of life in common, a net of shared love that will support and strengthen us.

When worship is real and I can pray and sing and ask God for forgiveness, eat with many people, and hear the word of God, worship becomes a way of building a paradise in hell, a wall against evil forces, a way of holding on to dear life, a way of creating forms of life against agents of death, a way of imagining life in its fullness, a way of creating a world that is yet to come.

Rebecca Solnit writes about communities that arise in the midst of disasters creating a paradise in hell.[12] When everything is gone and there is nowhere to go, communities find a way of solidarity to rebuild themselves and what was destroyed.

This is the function of the worship of word and table, brothers and sisters, to create a world of care, inside and outside the walls of the church building. Worship services can build healthy places where people can not only survive but also thrive for the abundant life Jesus has promised us. So it is fundamental for us preachers to recognize that our preaching is inextricably related to the liturgy of the church.

The task of preaching must lose the arrogance that it can do it all alone! It is the precious task of preaching with singing, and offering, and washing, and receiving forgiveness, and anointing, and eating together that can facilitate a much larger spectrum of God's healing and transformation to the life of the church and the larger community. The worldview of *Ubuntu*—marked by the African adage, "I am because we are, and we are because I am"—is what makes our church village find life.

Preaching is this unending remembrance of our life together and the obligations we have to each other under God's direction. We will only capture the art of preaching if, along with other worshiping things, we are able to guide each other into paradise, into that space where God visits us with wonders.

But there isn't only the liturgy of the church for us to consider, there is also the liturgy of the world.

The Liturgy of the World

When we praise and preach we are in the midst of the world. The world is very much inside of our worship services. We try to avoid the world with our stained glass windows, but the world is inside of our churches, forcefully defining liturgies that are foreign to our faith. The liturgies of the world are about economic Darwinism, money, and consumerism. Business!

We are told we will only survive if we can afford some things and that means that we are in direct opposition to somebody else who becomes not my keeper but my competitor. Thus, I have to exclude those in need for they can bring me down. Since our life's itinerary is controlled by consuming something at the mall, we are what we can buy and the ability to travel those itineraries is what makes me worthy.

12. Solnit, *A Paradise Built in Hell.*

Within this all-encompassing system of self-enjoyment, it is hard for the preacher not to concede to what her/his community desires. Sermons nowadays run the risk of becoming a sort of commodity that must deliver the goods that the congregation demands. However, it is important to make a distinction between preaching in a poor community where people barely have enough to keep going and preaching to those who are somewhat well off. In both situations, the preacher must discern and distinguish between desires that bring life and desires that feed detachment and sheer individualism, between the desire for God and the desire for things, between the wants created by the market and the needs originated in the Spirit.

Thus, instead of making preaching a commodity, preaching must keep its prophetical detachment from the lures of business-entrepreneurial-marketing-like understanding of the faith that turns the gospel into a product, worship practices into detached goods, prayers into obligations, preaching into no more than a feel-good deliverance, members into consumers, churches into enterprises, the study room of the pastor into an office, session meetings into business gatherings, church resolutions into minutes, mission statements into propaganda, and the pastor-preacher into a CEO.

Business is everywhere in theological seminaries as well. Many seminaries live off student loans to pay for classes, making student debt their biggest beneficiaries. Other seminaries that are dependent on endowments are not off the hook since they survive by the exploitation of the market. We all embody the ideology of the market! Not long ago I heard a seminary professor say, "Only thirty percent of churches out there in this denomination are in very good financial health and can offer a good salary package and we are here to prepare you to go to those churches." But what about the other seventy percent of churches that cannot support themselves fully or can't offer pastors a better package? What should we do with them?

The liturgy of the world has been taken hostage by the economic Darwinism of the market—the economically fit will survive—and this view is getting inside of our churches. If we do not preach against it, we will end up preaching to empty pews. Our theology of proclamation must entail a liturgy of the church that heals the nations and continuously tells us that the *joie de vivre* is in our life together and not in the freedom to acquire.

The liturgies of the world must be infused by the gospel, and the preaching of the gospel should help us not become hostage to money values or the culture of things we should have. Instead, preaching is a lifeline that reminds us both who God is and how we should be. In the midst of this ongoing social, cultural, political, and theological wrestling, preaching helps us create bonds and communitarian aspects that will sustain our lives together.

Thus, praying, singing, eating, and bathing together, along with the preaching of the gospel, must continue to offer a cultural model of life in common. The liturgy of the world in this sense is a cosmopolitan offering of the *oikos*, the *oikumene*, the house of God in the world. But more than that, we must expand this house by including the structure of this *oikos*, the *ecos* of the *nomos/mene*. Unless we start with eating locally, and know that we cannot eat whatever we want in whatever season but must follow the limits of the earth, we have a rupture between our singing to God and the God who created the earth. The art of preaching then would be the ability to discern the liturgies of the world that are destroying our life together, including the eco-system, and help people replace detached worship styles and lifestyles with the liturgies of the world that can sustain our communities by providing a local ground to sow, to plant, and to eat so we can offer a better future for our children.

Preaching must be an essential part in this discernment process to awaken us and help us see how far we have gone away from the gospel. In this discernment process, our preaching will restore altar calls for us all to repent from engaging in liturgies of death. The art of preaching would then empower us to imagine liturgies of the world that will create bridges and build people's trust, communal strength, and general relief. The art of preaching will help us see the beauty of our diversities, and divergences, and complexities and help us figure out how to live this life together.

Also, the art of preaching is about making theological/social choices. So what do we say about the wall of shame between the US and Mexico that is another liturgy of death that is breaking us apart as it rises as a symbol of hatred, xenophobia, and fear? Annually, the Catholic Church celebrates the sacrament of the Eucharist on both sides of the wall in Tijuana saying, "This is not right and we will continue to celebrate a liturgy of the world that will gather us together until this wall comes down." This celebration is a message preached in a very loud way. Sacrament that equals preaching that equals public theology, denouncing death, separation, class struggle.

If we don't keep our ear to the ground to see the directions that our culture is taking, in no time we will lose our ability to be critical to it, and we will reinforce mainstream values of narcissism, success at all cost, money dependence, and turning education and faith into commodities that will continue to kill us.

But we will not let it happen! We will continue to invent liturgies of the world that will create life and sustain the world as the creation of God. Our goal will not be to create a better market but to proclaim God's justice and to give God the glory. We will not prepare pastors to go to tall steeple churches but to serve the poor and strengthen people to embrace a more expanded and powerful mission of God in the world of many liturgies of justice.

And now, the last part, which is the liturgy of the neighbor.

The Liturgy of the Neighbor

The liturgy of the neighbor is the way in which we frame the second part of the Great Commandment: love your neighbor as you love yourself.[13] And by doing that we are also framing the world around us. Increasingly, we have been challenged with the presence of people who do not look like us or have the same origin, history, and perhaps the same future. Immigrants!

Damnian, "Ha (House [Mayan dialect])"

Damnian is ten years old, from Guatemala. In this picture he drew his family's home. With the help of his father, they both remembered together details of their home and its surroundings. After each detail, the father gave its indigenous name to the volunteer (*koostah,* "flower"; *ich,* "sun"; *itsch,* "dog").

The invasion of immigrants into US feels like the eleventh plague of Exodus for some. Immigration is changing the face of this country as it has always changed it, and we have only two ways to respond to that: either to feel like we can throw away people we don't like or work hard to figure out

13. Matt 22:35–40.

how we can find a place of peace for us all to live together. Most people come here not because of the North American dream but because possibilities for life were taken away from them in other places; and since money is concentrated here, people come to survive and feed their families.

Considering the Protestant churches, the presence of immigrants is deeply connected with the constant loss of members and the sense of loss of power within the culture. The combination of these factors has an enormous impact in our living together as neighbors and churches. Part of the church is acting in xenophobic and violent ways against that which they do not know. As an immigrant within the church I can be sometimes a target of this fear-hatred. In my classes, I have to keep telling my students, "I am with you not against you. I want to see the church do well the same way you do."

In our preaching, we must engage these fears and give people better tools to deal with them. Instead of keeping silent or pretending it is not there, we must act upon it with ways that will otherwise strengthen us. Thus, when we consider the liturgy of the neighbor we must think about offering a model of being church *with* our neighbors. When we think about our neighbor, we must consider what Slavoj Žižek said—that the neighbor presents himself/herself to me when he/she does something I really don't like, that disturbs me, that horrifies me, or leaves me without ways to understand it. In other words, the neighbor is this toxic part of the other I must love.[14] But how are we to love the toxic aspect of someone we don't like? Without putting too much pressure on worship, I do believe that it is in worship services that we can offer a model for a diverse society to live together. Let me propose this: we must become radical ecumenists!

The more I go to other churches the more my life of faith expands! I wish we could all go to each other's churches and bring home something we learn from others, and when we use those sources we do so because of the relationship we have to that church and not for my own sense of pleasure. I was in a white church not long ago and it was right after the killing of Freddie Carlos Gray Jr., a twenty-five-year-old Black American man, by the police. The country was in racial flames! During the service there was not a single note about the event and not even a prayer for the people suffering. However the most striking thing in that service was that the worship ended with a rendering of a Black Spiritual by two white people, and the whole congregation gave a standing ovation to the musicians. Why were they allowed to use resources of a community for which they don't care? That was appropriation! However, had this church been in relationship with a local Black church, they could have done a joint service and offered each

14. See http://www.youtube.com/watch?v=b44IhiCuNw4.

other challenges and consolations. They could have sung from each other's hymnals and prayed each other's prayers.

If we only stay with our own group we will not survive. We are all called to a great cloud of witnesses, an ethno-doxologically complex diverse cloud of witnesses to support and protect each other. This should be our beauty, and the power of our common faith! To be under identity construction, in our ever-unending becoming of a more expansive humanity in order to live better. We follow the Apostle Paul, who said,

> For though I am free with respect to all, I have made myself a slave to all, so that I might win more of them. To the Jews I became as a Jew, in order to win Jews. To those under the law I became as one under the law (though I myself am not under the law) so that I might win those under the law. To those outside the law I became as one outside the law (though I am not free from God's law but am under Christ's law) so that I might win those outside the law. To the weak I became weak, so that I might win the weak. I have become all things to all people, so that I might by any means save some. I do it all for the sake of the gospel, so that I may share in its blessings.[15]

Due to the love we must give and share, we go beyond who we think we are, knowing that we are limited to what we don't know and haven't experienced. Until I learn what it is to be and to feel like somebody else, until I don't fear to be somebody else, until I am not afraid to be with and fight somebody else's struggles.

If my identity is multiple, I can relate better, I know the limits of my experience, I try to appreciate what is not mine, I can save a space for someone else, expanding my identity by holding and losing who I am and what is important to me. This way, adding what *an-other* might be to my own identity, makes me stronger and prepares me better to deal with differences. Moreover, it makes clear the abyssal distance between you and me. Thus, the liturgy of my neighbor depends on what I understand not only of who my neighbor is but also how I see myself and learn to relate to him/her.

But also, we are challenged to engage other religions. It has to start with the preacher, dealing with fears and an often self-referential faith. Feelings have to be addressed, theological thinking will be necessarily engaged, and forms of welcoming and embracing creatively imagined.

Preaching here brings forth a challenge because it would have to deal more often with paradoxes, ambiguities, and parables than assurances and fixed univocal meanings. I will have to preach not only from what I know,

15. 1 Cor 9:19–23 NRSV.

but from a place that is not mine. As Latin American, I have to preach, with fear and trembling, about my African-American brothers and sisters, or indigenous people, or gay, lesbian, or transgender people while trying to listen, read, and share life with them so I can begin to understand what it means to preach with them from where they speak, live, and do their theologies. In that way I am always vulnerable, having to learn and correct myself all the time, since I preach always from my own people, whom I also do not know or fully represent. The place I preach must be a place in between: between me, other parts of me and somebody else's self, placing other people in relation to my many selves, their traditions in relation and contrast, in correlation and challenge to mine.

As a consequence, my reading of the Bible must be affected deeply as well. I must listen to other voices interpreting the text and be aware of the ways in which this text shapes people differently. At the table/altar, I am stretched to hear somebody else's stories, to serve and to receive bread from those whom I don't know, from a God unknown to my faith. In these movements of challenges, difficulties, and blessings, there is mutual learning, and the preaching of the Gospel gains in potentiality, in power to open spaces for encounters between us, ourselves and strangers, where the word of God fills the cracks of our disjunctures and holes, strangely warming our hearts as Jesus warmed the hearts of the disciples on the road to Emmaus.

On that road, strangers had their hearts warmed by someone they thought they had not seen before. A word spoken on the way warmed their hearts, prepared their ways into a table of *koinonia* and mutual care. The word was so powerful, so evolving, so filled with life that the gathering, the visit had to continue. The notion of a stranger gave space for a life of communion. "Don't go!" They said, "Stay with us, the night is upon us and it is dark and dangerous out there. We don't want you to be hurt or to stay on your own. And we are afraid of the darkness. We have warmth, shelter, and food. You, whoever you are, you have blessed us so deeply in this path that we couldn't even imagine! You, whoever you are, came unexpectedly to visit us on our sorrowful journey and brought us joy. You, whoever you are, come inside, stay with us, you are our family now, you are ours."

When they finally broke the bread, they became one! In their own singularities! Jesus went inside of their bodies and their lives were surely transformed forever.

That is the work of the word of God, to warm our hearts, to create a wiggle room of warmth, of welcome, of possibilities, of potency! The work of the preachers in the liturgy of the neighbor is to help people feel about each other what John Wesley felt when he was hearing Luther's preface to the Epistle to the Romans, "I felt my heart strangely warmed."

Conclusion

With hearts strangely warmed, we will embrace the powerful movement of preaching. The locus of enunciation is about Jesus Christ and us in this time and place dismantling structures of coloniality and oppression, expanding knowledges and perspectives, connecting people with people, people with all forms of life, people and the earth, and the universe. In this proclamation, sermons are acts that orient us, that make us dream, touch the ground, feel the sun when we eat, hoping from places of no hope, fighting with and without strength, working and praying, being changed and transformed.

My preaching is about trying to figure ourselves out in this act of worship, together. In my preaching, I will engage you in ways that are only possible because in my speech you recognize yourself, who you might be, either by affirming or negating what I said. Judith Butler says that, "One comes to exist by virtue of this fundamental dependency on the address of the Other."[16] Language is action, sermons have the power to measure human life, and preaching does shape communities. In her 1993 Nobel lecture in literature, Tony Morrison said that language is a "living thing," and "We do language that might be the measure of our lives." [17]

Yes, our sermons are living things, and they are vulnerable and powerful. Preaching sets potentialities in motion, where the people who, by the grace of God, do the healing and move mountains go from here to there. Our sermons are enunciations only, and it is the Spirit who goes not only to the heart of people but also to their guts. That is why we have to be very careful with what we preach. Unchecked speeches can also go, without the Spirit, to the guts of the people, destroying lives of individuals and entire communities. As preachers we can only do this in fear and trembling.

16. Butler, *Excitable Speech*, 5.
17. Morrison, "Nobel Lecture."

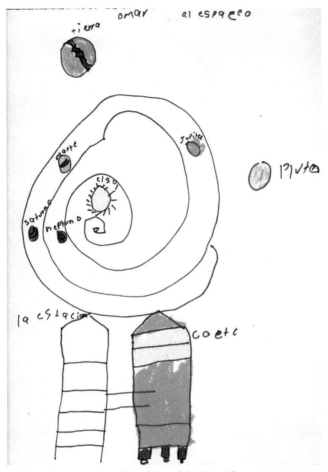

Omar, "Las planetas (The planets)"

Christine [volunteer]: "Omar was teaching me Spanish during this drawing."

The church is marked by the actions of our sermons and people will work in between the words uttered by the preacher and their social locations and individual struggles.

Also, our sermons not only try to describe and define what we are talking about but also announce what is to come. What is it that we are announcing in our sermons that it is to come to the church of Christ and to the world? What is it announcing that comes from the past, from the present and from the future? In what ways have we portrayed the church, the world and the neighbor in our preaching? In what ways are the tensions and outright conflicts between culture and gospel conflicting with one another? How do we examine it all with the least damage possible, always caring for the well-being of others, especially the poor? In our sermons, what is lifted up and exposed/offered in your preaching?

Singing each other's songs, praying each other's prayers, and hearing each other's sermons might be a way of creating a space between us for dialogical engagement with others so that we can figure out ways to strengthen, enrich, and deepen our living together. But don't forget that to create these spaces and this kind of church and society will be messy, very messy.

There are several good examples of this clear relation out there. I will mention just one. During the ministry of Pastor Donald Mier, First Baptist Church of Fall River, Massachusetts, was a diverse, wonderful, messy place. In this church, there were people who were poor and people who were rich, people who could read and people who could not read, people who occupied high ranks in the city and people who had been in prison, whites and blacks and foreigners. They had people with good health and people without health insurance, people with mental and physical challenges, traditional people and people who wanted to experiment with things. They were mostly Christians but some new immigrants were from other religions: a messy place. Many people couldn't take it and left. Others stayed and created/lived this utopia of the Kingdom of God. It was not an easy job for Pastor Mier, but his preaching and ministry helped sustain that place with love. It was not about him or his preaching alone but about trying to create a space for complex diversities. It was his preaching and his relational ministry and the work of the community that made the liturgy of the world, the liturgy of the church, and the liturgy of the neighbor one mission event in this city.

If preaching can help us create this space between us, enhancing people's lives and giving people such immense experiences, a powerful ecclesiological/pneumatology can happen. For this is what the Spirit is doing, building the forces of life everywhere, taking us from our individualistic liturgies and ego-sufficient habits of being, by creating threads that connect the body of Christ with the entire world. In order for that to happen, we must fundamentally depend on the Spirit to do something important with this precious and powerful art of preaching.

11

Praising God between the World and the Altar

I look on all the world as my parish.

—JOHN WESLEY

Introduction

The question that Paul Hoffman brings to us from the Rite of Affirmation of Baptismal Vocation in the World goes to the newly baptized—"Friends in Christ, will you endeavor to pattern your life on the Lord Jesus Christ, in gratitude to God and in service to others, all the days of your life?"[1]—is the question that comes back to us at the end of every worship service. And for us today, what does that mean? How do we pattern our life on our Lord Jesus Christ, in gratitude to God and in service to others, all the days of our lives? What does worship tells us about this connection?

This question to the newly baptized establishes the juxtapositions of various poles of forces and energies where we live our faith: the porous relations between the world and the liturgical places, the in-betweenness of our daily lives and what we call sacred symbols and practices, the inside and the outside of our worship spaces, the ways in which we relate to God and to the world. In this chapter I will connect the ways in which we praise God with the ways we live, relating some of the multiple religious and cultural

1. Hoffman, "The Rite of Affirmation of Baptismal Vocation in the World."

cross-pollination. In this way I will mention three different forms of worship that can be either cultural or countercultural forms of support or resistance to the ways in which we live.

The rapid decline of membership in many Christian churches in United States has made us tired of trying to figure out more intensely why it is happening to us. Consultants are out there trying to sell the magic potion that will turn us around and bring people to our churches. Specialists in "generations," worship practices, Internet use, online projects, use of music, new administration, new buildings, and so on are offering us six steps to become a new congregation, seven ways to regain our vitality, ten things you need to change in your worship service, the five music trends in Christian churches that are successful, eight signs of a church open to millennials, and thirteen ideas you need to know to survive the death of your church. From advice that goes from "change everything, you got it all wrong" to "do not change anything because this is the gospel and let us die faithfully," we are trapped between a thousand tongues speaking in anxiety and a thousand and one hearts filled with fear.

Our current situation is a result of a complex history made of colonial forms of exploitation, Protestant allegiances to capitalism, adherence to a future truly manifested and provided by God, a clear sense that this country is exceptional, commitments to the ways of living in the Empire and a community made of white, middle-class people. This is all related to certain forms of worship that organize the social structure of the people.

However, the cultural-social-economic structures of our lives have changed, and Christianity has lost its power in the main places of power. Our culture does not respect Sunday morning worship services anymore. Socially we are way more diverse and economically we are losing our place as a middle class. During its existence, Christians for the most part have not made bridges with other cultures and classes, have not shared its liturgical spaces, its liturgies, or learned with others but instead, tried to stay put inside its own traditions, while trying to save their own religious identity.

What we are facing today is the increasing inability to engage with one another generally, either in church or society. A new order of thinking is upon us: we are not responsible for others but to ourselves only. Our tax payments to the government are to protect ourselves and not to give money to lazy poor people. Social welfare is about my needs only.

If we use broad strokes in analyzing our society, we can name the assault of the neoliberal economic market on the political sphere, owning the political sphere and thus destroying and creating policies that facilitate the flow of money from social services to the private sector, the consequent need for free market without government limits, the demonization of the proletariat, the exhaustion of living in fear, the inability to feel solidarity with those who suffer, the anger with the poor, the deep-seated forms of racism, the common understanding that individual freedom as noted in the US Constitution is exactly it: an individual demand and not a social conquest development, and the replacement of social ethics with the ethics of the individual.

The dismantling of long-term structures that sustained the threads of social life, the destruction of labor rights obtained through so much sweat and tears and blood, the power kept by few families and the shift of the wealth from the 99% of the population to 1% of our people. The turning of health and education into profit enterprises is at the core of its disaster! The abandoning of projects for school and a new emphasis on prison systems shows the priorities of this society.

With Congressional representatives being mostly white, wealthy males and the vote of people not really mattering in the choice of president, the very notion of democracy is clearly in danger. And worse, when the two parties in place don't really care about the poor, but are only shaped to continue its "empire" power across the globe, leading wars with drones and owing more military bases across the globe while completely abandoning its poor, there is something to say to the thread of life in United States.

The current play of politics and economy, and the ways it makes us live in the *polis*, is what is destroying us all. Because what is at stake is the sense of life that permeates our societies, the sense that life is measured by abundance and enjoyment. As Jon Sobrino says, "The first world continues to put the meaning of history in accumulation and the enjoyment that this accumulation allows."[2] And we the church often do the same or allow that process to happen. I don't hear anywhere that accumulation is evil, that we are not supposed to accumulate things personally and as a social group.

The movie *Hunger Games* is a metaphor and a parable for our times: an elite decide to have fun and choose two individuals of thirteen communities to fight for their lives. There is only one rule: the competitors, who are never the rich, must kill to survive. During the game, rich people bet on different competitors and produce enjoyment for the social elite. The one who wins is invited into the social life of the rich. Isn't that exactly what is happening now? We are in a savage capitalist world but that is fine, this is what made us who we are. The Hunger Games must continue! Whoever can fight and win survives; those who can't afford to keep themselves alive will surely die. And this is their fault.

---

2. Sobrino, "A Igreja costuma se distanciar de Jesus para que ele não incomode."

Working from this background, let us think about our worship services. The way we live together has indeed to do with the ways we worship God, and vice versa. Our life in society is marked by individual commitments to our own happiness and the well-being of somebody else should only be a concern, if a concern at all, after I have my problems solved. How can democracy be seen in our worship services? Who are we serving? How concrete is our love?

Worship Services as Proposals to Shape Society

It is within this scenario that we need to think about the oath at the rite of the Affirmation of Vocation of the Baptized: "Friends in Christ, will you endeavor to pattern your life on the Lord Jesus Christ, in gratitude to God and in service to others, all the days of your life?"

How have worship services dealt with this alienating, desire-driven, narcissistic society? What kind of society do we propose with our liturgies, actions, symbols, where prayers, theologies, pastoral care, biblical readings and so on give a clear sense of what to be human is all about? How do our liturgies offer frames for our life together? If we look at the church today, we have several liturgical possibilities with different responses.

Pentecostal Services

We have *Pentecostal services*, which appeared as a response to historical Protestant churches and their traditional services. Serving as a critique to the hermetic way of relating to God in historical churches, Pentecostal services brought to the center of the liturgical spaces emotions, bodily motion, and feelings as tools to do theology, to relate to God and one another. These are worship services where feelings are allowed, the body authenticated as a site for God's revelation, and in some churches, women serve as leaders of the church. However, the theological organization of our lives together was disconnected from the larger social world, where economic events were always disconnected from the services. For the most part, moral issues related to the proper use of the body and sexual behaviors were considered in sermons.

Prosperity Gospel Services

We have the *theology of prosperity* forms of worship.[3] "Theology of prosperi-ty" denominations and churches were developments of historical Protestant and Pentecostal churches. These communities use, as well as dismiss, a mix of different sources—some religious, some not religious—according to their need. There is no connection with a tradition or desire to be accountable to a denominational body. The Universal Church of the Kingdom of God in Brazil, for example, uses cultural and religious symbols from the Roman Catholic Church, from Protestant churches, and also from African Brazilian religions to compose a faith deeply marked by the most common elements of the conscious/unconscious psyche of Brazilian religious culture.

Creflo Dollar and T. D. Jakes mix African-American culture and white, middle-class, conservative religious family values. In worship, what is at stake is the hope to get rich, and to find a better life. However, the change is solely in our comprehension of the gospel. If we only learn that we follow a king, we would know that we are supposed to live as princes and prin-cesses in this world without lacking a thing in life. Social change is never an issue but rather, the giving of our money to try to bribe God and make God do and be what God has promised in the Bible. These churches often have no membership—meaning no commitment to anybody—rely on the shifting movement of people in the pews, and make promises that prevent their leaders from being accountable to them. The main line is: if you have faith, God will give you this house or that car. If you don't get it, it is not the pastor's fault but your fault for not actually believing in God.

Joel Osteen's church is one strange example of prosperity theology—a kind of inner/outer prosperity by a mix of positive thinking with the "best practices" of a nice God. In his church, he tells his flock not to worry about anything and that we can change if we are positive about people, relations, and God. No challenges, no cross, no sin. These churches do not develop a sense of community since they are all dependent on their leaders, indi-viduals who run the ministry by a very personal imprint that depends on their names to exist. Fruits and results are our present economic model; these ministries depend on the development of this economic model and authenticate the neoliberal market that rules our social life without ever be-ing challenged.

---

3. Creflo Dollar Ministries and T. D. Jakes Ministries in the United States, and Universal Church of the Kingdom of God around the world, are good examples of liturgies/theology of prosperity. For the positive preaching of the gospel, the ministry of Joel Osteen is well known.

These churches are a result of the neoliberal market mostly without regulations, or limits for wishes, desires, and impulses. These worship services carry a theology that submits itself to the sacrificial mode of the market: you must sacrifice in order to gain good results. Give and wait, and through this sacrificial act you will receive. Moreover, these churches work on the endless desire of the people, it feeds the desire of the market: don't you want to have everything? Aren't you the son and daughter of the King of gold and silver? Desire all you want and God will give to you if you are faithful to the theological notions of the market-reading of the Bible. Also, since there is no sense of agency, that one cannot change the system as it is, the church becomes a spiritual lottery where people go to strike a fortune, without work, without real gain or losses. Thus, as part of the system, these churches feed a passive society that does not, should not, offer any critical tools to inquire of the powers that be much less challenge the status quo.

For this chapter I will work with only two liturgical frameworks: the so-called Emergent Church and its new ministries, and especially the traditional worship of historical Protestantism. While these two movements warrant a much deeper consideration, I am raising some issues to help us have a general idea of both of them.

Emergent Church

John Buchanan says that the emergent movement is "more practical, a movement that is more interested in a dynamic life to be lived than a set of beliefs to be affirmed."[4] Harvey Cox says that it is "less hierarchical, dogmatic, patriarchal."[5] If what Buchanan and Cox say is true, the emergent movement brings very important and critical aspects to our way of worshiping God. This movement appeared as a response to the stiffness of historical worship services and their fixed resources that seem impossible to change, to engage modern life, challenging (a) hierarchical structures, (b) limited participation, and (c) developed passivity. We surely must pay attention to those challenges.

However, for all its very important challenges, the emergent church seems to fall too quickly into the same shining hole of the economic market as other churches mentioned here. That is because this movement runs the risk of turning this ancient faith into the image of whoever creates its worship. Whatever one does not like in the order of worship one can take away.

4. Buchanan, "Entry Points."

5. Harvey Cox, *The Future of Faith*, 223, Quoted in Buchanan, "Entry Points."

In response, something new is created in order to make it trendier, more comfortable to the new hipster standards of new artistic creations, sophisticated poetry, and a sense of coolness. Thus, if we don't like the pulpit, let us have a lawn chair and a table on the chancel, if there is a chancel anyway; if we don't like the confession of sins, let us get rid of it.

New liturgical objects and creations give the sense of a new freedom and perhaps a closer proximity with God. However, in this eternal recurrence of the new, the gospel can lose the critical edge of its old challenging demands. Instead of challenging people, the gospel has to produce enjoyment or a sense of coolness. Instead of taking a hard look at the biblical text and the necessary contexts, it offers easy reflections for the daily consumption. In some churches, passivity is also key to its life. Few creative people will create everything and the rest of us will watch them play, sing, preach, do art. This is how the economic market also functions: some people will take care of the whole social life, beautiful innovative movements without social change, daily consumption and profit/enjoyment/coolness as much as possible. Besides, this movement has been marked by a massive participation of white people only, which is also symptomatic of the locus, the status quo, challenges, and the difficulties it carries.

Traditional Worship

Historic Protestant churches are trying to keep the ancient, historical liturgical practices valid. They work (and I include myself in this group) from worship books produced for the entire denomination. These books carry proper worshipful values. In spite of the fact that many local churches don't follow these books, we will work with the general assumption that these books carry the wisdom of the past, the proper liturgical practices, and words that assure a proper worship service. In this assumption, we see a couple of things: one is that this group holds on to an amazing wealth of historic traditions, and two, they tend to see worship as something that has intrinsic value and a given meaning; thus it only needs to be performed properly. Once proper time, proper space, proper leadership, and proper actions are kept the way they are given in the rubrics, proper worship will simply happen, and meaning, power, and transformation will flow "naturally."[6]

6. Some people will say that this form of worship is described in Latin as *Ex opere operato,* meaning "from the work done," which tends to say that the efficacy of the sacraments is in the proper rite performed and not on the celebrant. Rejecting this description, some liturgical scholars will say that the given order of the worship is not based on the *Ex opere operato* but rather on the *Ex opere operantis* that is grounded on the Church's sanctity, on the faith of the assembly and not in the way the sacramental rite

The problem with this way of thinking and practicing worship is that it runs very close to idolatry, since the order of worship is sometimes more important than the actual gathering of people to worship God. Also, it runs the risk of elevating what was chosen as *proper* into such a higher position that change can never occur. As a liturgical scholar-friend of mine has said, Jesus did not send his disciples with the worship book in hands saying go and do likewise.

This group of people—and again, I am including myself here—have grown up following an order of worship faithfully, and I have it all in my bones. However, we have made proper things be more important than people.

A pastor of an historic church was leading worship looking at the altar/table. One day, after the service, I asked him, "Why did you keep looking at the altar almost throughout the worship?" And he answered, "Oh my son, it is much better to look at God than to look at people!" Indeed, sometimes it is! Here are a couple of examples:

- *Time as a proper aspect of worship.* Time rules us, time controls worship. Worship done properly has to stick to a certain time—usually one hour. We are bound to time and not even God can leave this time-frame. Time defines the limits of our prayers and singing and preaching, and not the other way around. In this framework, one can't afford going five minutes over the limit of worship; otherwise we will hear interminable complaints about the lack of respect or lack of proper preparation. But here is the paradox: when people go to a restaurant right after the church service, the waiter will say, "I am sorry you will have to wait thirty minutes to have a table," and we say without thinking, "That is just fine." This anthropological way of engaging with time encounters great problems when we meet people who use time more loosely such as some African-American, Pentecostal, African, and Latina-American churches. In this way of worshiping, it seems like our faith is made for time and not the other way around.

- *Space and things as a proper aspect of worship.* We are made for space and not space for us. However, we have become prisoners of the spaces we have created to worship God. We cannot touch, change, or move anything in our liturgical spaces. Things have more sacred weight than the very people who worship in those spaces. Space is so important that sometimes I feel that our faith was made to honor the space we worship and not to help us honor God and each other. Once I tried

is performed. Nonetheless, this group cannot see the liturgical orders change, which seems like the belief is more on the efficacy of a proper rite than the actual presence of the people.

to remove the pews from a chapel in order to help us find many ways to worship God but the conversation went nowhere. We must not forget that space and pews are theological statements, and we cannot touch them. Once we have placed our organ on the main wall of the church, it gains a higher sense of the holy, and other instruments become mundane. Meaning is attached to spaces, and again, we can't move anything anywhere without changing the meaning of spaces and things.

We forget that the major aspect of our faith and the power of our spaces, things/objects, actions, and bodies are in constant movement, repetition, and creation of possibilities for worship and communal life, and not in keeping the holy things away from people, uncontaminated by our improper actions, or trying to save its holiness from our secularized world. Instead, we are to use these things as open gifts that we go back to time and again in order to find God in the old and in the new. A radical participatory democracy in worship, using holy time, things, actions, and the presence of our bodies would help us always find old and fresh expressions of a grace unbounded, a gospel that makes us free, an invited shared governance, and a responsible faith.

Nancy Cardoso Pereira proposes a hermeneutics that sees God's presence in the used, the shared, and the lived together. Better are the old, the rustic, and the torn apart things that accompany us through life. She says, "The use of many (people) transforms and perfects forms, so many times visited. When moved, used, objects become precious. They become noble and precious not because they are new and innovative. Rather, objects become noble and precious because they persist, insist, reminiscent of something."[7] Meaning is to be discovered together: the social context, the wisdom of ages, the sacred objects and ourselves, all of it together, figuring it out together for our time, for the demands of our situation and for the glory of God.

The problem with this group of people—my people, the people of tradition—it seems, is that the operative assumption that underlines its structure is that meaning in worship is not constructed, but enacted from something already given. The doing of the proper thing, be it time, space, or the practice itself, will inherently bring the proper meaning of our faith. If we only name the holy things properly and do them accordingly, the gospel will surely be lived, God will surely be honored and the people of God will surely be renewed. Again, worship has to do with learning how to enact a meaning that is and always has been there. The possibility of constructing

---

7. Pereira, "De todos os objetos . . ."

another meaning while we worship runs the risk of altering, shifting, or even erasing what is proper.[8]

The main thing about this understanding of worship and the market is that worship orders can (not necessarily will) contribute to making people learn to be mostly passive spectators in worship. Thus, the problem with keeping worship as an operational system performed with a strict meaning that is already established is that it can get stuck in an ideology that nothing can be done differently without losing our faithfulness to the tradition proper. Otherwise, we run the risk of losing our faith entirely. This is a critique of rationalist/modernist perspectives. Here's the meaning—follow it.

Thus, we risk creating passive people who will mirror this behavior in society. In a way, this worship style says that a new world is only possible with the keeping of its present order, and that the present order is the only possible and available one. Also, this worship framework has connections with our desires. If in the emergent church desires are mostly unregulated, here desires are not desirable but can only be framed properly. Thus we have de-regulation versus over-regulation. If on the one hand desires are not often welcomed, because they are seen as dangerous, on the other hand, by imposing regulations on our desires, it also regulates the unending wheel of desire and the empire of the new.

As I describe these two fields, I am aware of the generalizations I am making and that I am not being completely fair with either side. What we can see clearly, however, is that these worship services propose different ways of organizing society and the use of power. These worship services also compose the organization and provide the maintenance of social classes around specific notions of identity. As churches of Jesus Christ we are called to break these boundaries and create a space for the mixture and blurring of these class/ethical lines. However, to break these notions of identity into a possible movement between people of economic status, cultures, and ethnic differences is as easy as a camel going through the eye of a needle.[9]

All that being said, the question for us now is: does the death of democracy and total lack of people's participation in the political arena; the control of the economic market over nation-states and public policies; the massive movement of money towards one percent of the richest people and the consequent demonization of social movements and the poor; the trap of the unregulated flow of personal desires; and the narcissistic cultural framework based on accumulation as enjoyment that invaded our churches and

8. Graham Hughes has delved deeply into this discussion. See Hughes, *Worship as Meaning*.

9. Matt 19:24 NRSV.

turned into a religion of sacrifice, offer a liturgical-missional response from our churches to the world now and in the future?

What kind of worship are we going to struggle for, and how are we to negotiate (another economic term) the traditions we carry, the liturgical practices we perform, the life we carry into the liturgy of daily life after the liturgy of worship, and the very definitions of the sacred we invoke in a world that makes us think that everything is holy and nothing is holy? How are we to regain the edge of a demanding gospel that challenges us day in and day out to live simply, to give what we have, to fully commit—to love one another?

The best liturgies and places of worship are located in the relation between the sources of Christian tradition and the use of wisdom from people of different places, be it other religious traditions, cultural, social, health, play traditions, and so on. Perhaps we should start looking at other forms of worship services and church life. Other, perhaps, non-four-part worship that can also be called worship. We might learn from Black churches that have kept their prophetic tradition alive, where worship means "having church" and to miss church is losing the ability that we can keep going for another week. Or perhaps we need to learn from non-documented immigrant churches and their "simple" worship, living under the radar of the government, finding church to be the only solace for rest and worship the space for healing and renewed hope. In these churches, they worship God together not to keep an order of worship but because they need each other to survive. They are more committed to each other's survival than to any commitment to a certain theologian or a need to keep their cultural background. I will now turn our attention to some liturgical practices in the early church as a way to bring ancient wisdom to the practice of our faith.

Social Liturgical Practices in the Early Churches

Searching for some liturgical practices can strengthen our life together. Going against the massive individualistic discourse of our culture, the attack against the poor, we should find ways to engage in even more communal liturgical activities that promote neighborliness and togetherness around our worship of God, breaking the social divisions that set us apart from other people. The attempt is simple: find ways to connect the wealth of our lived traditions to new liturgical practices of togetherness that create possibilities for new and old encounters, and deep social bonds. In this movement, worship's meaning is received as it is created. What follows now has a somewhat Barthian flavor, even though in many ways Barth saw the Bible prescriptively as a way to fix the ills of the modern world. His assertion was that we must have in the one hand the Bible and in the other hand the newspaper. I intend to look at the Bible and some liturgical actions done in the early churches, and on the other hand I also intend to look at our world today for hints of how we can learn to live together from our present realities. The idea here has to do with the creation of meetings, fostering a variety of encounters, so life in its expansive possibilities can happen within these spaces of connection.

I will start by looking at the Bible to see threads of communal liturgical practices that can help us gain a more heightened social and communal sense of worship. I will name briefly what Paul commends in Romans 16:1–16, namely, *greeting* and *holy kissing*, as just two examples.

Greeting

The Romans text is filled with names of people for whom Paul cares deeply. It is fascinating to see how Paul regards each one and the effort he takes to make sure that the community in Rome will care for each one of them. Let me mention just three of these names here.

In verse 6 Paul says, "I commend to you our sister Phoebe, a deacon of the church at Cenchreae."[10] Phoebe was a person of social standing, who had business that called her to Rome, where she was a stranger. Therefore Paul recommends her to the acquaintance of the Christians there: an expression of his true friendship for her; as a servant to the church at Cenchrea: *diakonon*, a servant in acts of charity and hospitality, especially to strangers. They most likely used to meet at her house, and she undertook not a minor role but rather, work as a deacon that was comparable to the work of leadership offered by male leaders. And Paul says, "help her in whatever she may require from you." See that Paul is not saying, "Help her with whatever you can, but instead, help her in whatever *she may require* from you."[11] Greeting is always more than saying "Hi."

Verse 3 also talks about a deep bond between Paul and Priscilla and Aquila: "Greet Prisca and Aquila, who work with me in Christ Jesus, and who risked their necks for my life, to whom not only I give thanks, but also all the churches of the Gentiles." A famous couple for whom Paul had special fondness, they were originally from Rome, but according to the book of Acts were banished by the edict of Claudius.[12] Aquila and his wife, Prisca, cooperate with Paul's ministry. After the edict was retracted, they returned

10. Rom 16:1 NRSV.

11. Rom 16:3 NRSV; emphasis mine.

12. Acts 18:2 NRSV.

to Rome, and now Paul sends commendations to them. He calls them his, "helpers in Christ Jesus who have for my life laid down their own necks."[13] They exposed themselves to secure Paul, hazarded their own lives for the preservation of his life. Paul was in a great deal of danger in Corinth, they sheltered him, even though it angered others.[14] Are we ready to lay down our own necks for somebody else? Greeting someone is never only about saying greetings.

In verse 16 Paul says, "Greet one another . . ." The word for "greeting" and "saluting" is the same word, *aspasasthe*.[15] It means something like "Let them know that I remember them, and love them, and wish them well." How do we then greet, or let our people know we remember them, we love them, and wish them well in our worship services? To greet people is to get to know them, it's to listen and engage in their stories.

To greet is to move away from centeredness in our own self and into someone else's perspective. To greet is more than shaking hands or listening to someone's name. To greet is about sheltering, welcoming into our midst, offering our resources, giving our belongings, dedicating our very best. To greet is not only a personal thing, it is the work of the whole community who receives strangers and takes each other into their very arms. When we greet somebody in the local church, one of our communities, the global church of Christ greets them as well. It is not just a generic greeting that I am speaking of here, but rather greeting that entails making space even for what is difficult or obnoxious about people and their articulation of their selves, needs, theologies, beliefs, etc.

The challenge for us might be the reduction of the complainers to a caricature and the greeting and the extension of welcome to a trite or easy acts, and not necessarily hard acts, ones that require overcoming of possibly legitimate or at least initially defensible worries. Greeting is a communal liturgical action that strengthens the core of our community life.

The Holy Kiss

In the same verse Paul adds "the holy kiss" to greeting, "Greet one another with a holy kiss." All the churches of Christ greet you. We have good resources on the holy kiss now. Our passing of peace is the legacy of the holy kiss. A church in New York spent a whole semester discussing if they should

13. Rom 16:3 KJV.
14. Acts 18:12, 17 NRSV.
15. Rom 16:16 NRSV.

have the passing of the peace, and after much debate they decided not to do it since that would *interfere* with each other's lives! Imagine interfering in each other's private lives!

The holy kiss proposed by Paul[16] was an activity of bonding, a warm exchange of love to one another. That is why, here in this text, the holy kiss comes after greeting. I hear about you, I learn you are my brother or sister, and then I kiss you. When I kiss you, I seal what greeting first did: the showing of my love. The holy kiss is a kiss of truth and genuine affection.

We learn from the Mennonites that the holy kiss is "a symbol of love and fellowship in the history of the Christian church. It was not the same as the common kiss among friends in the Roman world, nor the common Jewish salutation among friends, for it was a 'holy' kiss observed only among the members of the church." It was often practiced at baptisms! Cyprian reported that the newly baptized were greeted by the entire church with a holy kiss.[17]

In one of St. Augustine's sermons, we read the following: "Then . . . when the [Holy Sacrifice of God] is finished, we say the Lord's Prayer which you have received and recited. After this, the 'Peace be with you' is said, and the Christians embrace one another with the holy kiss. This is a sign of peace; as the lips indicate, let peace be made in your conscience, that is, when your lips draw near to those of your brother, do not let your heart withdraw from his. Hence, these are great and powerful sacraments."[18]

Michael Penn, assistant professor of religion at Mount Holyoke College, performed great research on the place and meaning of the kiss for Christians in the Late Ancient Church. He says,

> Just as kissing had many different meanings in the wider ancient world, so too early Christians interpreted the kiss in various ways. Because ancient kissing was often seen as a familiar gesture, many early Christians kissed each other to help construct themselves as a new sort of family, a family of Christ. Similarly, in the Greco-Roman world, kissing often was seen as involving a transfer of spirit; when you kissed someone else you literally gave them part of your soul. The early church expanded on this and claimed that, when Christians kissed, they exchanged the Holy Spirit with one another. Christians also emphasized the

16. But not only by Paul; see these passages in the New Testament: Rom 16:16; 1 Cor 16:20; 2 Cor 12:12; 1 Thess 5:26; and 1 Pet 5:14.

17. Bender, *Mennonite Encyclopedia*, 3:181.

18. Augustine, Sermon 227, in *Sermons for the Liturgical Seasons*, 197.

kiss as an indication of mutual forgiveness (it's from here that we get the term "kiss of peace").[19]

To kiss you is to draw my heart into yours; it is to receive your breath, your very life into my body. To kiss you is to establish a bond of peace and I cannot withdraw my body and myself from you. I am bonded to you now. That is why this is scary, especially when we are trying not to interfere in each other's lives and being civilized and respectful. When I kiss you I give you a part of myself that only you will know, and therefore, you become responsible for it. The holy kiss is a bond, a gesture of deep commitment, of forgiveness, a familiar gesture, an affirmation of belonging, an act of love, social and communal love. The holy kiss is a collective practice that goes against the tide, one that perhaps can challenge this narcissistic culture that pushes people into withdrawing from one another.

Social Practices Today

As we have looked back, we must also look around the world now and at our recent history. When we look at the world, we must look for practices that can help us dialogue with our traditions and enhance our liturgical actions and communal living. Let me mention very briefly a few movements and churches.

The Landless Workers Movement[20] is the largest social movement in the world. This group of peasants, homeless, rural workers, and poor people organized themselves and fought for agrarian reform in Brazil, the only country in the world that never had agrarian reform. In thirty years, they have provided a piece of land for more than 370,000 families! They provide land, organization around biodiverse planting, no use of agrotoxins, and respect for the land. They create cooperatives made of the people of the land that become strong through empowering each other. From the words of one of the most important theologians in Latin America these days and Bishop Emeritus of São Felix do Araguaia (MT): "We know that we must rely on the light and strength of the Spirit, who renews all things. We are a movement of rebellion and utopia. We fight with our hoe, planting clean seeds, and doing the possible popular agrarian reform every day. Thirty years of walking up to free the land and taking the land with the people."[21]

19. Penn, "On Kissing: A Q&A with Michael Penn." For an in-depth look into the meaning of the kiss for Christians, see his book *Kissing Christians*.

20. For more information, see http://www.mstbrazil.org.

21. Dom Pedro Casaldáliga in *In Depoimentos em homenagem aos 30 anos do MST*, January 22, 2014, https://acervo.racismoambiental.net.br/2014/01/22/.

From this movement, the church could learn that struggle for life creates community, mission, and a sense of life that is grounded not in accumulation but in providing for one another. The communities that continue to live together have this sense of many forms of belonging, of gaining a sense of full citizenship and full humanity. To take the land is a work of justice, to plant without the massive destruction of agribusiness is a work of resistance and care.

My second example is the life and work of a man in Brazil who was known as "Prophet Gentleness." Prophet Gentleness, or José Datrino, was born in São Paulo State and went to Rio de Janeiro when he was twenty years old. In 1961 a circus in Rio de Janeiro caught on fire and killed about five hundred people, including many children. Mr. Datrino said he heard God's voice telling him to abandon the material world and dedicate himself to the spiritual world. He sold everything and gave it to people. Then, Prophet Gentleness got his truck and went to the place where the fire had happened. At the place, where the ashes of the fire remained, he planted flowers and a raised a garden. He lived in that neighborhood for four years comforting the families who lost beloved ones. Prophet Gentleness's mission was to write about spiritual lessons and spread gentleness. He actually wrote many words of love and gentleness all over the city, on walls and bridges, trying to tell people that the way into a new society was to create a space for gentleness to each other. His best-known phrase was "gentleness creates gentleness."

When people called him crazy he used to answer, "I am crazy to love you and stupid for wanting to save you."[22] His proposal was not only a handshake or a hug but a deeper philosophical/ethical proposal that would create space for relationships as a way to build a new world steeped in gentleness and love for each other. His work offered a new aesthetic, and a new ethical urban format to relate to each other. In the chaos of Rio de Janeiro his call was to spread gentleness around that city. He would get flowers every day and walk around the city giving flowers to people. The city of Rio de Janeiro rediscovered him, and his works are public theologies on the walls of a massive flyover.

Another example is a church in Minneapolis that tried to create a shelter for the homeless, but the social regulations were such that this small church couldn't afford it. What they did instead was to create vigil services throughout the winter. So homeless people could come and pray while sleeping. Another church created a common public garden and created a farmer's market to feed all the people around the church. They created jobs

22. Datrino, "Gentileza gera gentileza."

and a sustainable community. Another church outside of the US was giving baptism certificates as an official document for people to get their passport. Another church made its space into a sanctuary building and was holding immigrants who were supposed to be deported, provided lawyers and shelter until their case should be properly heard. Another church created a circus to gather kids from the streets and teach them artistic tools to survive and create income. Another church celebrated their Christmas not in their building but with incarcerated people, bringing them cakes and songs, and hugs and gifts.

Finally, during the most difficult years of the war in El Salvador, the powers that be, supported by the United States, were repressing the people, going after rural workers, peasants, priests, and bishops, killing them in order to stop the revolution that the people had started. The church interposed itself radically and fundamentally in favor of the people and against the military powers of oppression. Óscar Romero, Ignacio Ellacuría, and many priests were killed because of that. Rural farmers, peasants, and poor workers were killed, too. Don Romero, a few weeks before his death in 1980, said that "a Christian who cannot live this commitment of solidarity with the poor is not worthy to be called Christian."[23] He was not afraid to make these bold affirmations. He was not concerned with hurting some people or leading people away from the church. On the contrary, by saying so he was making a bold affirmation about Christ, about the place of Jesus Christ in that battle, and at the same time he was caring for the church as he was caring for the oppressed. The struggle was so great that the political right placed a slogan on the streets, "Be a patriot, kill a priest."[24] The oligarchy, the people with money, told the priests: leave the country or you will be killed. They didn't. And that is why Don Romero, Ellacuría, and others were killed. In that movement, we can see how radical the church was, taking sides with the poor and against the powerful. A church that is so bold is a church that inspires its people, making them dream, empowering them with tools to protest and find a new and more just life. There is so much that we can learn from that church at that time.

The relation between the altar and the world entails a double movement. First, when our traditions and songs, prayers and profession of faith, healing and reading the Bible, baptism and Eucharist are living possibilities of justice and grace, marks of a church that will deeply challenge and change the life of the streets, of the cities, of the markets, of the life of the poor. The other movement is when the world is begging us to change, to renew

23. Ruíz, "Romero."
24. Ruíz, "Romero."

ourselves, to go through a conversion to remember the poor again and again. That is when we, the church of Jesus Christ, leave our buildings to be the church in the world, living the liturgy after the liturgy. If our faith is to be lived in the world as Paul Hoffman powerfully said, "You have been formed in Christ for the sake of the world,"[25] and Douglas John Hall reminded us, "Faith is a journey toward the world."[26] Then we must go out and find Jesus on the streets and come back with their lives and concerns in our heart, perhaps even bringing them to our worship, and changing our prayers, our songs, and the ways in which we worship God and live this gospel.

Conclusion

Abraham Heschel said, "Religion is a critique of all satisfaction. Its end is joy, but its beginning is discontent, detesting boasts, smashing idols. It began in Ur Kasdim, in the seat of a magnificent civilization. Yet Abraham said, 'No,' breaking the idols, breaking away. And so every one of us must begin saying no to all visible, definable entities pretending to be triumphant, ultimate. The ultimate is a challenge, not an assertion. Dogmas are illusions, not descriptions." [27]

Moving within this challenge, we should see our liturgies as breaking with the sources of capitalism and a system of exclusion. Our liturgies should be tools and resources for the those who suffer economically, politically, with illnesses, those who cannot eat, who are under national threats, mothers who do not have enough to raise their kids, people who cannot afford proper treatment. Our liturgies should hold out signs of our preferential option for the poor, a radical siding with those who are marginalized. In that sense, our liturgies must learn constantly from what is happening at the ground, with grassroots social movements of the poor so we can engage the liturgical movement into the liberation of the oppressed. Thus our glorias will hold hands with the dispossessed, our alleluias will proclaim freedom to the captive, God's love will give us the strength to look up, and God's grace will empower us for the struggle that is ahead of us! As Heschel says, "The liturgical movement must become a revolutionary movement, seeking to overthrow the forces that continue to destroy the promise, the hope, the vision."[28]

25. Hoffman, "The Rite of Affirmation of Baptismal Vocation in the World."
26. Hall, Cross in Our Context, 55.
27. Heschel, Moral Grandeur and Spiritual Audacity, 262–63.
28. Heschel, Moral Grandeur and Spiritual Audacity, 265.

Mainly, what I am proposing here is that instead of having to recur endlessly to the nauseating newness of the new, and instead of believing that the proper way of worship brings the proper meaning of life and God, we might be able to find tools to fight against the empire of consumerism and self-enclosed detachment from another kind of life by enhancing ancient and new practices of common love that can answer the current needs of our society and help us produce meaning in the encountering of people, in the relation with one another in our local forms of wisdom. Then, if we start caring about those who hurt in our neighborhoods, it actually doesn't really matter what liturgical frame we use. Once our theology of praise is fully intertwined with the liturgy of the church, the world, and the neighbor, serving those in need, we will begin where Jesus began. And our worship will praise God wholly, fully, and attend humankind and the earth abundantly.

Greeting, exchanging holy kisses, spreading gentleness, standing on the side of the poor, sharing our resources, supporting black communities, visiting immigrant churches, caring for indigenous communities will show how we are each other's keepers, producing encounters with one another that will last. In these encounters we should be open to the breaking of our classes, the embodiment of our various cognitions, borrowing from each other different *senses* to approach our (dis)belief, so we can stretch our horizons and ultimately, our faith. God's senses rest in our bodies and through these encounters and exchanges, we can certainly see the manifestation of God in and through us. How do we walk through these encounters with God, between traditions past and present, the economic market and the sacramental table, between the struggle of the poor where life is at stake and the dealing of our budgets? It is between our relations that God manifests Godself to us powerfully, helping us sort through our cultures, our differences, our languages, our liturgical actions, our likes and dislikes, and moves us towards that which we might not want, but will give to us a better sense of community, of living together.

Paul Hoffman made wonderful connections for us to wrestle with. He said,

> A word of Eucharistic selflessness offered in an ethical word at the corporate meeting.
>
> A sense of justice spoken to a five-year-old in our vocation as parent when teaching the difficult lessons of sharing.
>
> A heaping helping of the same hospitality we have received at the Lord's—the Lord's!—table offered to the poor.

A promise of life renewed to those who have no hope,
whether "those" are a dying great uncle in a distant city or a
newly divorced co-worker in the next cubicle.[29]

And we continue endlessly praising God:

Between the altar and the world, our daily lives, boredom, anger, and
dreams.

Between the altar and the world, our sons trapped in drugs, our
daughters wrestling with eating disorders.

Between the altar and the world, an economic system that is killing us
brutally day by day.

Between the altar and the world, a world made for the 2 percent of the
richest people.

Between the altar and the world, a massive number of people going
hungry every day.

Between the altar and the world, the incarceration of minorities as a
way of erasing them from our sight.

Between the altar and the world, the deporting of people who are here
to survive, also as a way of erasing them from our sight.

Between the altar and the world, our desire to love and be loved.

Between the altar and the world, the demands of a gospel of justice and
a world made of injustice.

Between the altar and the world, the demand to be thankful when
there seems nothing to be thankful for

Between the altar and the world, the need to keep on going with our
glorias and alleluias! Even during Lent!

Between the altar and the world, you and me, wrestling with this gospel, with a thousand different understandings of this faith.

Between the altar and the world, Luther, Calvin, Wesley, and sometimes our fidelity more akin to these European men than to the poor in our
neighborhood and to Jesus Christ.

Between the altar and the world, my God, our God.

Between the altar and the world, Jesus Christ.

Between the altar and the world, the Holy Spirit.

Between the altar and the world, the poor.

Between the altar and the world, a mission given to us by Jesus to go
announce this gospel for the transformation of the world.

---

29. Hoffman, "The Rite of Affirmation of Baptismal Vocation in the World."

12

And the Word Became Connection

Liturgical Theologies in the Real/Virtual World[1]

The Router is my Shepherd and I shall connect with everything . . .

I turn my eyes to the walls, where does the strength of my power outlet come from?

In a recent long trip I made with my mother in the United States, we were on the road when the service of her home Independent Presbyterian Church in São Paulo, Brazil, was happening. My nephew sent me a WhatsApp message saying that the worship was going to be streamed online. I got my phone and connected to the worship. For one hour and a half, she worshipped God as if she were present, there with her people. She described the service to me, prayed, sang, listened to the sermon, and she cried when she saw her son-in-law singing in the choir. She had been praying for him for a long time and finally he was back in the fold of the church. She gave glory to God raising her hands inside of my car while we were driving across the US. A real/virtual worship service for her!

Here we are again, Christians having to adapt our faith to our current times. Current issues such as global warming and the accelerated destruction of our planet, the economic devouring of the middle class everywhere, hatred against the poor, neo-imperialism in full force, the shifting of cultural

1. A shorter version of this chapter was published in *Liturgy* 30.2 (2015) 26–35.

patterns of living together, new ways of being church, and the virtual world we have been thrown into are only some of the main issues that are at the cusp of our needed renovation as Christians. In this article we will focus primarily on the virtual life, the e-life. In this needed adaptation, the virtual world is challenging the church of Jesus Christ in many and unprecedented ways.

Traditions do change, all the time. Traditions are continuously challenged and being kept alive in many ways: by ways of betrayal, inner renewals, break ups, migration, ethnic and multicultural participation, theological shifts, and so on. In the midst of our fears and uncertainties, another challenge is upon us who live in the digital era. How can we face the new challenges of the virtual world, surely a new language, with openness, love, and justice?

This article offers theological insights to begin thinking about the strange presence of the virtual in our midst in ways that will empower us. To do theology is to theo-login, i.e., to enter/log into God's virtual world, theologizing the real of our login/virtual life, to think/live/experience God in a new language and dimension, to get our faith plugged into this wireless net of information and people where we are connected with a world known and unknown that is unfolding before our eyes. To theo-login is to provide tools to navigate this sea of possibilities to find ethical responses and to continue to live God's love in this new dimension. The hope is that by delving into the theological/theo-login, we can think/practice our liturgical theologies in ways that foster a vigorous Christian mission. In this process we must have imagination, a prophetic voice and a free spirit to face the challenges presented to us.

The Real and the Virtual

As we get into this new language we start to learn both the possibilities of connections and their limitations. How are we to think theologically about the virtual world? How is the virtual related to the real and what is real and what is virtual? Does the virtual erode the categories of history and materiality? Does the virtual destroy our real gatherings?

What is the virtual? The virtual is that which we can't quite locate. Things are in the cloud and there are no physical, real places where we can go. However, it is *there*, there meaning a place with no bounds, a there that is always elsewhere. Our bodies are extensions of gadgets, electronic machines and our minds are wired in very different ways, transforming our cognition, the way we think and also the way we relate. Some people say we are in the post-human era. We are all bodily, emotionally and fully involved in it, one way or another, creating new forms of life and new spiritualties are being birthed, alongside ancient traditions.

Mark C. Taylor gives a definition of the real and virtual using a theological frame. He says that, "The real, however it is conceived, is other, wholly other, or, in Kierkegaard's words that continue to echo, 'infinitely and qualitatively different.'"[2] The real is also the virtual, an-other dimension, place, "infinitely and qualitatively different" within and beyond us, deeply related to who and what we are and are becoming.

The virtual is the new religion. A new psalm could be composed: "the virtual is my shepherd and I shall lack and be fed." The virtual is a void filled with a presence to be reckoned with. A new re-cognito, new ways of thinking and being, framing our times, defining us endlessly, shifting our beings and leaving us with this way too real and uneasy and ongoing sense of unfinished identities. Our time can be defined by M. H. Abrams, cited by Taylor:

> To put the matter with the sharpness of drastic simplification: faith in an apocalypse by revelation had been replaced by faith in an apocalypse by revolution, and this now gave way to faith in an apocalypse by imagination or cognition. In the ruling two-term frame of Romantic thought, the mind of man confronts old heaven and earth and possess within itself the power, if it will but recognize and avail itself of the power, to transform them into a new heaven and new earth, by means of a total revolution of consciousness.[3]

This new cognito is shifting our ways of living, new traditions on the horizon, with new few forms of cognition, relations, and movements.

The Real and the Virtual Word of God: Theo-login

The ways in which God manifests Godself in our midst has been a major theological thrust in the life of Christian communities. Jesus coming to live in our midst, word made flesh, God with us, is the apex of our connections. For Jesus connected us with God, the source of our being, intersected our lives with the threads of life found in God, minded the gap of our many separations, splits, and brokenness. Jesus redeems us from all sorts of disconnections, saves us from ourselves so we can find ourselves, liberates

2. Taylor, *Rewiring the Real*, 5.
3. Taylor, *About Religion*, 171.

us from bonds of injustice, transforms our stories and relations, heals our wounds, wires us into God's own life, and streams us alive and nonstop into the aliveness of God's present really/virtually in Jesus. Our Christologies must give an account of the Emmanuel in the virtual world.

As the mediator between God and us, Jesus was the link, the connection, the bridge, the gathering between us and God. The sins of disconnection were redeemed! The wired bondage of slavery, poverty, and patriarchalism were unbounded and made free, wireless in Jesus, whose deep connections broke the chains of connection that killed us and were made now stronger through deeper bonds/wires of love, patience, mercy, hope, and justice. The tree of life is now spread through rhizomes of many roots giving fruit in many other trees, covering a much vaster territory, invading realms of death and producing a wireless connection throughout the world and even beyond the universe, in time/place capsules that contain the fullness of the eternity, with Jesus Christ being manifest in each random bit of energy and pulse of our bodies and local communities.

In Christian histories, the most accepted mediations have been the Bible, God's revelation in nature (in Calvin's words: common grace), and in Jesus (special grace), tradition, church documents, ecumenical councils, preaching, and the sacraments. Now we must deal with many other wired and wireless connections.

The Word that was there at the beginning and continues to need to be interpreted by our communities is now becoming something else in our day, also for the sake of the glory of God and the fulfillment of human life. The word that became flesh and bones is now metamorphosing itself into the virtual world, a world unknown to us in many ways, but a world that can carry both healing and transformation as well as injustice and corruption. The virtual world carries power and needs to be challenged. A world that can expand the possibilities of life but also one that needs vigilance by the people of God since it can easily spread sin and death. The real wor(l)d of God must enter into the virtual wor(l)d we live in so it will continue to be liberated and transformed.

As we continue to engage our traditions, we must deal with the virtual world and social media as we add this new source to the formal and former sources of theology. We see now that the word has become connection and connects us all into a web of relations and unthought-of possibilities.

God's love in Jesus continues to be expanded by new sources of life, and death, namely the virtual world. In this virtual world Jesus is the e-life, the e-way to God, still in its fullness. We the e-church, must continue our e-vangelism spreading the good news of Jesus Christ, who continues to connect us to God and one another, being the e-bridge within a disconnected world. The e-life, e-death, and e-resurrection of Jesus Christ are the spaces in which the conditions of the possibilities of God's manifestation are manifested. The Christian life is still about experiencing God, and now we must learn how to experience God in the virtual world.

As we start to open ourselves to the possibilities of God's manifestation, we must see how real the virtual world can be. People begin relationships, have sex and orgasm, experience pleasure and pain, feel loved and hated, step back from suicide, find reasons to murder, learn how to love and make bombs, become aware of things and forget reality, make wise and stupid decisions, and live their lives in the virtual world. At the heart of the virtual world lies an unresolved ambiguity. And yet, the embodiment still remains at the center of all the virtual experiences. The virtual world is elusive and clarifying, empowering and destructive. Just like our real lives.

To deny the presence of the Spirit in the virtual world is to deny the wondrous and multiple ways God's grace manifests. God is with us in this virtual world as well. Virtual space, like God, is a place that none of us can control, tame, or define properly. It is a borderless place that does not give itself to limits, creeds, and traditional worship rules. However, this world cannot be conflated with God since it is human made and must be developed, limited, apprehended, and organized.

How are we to do theology in this place? How to figure out the unfigurable, that which cannot be known, controlled, grasped, figured? Perhaps the same way we do with our theologies, creating formats, expressions, and concepts. In one phrase: finding borders within this borderless world. In this space Jesus's promise of abundant life must be held high. Jesus lived and promised us life in abundance and that is the life we are called to live in the real/virtual world. In his day, Jesus was very careful to work within the tradition, with the Torah and the cultural ways of living faith in God. By reinterpreting all of it, he was searching for the fullness of life for the sake of life. Life comes first—before any theology or worship! First God's love touches us, then we gather together to worship God. First life is breathed in us then we try to understand this awe striking breath that keeps us alive!

We could say that the same way reformed people believed that God would accommodate Godself into the language and limitations of human beings, God might be now accommodating Godself into the usage of online media so that we can experience God's grace within the virtual world. The virtual world is the new theater of human possibilities and it also needs the glory of God to be found, chanted, and lived.

Nonetheless, these borders are always prone to the borderlessness of Jesus Christ, the event of God. It is God's borderlessness in Jesus Christ that breaks down all of our borders time and again so we can get closer to the fullness of God's glory and life. Thus, if we are to do God's will on earth as it is in heaven, we must also make sure that the will of God is lived fully in the real/virtual world. The daily bread has to be present—a presence that provides the possibility of a just life available for all. The virtual, as the real, must be a place for justice and inclusiveness. The virtual world alone should never be understood as enough. If the virtual world proclaims that life by its own measure is enough, then we are seeing the powers of death taking over. If a life connected by the wireless connection is enough then we are talking about a fully disconnected life that has been trapped into the virtual worlds of utter disconnection.

In order to avoid the individualism (not individuation) that promotes a world of me, me, me, we must call each other to gather together time and again. The virtual world is the new psalm of David, who said, "I was glad when they said to me, 'Let us go to the house of the Lord.'"[4] The call is the same, and the virtual is one of the spaces we meet and share. However, this is a space that must create conditions for our meeting together face to face, where we rub each other's shoulders, smell each other's smell, breathe each other's breath, kiss each other's cheek, and hold each other's hand.

The word of God in the virtual world is also a prophetic word, a word of love, justice and liberation that responds and reframes this very real/virtual world in order to show the glory of God in the real lives of the poor. The word that was, and still is real, way too real, is and must be fundamentally real to the lives of the poor, especially the disenfranchised, disconnected from the material resources of life, those who lack access to the virtual world in terms of computers and Internet.

Some Liturgical Theological Themes

Beyond the christological perspective, here are some liturgical theological themes that we can think about when we think about the virtual world

Church

From a theological/accommodation/mediation of the virtual world perspective we can continue to think of the church with the metaphor of the cloud of witnesses. The church has two thousand years of history in its visibility and invisibility, and lives at the same time in the past, present and future. We are all a cloud of witnesses inhabiting the virtual and real world, as well

---

4. Ps 122:1 NRSV.

as gathering together to worship God. The ways that we now organize information are changing the ways we organize ourselves. Before the digital era we had owners of the church in the same way that the media had its owners, too. Now information has been pulverized and monopolies of power and control cannot hold their hegemony the same way they used to. The advent of the digital era expanded the ways we hold and share power and facilitated a democratization of the world where nobody can hide information anymore. We are much more accountable to one another in our digital era, and this is great news for the church of Jesus Christ. Here every one is accountable to one another and power is something to be shared from the bottom up instead of being held in hierarchical structures. And yet, because anyone can create a website the truth of what they write is not monitored. Thus they can deceive people, they can make up their own identity without any proof, and they can make statements that are not facts. We are the real and the virtual church where borders have been shifted and reinforced, with worlds of connections between people opening up and closing. How do we talk about the cultural, ethnic, sexual, gendered, economic aspect of the cloud of witness when we are also talking about the virtual world? How do we live together in this world with that which we have received? The power dynamics persist!

Holy Spirit

We have been living in this virtual world since Jesus's ascension to heaven. The Holy Spirit is our real/virtual Wor(l)d, the digits of our shifting identities. When we talk about the cloud of witnesses we are talking about archives and communities. Now our archives, files, texts, photos, and memories are placed in the cloud, as a proxy of the Spirit. It is a virtual place that holds our histories and connections. We can't see this place, and nobody knows where it is, but it is surely t/here, somewhere. The tangible archive is becoming a thing of the past, burned into the ashes of our memories and now located somewhere else. To be a Christian is to go elsewhere where the Spirit might be, often away from high-class churches and institutionalized power, and more clearly within the pariahs, beggars, the unemployed, the sick, the miserable, the outcast, the downtrodden, the ones outside of the system. There, the real is more than virtual, it is so real that it is surreal! Do we have a gospel for them/us–we?

Fredy, "El barco (The boat)"

Fredy is five years old, from Guatemala. In this picture he drew the boat he and his mother rode
in crossing the Usumacinta River (Guatemala-Mexico Border).

Sin

We live in a time that begs for connection, and connection comes from the
incarnation of God in Jesus Christ, "The Word became flesh and blood, and
moved into the neighborhood."[5] This is the key aspect of this world: connection. The Internet is connecting people in a variety of new ways, and
connection has become the most important value of our time. Nowadays

5. John 1:1 MSG.

people are not looking for meaning but for connection, and whoever can provide connection will gain people's attention. Our sin today is to be disconnected and disconnection has become a disease. People have been so afraid of losing connection that new illnesses have appeared in our society such as different forms of depression, rage, loneliness, social phobias, body pain, stress, anxiety, addiction, and so on. To lose connection is to be utterly alone and in danger of disappearing. The church must offer possibilities of interactions, but we are often missing that point. One goes to school to be connected more than to receive "education." That is why some schools cost so much, because they can offer more lucrative connections to the richest parts of our societies. The sinful nature of the current neoliberal economy is to keep on top those who already own the game, and to keep on the bench those who can only watch it, and to keep away from the stadium those who cannot afford to buy a ticket. This is the structural sin that pervades our culture and prevents the possibilities of God being manifested. It is against this sin that the church should push hard, bringing the connectivity of God's glory in Jesus Christ, reminding us of the death and resurrection of Jesus Christ, and the healing power of the Holy Spirit. To defeat disconnection we have the *word* of connection that comes from God and marks history with materiality and justice, holding on to life that is real, all too real.

Sacrament

The Eucharist is the celebration of the transubstantiation, consubstantiation, the real presence, and symbolism of God in our midst. In all of these possibilities of connections with us, Jesus is fully present by way of his absence. The virtual presence of God in the real is such that the real gets transfigured, transformed into life anew! The absence of God is made present by gestures of faith, vivid demarcations of a territory both virtual and real that points to Jesus, the one who is there and not there at the same time. The famous definition of the sacrament by Saint Augustine, "The outward sign of an inward grace,"[6] is the epitome of the virtual in the midst of the real, not exactly knowing what/where is the real and what/where is the virtual. In the real and virtual world, the place of memory is fundamental. The Internet is replacing the location of our memory: we now don't remember things but we do remember the places where things are, what part of the virtual world we can go to remember something. Google/Finder are technological tools functioning as proxies for our memory. What would we do without Google/Finder? Would we remember ourselves? The subversive memory of

6. Fitzgerald et al., *Augustine Through the Ages*, 159.

Jesus Christ is in the archive, in us, and in the virtual world, connecting communities and movements of change.

Symbols

In the same way, the churches of Jesus Christ have utilized symbols throughout their history: fish, bread, wine, lion, boat, cross, empty tomb, dove, serpent, lamb, and so on. We have accumulated many symbols in these two thousand years. Now, as we continue to work with the traditions of the church, accommodating the traditions to our cultures, we might need to add phones, iPads, and routers to and of our faith, worship spaces, coffee shops, and etc. One example: the long-distance healing that Jesus effected in the transformation of the daughter of the Canaanite Woman.[7] Jesus was already healing from a distance, virtually! Now the same distance healing is brought to us through cups of water on the tops of radios and TVs or through the Internet by participating in a rerun of a worship service that was recorded a week ago. The altar call where people would come to the front to accept Jesus is now possible through pressing a button on the computer. People watching the worship service online that happened last Sunday can still affect other people's lives around the world in the same way as books traveling to different places have changed people.

Evil

However, this virtual world is also a place deeply marked by power and the possibilities of evil. We all must be aware and careful about the ways in which power manifests. This world is made of billions of dollars with a moral agenda, as well. The virtual world has monetized and globalized our economy, dissolving and hiding powers in ways that are difficult to be accounted for. This is where liberation theologies come to the fore. The virtual world is prone to injustice, greed, and exploitation just as the "real" world is. As a matter of fact, the virtual world has become a privileged place where people are abused and degraded, where the rich protect their money and make alliances against the poor. There must be a call for justice everywhere and a virtual liberation theology is needed now to issue a prophetic call against the imbalance of power and against those who perpetrate evil. When we talk about the virtual world we must remember that a huge part of our population has no access to the Internet and those who are outcast

7. Matt 15:21–28 NRSV.

and poverty-stricken cannot afford even a cheap cell phone since they can't afford a meal a day. Suffering is everywhere and is a consequence of our disconnection. Who can connect? Who is this church? I hope to live in a church with the poor, and even if there might be high speed Internet in many poor areas around the globe a vast majority of people have no access to it. The virtual exclusion of the poor is also a fundamental aspect of the sinful/disconnected world we are living now. A real/virtual church is one that makes sure people can eat, can have access to health care, have shelter and the possibility to live well.

Spirituality

Our spiritualties happen in the real and virtual world. Clement Greenberg's expression "Kingdom of the abstract"[8] is where we live. Keeping the binaries for a while, the virtual kingdom of God is now offering something that the real kingdom of God takes too long to accomplish. It is easier to live in the virtual than the real. The necessary illusion that would take us away from the real now has become a reality in itself and reality has taken the place of illusion. Reality is an illusion that we try to escape. The divide between immanence and transcendence has been enmeshed into one another. Consumerism is actually the new and most important spiritual practice. Bargaining with God and the world is our preferred lifestyle. Moreover, the real spiritual life, when Christians *read the Bible* daily and *prayed seven times a day*, feels like an outdated mode of spiritualty. Many of the Christian traditions are now part of a relic, something we go back to to remember who we used to be. And more, *service* today is almost an awkward word. To serve somebody we now have to ponder our limits, our willingness to do it, and be aware of the dangers and the liabilities when helping the poor. The *simulacra*, an image/representation/imitation of someone/something is more real than the real. Mark C. Taylor says, "In the world of simulacra created and sustained by complex networks of exchange, differences become indifferent until it seems as if nothing is special."[9] Virtual in-difference is easily translated into the material/real in-difference leveling out our love into whatever platitude we want to hide under. The result is that the poor become even more other, virtual, infinitely beyond, excess, garbage, simply to be taken and moved out of our glorious virtual/real lives. The quest for materiality, our bodies, and each other's real individual and social conditions will always be at the heart of our spiritualties.

8. Taylor, *About Religion*, 182.
9. Taylor, *About Religion*, 196.

Proclamation

The *kerygma* is already there but in a variety of forms and possibilities and expressions that makes the very homiletic event something hard to define and rather difficult to grasp. The differentiation of the gospel, once marked in the act of preaching, is now often swallowed by the constant new media and its endless novelty. The lonely master voice of a preacher is now interspersed with so many other voices, and her/his voice is now only one piece of information amidst many offers to see and interpret the world. The pastor, the one holding the truth of the community no longer exists. And this might be a great opportunity for us to move from a top-down structure of church to a bottom-up way of living in community. Knowledge is not a gift bestowed upon a wise person, but rather shared in solidarity. Pastors are just one among many who are given the gift to preach. Preachers are adaptive leaders who preach a gospel that connects people to people/places/events of life. Pastors are networkers who help people adapt to this world, able to work with people and their resources in order to search for life anywhere, elsewhere. Proclamation is a work of the community and not a sole action by one person. It takes a village to preach a sermon!

The Real and the Virtual

We are all intertwined, interrelated and interconnected. Our task as the church of Jesus Christ is to model the ways in which these interactions, connectivity, and interrelations can and should happen. Our end is not alone behind a screen but together with one another. While the virtual world is a real and fundamental part of our lives, we must use it for the proclamation of the word of God, healing, transformation, interfaith relations, and working for the sake of the poor.

Facebook, Twitter, Instagram, Flickr, Foursquare, and so on, are mediums of connection that empower our connectivity. They do not, and should not, replace our gatherings, our living together, our rubbing our shoulders together, our kissing and sharing the peace of Christ. Wiping each other's tears can be done over the Internet but it must also continue to be done person to person, the virtual empowering the real, the real being a sign of our need for each other—the same way the real must also empower the virtual, expanding ways of connection, of love, care, and presence.

Our history is still made of materiality, our people still need real food to eat and survive. Economic structures, understanding of work, and class relations are still marked and mediated by the virtual world. People's access to the virtual world is a marker of social inclusion. While many poor populations have some kind of access to the Internet through phones or LAN houses,[10] the extreme poor still have no way to access anything beyond the streets where they search for their daily food.

Thus, God's preferential option for the poor must continue, really and virtually. In order to challenge the mechanisms of injustice that are still present in the real and virtual worlds, our task is to fight for those who are outside of the system. We must create possibilities of economic, social and class mobility, resource communities with tools and wealth, fight against the hegemony of companies who own our natural resources and against the two percent of the population who own us all, and continue to be a model of resistance for all Christians.

How can we rewire the real? That is the major theo-login question for all of us!

Worship

Now that we have some glimpse of theological notions of the virtual/real world, how can we worship God? What is the task and mission of the people when they worship together? Worship is always a second act. The first act is God's love for us demanding that we love God and the neighbor. When we love one another we must gather and worship God. Our worship is our wireless connection with one another, bodies next to bodies, connected by something that is fully there and also, in some ways, isn't.

Our worship of God is a way of producing connection with one another, God and the world. A new world is created, a cloud of witnesses is present, a wireless router can bring us connectivity just as the songs of a hymnal sung by our ancestors. In the virtual/real world, my culture gets blurred with someone else's culture, and my social class is broken down for the sake of those who are at a disadvantage in social connectivity/life.

It is there, at the worshiping place, that we negotiate the ways in which we connect. The cliché "seven points for a healthy online church," or "how to use media properly," or "how to become welcoming" won't do the job. The use of technology in our churches is both fundamental and not important at all. Because in our worship services what matters is that we are together to worship God. With or without screens, iPads, and wireless mics, the importance is our life together, our empowered prayers with one another, and preaching done in a way—any way—that brings the gospel to the people.

10. LAN houses are stores with several computers where people use the Internet by the hour.

When we have the Eucharist, the eating of the bread and the drinking of the wine, face to face or with a loaf of bread on top of the computer, we are announcing that this sacrament is fundamentally, a heightened moment of connectivity, where we announce the death and resurrection of Jesus Christ and our mutual responsibility to one another.

Our challenge is to deal with unstable notions of time and space. Our buildings are not the sole place for worship and connections. Whether we are in each other's homes, on Internet chat places, on Facebook pages, spreading news on Twitter or sharing photos on Instagram, we are all connecting with one another. These are the new ways we must see church in our day.

Jesus used the Greco-Roman meals to share life with people, preached for the crowds, went to people's homes, met them on streets, went to where the people were, and used symbols and parables to allow people to know what he was doing. The Apostle Paul used the structures of his time, went to the Pantheon to preach about Jesus, and told us to preach both in time and outside of time. We must claim this adaptability as well, seeing and living a church that is not hegemonic, that is not an institution holding to middle- and upper-class behavior, but rather, a movement of connections, adapting to what we have, challenging those who have too much, and living for the glory of God and the sake of the poor.

Conclusion

As we think about our liturgical theologies, we can ponder the wonderful Jewish thinker Walter Benjamin's Angel of History. Benjamin was in awe of Paul Klee's painting *Angelus Novus*, a painting that shows an angel with outstretched arms moving forward but looking back. Perhaps he was trying to hold a tempest, this tempest being progress in the mind of Benjamin. The angel is looking to the past piled up with tragedies and horrors. He moves forward haunted by the past. The progress we have now is a sign of human genius and amazing abilities to create. However, this progress has also been a piling up of tragedies, people being killed and excluded. The present sense of greed, individualism, caring only for oneself, and living with unrestrained desire, is bringing forth more tragedies.

Our worship services are signs of our times and how we think about our humanity. It is our task as Christians to engage the virtual world seriously, to help create the conditions for God to manifest in our midst, and to live our faith fully, as Jesus promised us!

Conclusion

Towards a Liberation Theology of God's Glory

I looked at my hands to see if I was the same person. There was such a glory over everything. The sun came up like gold through the trees, and I felt like I was in heaven.

—HARRIET TUBMAN

Soldiers in the horror of battle offer solemn testimony that life is not a hunt for pleasure but an engagement for service; that there are things more valuable than life; that the world is not a vacuum. Either we make it an altar for God or it is invaded by demons. There can be no neutrality. Either we are ministers of the sacred or slaves of evil. Let the blasphemy of our time not become an eternal scandal. Let future generations not loathe us for having failed to preserve what prophets and saints, martyrs and scholars have created in thousands of years.

—ABRAHAM HESCHEL

The permanent condition of political emergency and cultural vulnerability we live in leaves no other choice. If our actions are not daring, inventive, and unexpected, they won't make a difference, and border reality, with its overwhelming dynamics, will supersede us in an instant.

—GUILLERMO GOMEZ-PENA

We need to be angels for each other, to give each other strength and consolation. Because only when we fully realize that the cup of life is not only a cup of sorrow but also a cup of joy will we be able to drink it.

—HENRI J. M. NOUWEN

It always seems impossible until it's done.

—NELSON MANDELA

Words are not things they are spirits.

—CLARICE LISPECTOR

I finish this book with two other stories, one from Jaci C. Maraschin, one of the most prominent liturgical theologians in Latin America who once told me this story. He was visiting a church on a Sunday morning and the priest looked at the altar throughout the mass. After the service, Maraschin went to see the priest and asked, "Why did you only look at the altar and not the people?" And the priest said, "My friend, it is much better to look at God than at people." The second story comes from my five-year-old son Ike. In my study room in our house I have a picture of an indigenous child, adorned in red and black. Ike looks at this child and asks, "Dad, what is her name?" I gasped and said that I didn't know. He was surprised and asked, "Why is her picture here if you don't know her name?"

In some ways, these two stories point to the reason why I wrote this book. Perhaps inside of me there is a quest for God to look at me and know my name. There I was, in poor health and God looked upon me through my church. If the liturgy doesn't have God looking at me and my people, as terrifying as it might be, or calling me by my name, I don't know why I am there. My desire for God's gaze and hearing God utter my name comes from my history; and it is not only for myself since God's gaze is upon us all. Fundamentally I am looking for God's presence in the midst of those who live in the shadows of our society, those who go bruised day after day, and those who live in an endless liminality of lacks, embarrassments, brutalities and abandonment. There is no reason for the Christian faith to exist if the liturgy of this faith is not a ritual of liberation, a space for the renewing of our minds (Rom 12:2), a time when hurting people are healed, when the outcasts are brought back into the fold through God's grace, when the wretched of the earth find consolation and an excellent place to live, when the names of those who are excluded are called back and they respond, "*Presente!*," and when the glory of God is a loud affirmation of life.

The assembly of Christians is this movement of people working together with God, celebrating, calling names (and with it their most diverse peoples and realities and sufferings) in the name of God, bringing their stories, pains, and hopes, making us sometimes shift, sometimes step away from something into something else. This work of the people with God is what liturgy does: look for the afflicted, tell the truth, hold life up high, give language to recreate worlds, restore dignity, rekindle faith, and construct meetings and networks of people and systems of life. Each time we gather to work together, we sing glory to God.

Towards a Liberation Theology of God's Glory

A liberation theology of worship starts where it hurts, where people are wounded, where life is threatened, where hearts have fallen to the ground, where hope is lost, where there is little singing. It is at these places of destitution that the glory of God can restore our humanity!

In the movie *Selma* we learn what the meaning of glory is all about! The movie describes a short period in the civil rights movement when blacks and whites got together to fight against white supremacy and apartheid in this country. It is so amazing to see how our brothers and sisters back then knew how scary it was to sing to the glory of God.

In that time, to shout "Glory" was a very risky endeavor. Every shout of "Glory" was a shout for justice! Every shout of "Glory" was a prophecy of a new world! Every shout of "Glory" was the struggle to honor every black person in this country! Black people and some white people became the holders of a new world right there! They were the chorus of a glorious future! Singing and fighting on our behalf!

They knew that to shout "Glory" could destroy their families, it could put them in jail! They knew that to shout "Glory" could get them killed! In the midst of the fight, God's Glory was something unknown, since the birthing of a movement had so many unknowns. And yet the glory of God was closer to them than anything else. For God was hovering over this movement with a cloud of God's own glory!

Their shout of "Glory" was a proposal for a different society! They opposed the glorias of the white supremacists. Don't forget that the KKK used to sing glory too! It was a glory that was a very corrupted glory, a glory that was based on a white theology of destruction. And yet, the "Glory, glory,

Alleluia" in the mouths of black and white folks broke loose the gates of hell. The marchers walked because they knew the glory of God! They crossed the bridge and went from Selma to Montgomery because the glory of God went ahead of them! The angels of God were singing along with the cloud of witness singing, "Glory! Glory! Glory!"

And they walked! In the midst of bullets, water hoses, and dogs, they walked! For all they had was the glory of God, and singing their glory to God was the way to keep themselves alive! They knew the very consequences of singing glory!

When they got to Montgomery, the journey wasn't finished. There were still way more glories to sing, to come, many more glories to be shouted so the fight could go on! And after fighting for years, after losing so many people along the way, they knew what to shout glory was all about! Martin Luther King, Jr., Malcom X, and so many others couldn't shout glory with their people when the laws of segregation were broken.

But now, you have your own history to teach your people and your sons and daughters what God's glory is all about! The forces that continue to kidnap the glory of God in the world are in full force! So don't go alone! Engage with other people, find movements of resistance, and never ever forget to sing glory together with other people! For if you hold to the glory of God tightly to your heart and mind and body, you will see the glory of God coming!

Sometimes you will need to go to the mountaintop to see the glory of God. Sometimes and more often, it will be amidst your people that God will show God's glory to you. Every time you don't know where the glory of God is, go where the poor people are, and you will see Jesus, and the glory of God shining in its full stretch. And if the church isn't there, leave the church! But never leave the poor! For there, amidst the poor, the glory of God is in full swing!

Capitalism in all its forms has taken away the glory of God and has stolen the glorias from the mouths of the people. As I mentioned elsewhere,[1] Jaci C. Maraschin was concerned about the lack of glory in the world. Maraschin argued, "The lack of 'glory' in the modern world is due to the mass production, which from economic domination, encompasses the arts and churches. . . . The notion of 'glory,' linked to the revelation of the truth, presupposes a ground to be revealed in the thing, in the context of a new creation and not in the technological culture where art is turned as repetition, following economic production and the stereotyping of successful models."[2]

1. Carvalhaes, "Multiplying the Glorias Around the Earth."
2. Maraschin, *O espelho e a transparência.*

The kidnapping of the glorias is seen in the lack of joy to go to church, in the lack of breath of people to sing, the lack of life and full lungs singing full force the glory to God. Capitalism is teaching us to breathe in short spasms, brief intervals of "breathing in the desires to get stuff," and "breathing out the frustration of not getting it yet." The lack of breath has to do with the "ground to be revealed in the thing," as Maraschin puts it. Instead of being grounded in the new creation, deeply connected with the earth, humidified by the humus of our existence, and closely connected to each other, we are constantly placed in individual worship at altars that sanctify everything but the glory of God.

When the Christian churches in the United States decided to adopt the flight to suburbia, a clear movement away from the poor, the glory of God lost its breath and shifted the ground of its spiritual existence. Insulated in their own worship spaces, fearful of everything, the churches fully enveloped themselves in the last breath of God's glory. By going to the woods, with new buildings, the church gained conditioned air that separated them from the thick air of the places where the poor lived.

For Christians to regain the Spirit, the *ruach*, the breath of God, the church has to take another flight now in the direction of where the poor live. Not a flight that produces gentrification, stealing, and expulsion of the poor from their homes as is happening everywhere so the rich can have a good house, but rather, by getting to know their lives and together breathe the air they breathe, Christians will regain the lost air of the Holy Spirit. By breathing some fresh air into our lungs, we will realize that the polluted political air we have been breathing is the religion of money that is toxic to our bodies and carries no beauty to make us fly and imagine.

The breath of God comes to us in the loving and beautiful movement of God in the world, through the aesthetics and ethics of our living. Discussing Karl Barth's connection between the love of God and God's glory when he says "God loves us as a God who is worthy of love. This is what we express when we say that God is beautiful," Jürgen Moltmann says,

> If after this brief excerpt, in the context of the biblical use of the term "glory," we rephrase the question from the point of view of the relationship between ethics and aesthetics, we must point out that the experience of God in the life of faith is inseparable. The power of God is felt at the same time as glory and its beauty as sovereignty. God's glory cannot be reduced to God's dominion or God's dominion to God's glory. The one interprets, and the other defends it from misunderstandings. What is beautiful

is what brings joy in God. . . . Without the free play of fantasy
and doxology, new obedience degenerates into legalism.[3]

This, the beautiful Gloria of God can only come from lungs filled with
the air of the Holy Spirit. In spirt and in truth, in joy and in beauty, in aesthetics and in ethics! A theology of worship that depends on the Spirit will
challenge the detached ways of worship from the world, will be critical with
a certain self-fulfillment of the ways we worship God, and will challenge the
conflation of the American way of life/American dream with God's grace. A
theology of worship will take awe, wonder, and beauty as a fundamental way
to expand the work of freedom and liberation of God in our midst.

The late Jaci C. Maraschin, an Anglican liturgical theologian from
Brazil, said this: "Every liturgical reform must also be linked to the mission and must be based on a new theology, a mission linked to joy and
freedom. Liturgy and mission are sisters dancing together for the beauty of
God's kingdom."[4] Citing the Report of the Inter-Anglican Theological and
Doctrinal Commission called "For the Sake of the Kingdom," Maraschin
notes how liturgy and mission are interrelated and notes the troubles in his
own Episcopal church in Latin America. His analysis fits well the general
historical Christianity in the United States:

> The pseudo-elite addressed [by the report] accepted with self-
> complacency and a certain veiled pride the image of "superior
> church" and did not bother to bring the gospel of Christ to the
> poor and oppressed of our Latin America. The liturgical ques-
> tion is actually a theological question itself. It has to do with the
> concept of church and the ecclesial life of the group established
> in time and space. . . . The liturgy is, in fact, what the church is.
> It is in the liturgy more than in any other activity of the church
> life that the church reveals itself as it is. If the church chose the
> life of social and political alienation, this alienation will reveal
> itself in its liturgical life. It will turn to heaven and to the soul
> instead of worrying about the earth and the body. It will appeal
> much more to forms of individual piety than to collective piety.
> She will be a foreigner and will be ashamed to speak to our land,
> which will be equally strange to the earth. Liturgy is the form
> of our life in this world. It can express the anticipation of the
> freedom of the Kingdom of God, the fullness of love and the
> transparency of faith. It is in the Church to be the sign of our

---

3. K. Barth, *Dogmática de la Iglesia*, II/1, 734, 739, cited in Moltmann, *Un nuevo
estilo de vida*, 147.

4. Maraschin. *Da leveza e da beleza*, 21.

hope. The criterion for judging this life, and for its consumma-
tion, is the future promised by God.[5]

Without the ethical freedom can't come! Without freedom the aesthet-
ical can't appear. The historical ethical-aesthetical judgment of our liturgies
portrayed by Maraschin is similar to that of Womanist theology. Delores
Williams says that one of the four methodological tenets of Womanist theology is *liturgical intent*. She defines it this way: "Liturgical intent . . . means
that womanist theology will consciously impact critically upon the foundations of liturgy, challenging the church to use justice principles to select
the sources that will shape the content of liturgy."[6] Linda E. Thomas says
that "liturgical intent means that black female religious scholars and clergy-
women will develop a theology relevant to the African American church,
especially its worship, action, and thought . . . In a word, black church liturgy has to be defined by justice."[7]

Any theology of worship must have a similar liturgical intent: using
the beauty of rituals, liturgies and symbols, and the history and experiences
of people, it has to work for justice![8] Embracing the lives of black women
and other oppressed communities and from their life experiences, their notions of beauty and the ways they live their larger cultural historical context,
there is a need to develop a liturgical theology that is relevant for the most
vulnerable in our societies in worship, action, and thought.

With this liturgical intent in our immediate horizon, any theology of
worship must search to know who we love when we worship God and must
answer several questions every Sunday. Who do we want to be with when
we worship God? Where is the ground from which we worship? What do
we need to have when we worship God? What are the liturgical things we
decide are holy things? Who can handle these things and speak the holy
words? What is the notion of beauty that spurs imagination and freedom,
and stretches the horizon of possibilities? What is the place and role of the
Holy Spirit in our gatherings? What kind of air is in our lungs? Is this common air breathed from the hard places on earth? Are the lives of the poor
breathing in our nostrils? What do we learn to desire when we desire God?
What anointing or forms of healing do we hold from traditions and our
communities that we can freely offer to each other as communities of faith?
Who has health insurance in our midst? Are the poor kids in the neighborhood properly fed, cared for, and taught properly? Where are the artists

5. Maraschin, "A antecipação da liberdade do Reino de Deus," 349–63.
6. Williams, "Black Theology and Womanist Theology," 64.
7. Thomas, "Social Sciences and Rituals of Resilience," 49.
8. See Walton, *Feminist Liturgy.*

who, in worship, make us imagine, dream, stretch our horizons? How are the rivers cared for in our communities? Who is crying and who have we, from our worship spaces, failed to hear? How many and how loud can our glorias be sung to dismantle evil?

There is a weight for the costly grace of God that comes with God's glory. For the glory of God happens in the pursuit of justice for the widow, the orphan, the poor, and the foreigner among us. The glory of God shines in the places where the people of God work hard so the destitute can be restored, the undocumented are offered a home, the imprisoned find freedom, the homeless find shelter, the sick find health care and those who are nobodies become somebodies! Just like the glory of God shone in the life of an undocumented peasant called Jesus Christ.

That is why this liturgical theology of glory must avoid being captive to a notion of the Holy Spirit as a supra power, a totalizing force that controls everything and everybody from elsewhere. This spirit can often be confused with the spirit of absentee colonizers, transnational companies and the financial market that dominate the globe hiding its true face and promising a fake perfect life. We must be aware that we can be captive to a theology of glory that lives in sheer transcendence, equating the Holy Ghost with the *geist* of our immaterial globalized world, spiritualizing everything, making us live in immaterial promises and a personal world of illusions. This theology of glory of this world takes us away from the materiality of our lives, from the historicity of our pains, from the voices of our ancestors, and literally detaches us from our immanent world, from touching the ground, listening to the birds, flowing with the rivers, paying attention to the flights of the bees, talking to the animals, connecting and grounding our bodies with the soil, with the air. As theologian Sharon V. Betcher says,

> Spirit has conceptually been made to collude with the powers of normalization and, therefore, has been read as a totalizing, colonizing power. . . . We overdraw transcendence, that physics of Spirit, when we lose track of the sociopolitical conditions of religious articulation. Pulling transcendence into a vertical scaffolding that supersedes the terrestrial, we anesthetize ourselves. . . . We habituate ourselves to our cordoned off in/security zones, rather than take responsibility for that which opens off the edge of our present.[9]

A strong liturgical theology of glory helps us move away from this spirit of the world and turns us close to our world, a world where the colonial state of violence that we are living in continues to weigh on us, leaving

---

9. Betcher, *Spirit and the Politics of Disablement*, 39, 38.

us barely breathing, or completely breathless like Eric Gardner in New York. How can we face our present time and still find breath to give glory to God? This is indeed a daily battle that we must go through with God's daily provision of manna. We must not forget that it was the glory of God that came to us once and changed our lives! God's glory, awe, and wonder that came to us through either a slow process of self-revelation or in a sudden strike. And we were changed forever! It is to that glory, that love, that awe, and that wonder that we must return to/go after continuously.

It is the awe and wonder of God's glory that allows us to see/feel the depth and width of God's love and continue to face the injustices and evils so present in our lives and in the lives of our neighbors, communities, and the world. Mayra Rivera describes the overflowing weight of glory in our realities:

> To perceive glory is to awaken to the weight of reality, to be exposed to its insistence and resistance. This is not just an intellectual process. While precluding neither doubt nor opinion, sensibility to glory entails an effective turn, indeed a conversion . . . [that] leads to a sense of self that is inherently marked by the responsibility to the human-Other . . . [which includes] the non-human world. . . . The cry is not a negation of glory, but the negation of its negation. The cry of a hungry person and the groaning of creation manifest the persistence of glory, the astonishing fact that all the world's callousness and violence have not overcome it.[10]

The glory of God is nothing less than the love of God for the world. "For God so loved the world . . ." says the apostle John.[11] The song "Yes Jesus loves me! / Oh, yes Jesus loves me! / For the Bible tells me so," holds the weight of the theology of glory; a glory that is marked by passion, suffering, violence, and death. A glory whose love now is not to reinstate suffering or vindicate glory through suffering, but rather to end suffering by way of its loving revelatory salvation.

10. Rivera, "Glory," 176.
11. John 3:16 NRSV.

Saul, "Casa y sol (House and sun)"

Saul is seven years old, from El Salvador. In this picture he drew his neighborhood. Living next door to his house is his uncle Luis, and then his grandmother.

The Christian message is grounded in love. Our faith starts in God's love and not in correct belief. *Lex orandi!* God's love/glory is this shining proximity through salvific darkness, the immemorial beginning of our self, the everlasting end of our lives. Thus, if you know you are loved beyond measure and beyond your own ability, then you know you can say, "Glory!" That is why we go to church every Sunday, to shout "Glory!" and find a measure of ourselves with one another in God. When we find out we are loved by God we cannot not shout "Glory!" To be known by this God of love is the beginning of our worship! We begin in God's love, in contemplation and practice! The itinerary is simply: from the contemplation of God's glory in the practice of our faith on the streets with the poor so that we can figure out what we believe. Gustavo Gutiérrez gives us an itinerary:

> God is first contemplated when we do God's will and allow God to reign; only after that we think about God. To use familiar categories: contemplation and practice together make up a first act; theologizing is a second act. We must first establish ourselves on the terrain of spirituality and practice; only subsequently is it possible to formulate discourse on God in an authentic and respectful way. Theologizing done without the mediation of contemplation and practice does not meet the requirements of

the God of the Bible. The mystery of God comes to life in contemplation and in the practice of God's plan for human history; only in a second phase can this life inspire appropriate reasoning and relevant speech. (Given the two meanings of the Greek word logos—"reason" and "word"—theology is a reasoned word or reason put into words.) In view of all of this we can say that the first stage is silence, the second is speech.[12]

The glory of God is contemplation and deed! A performative mixture of silence and deed, awe and act, pause and motion, holding back and moving forward, saying yes and no, moving through affirmation but also through negation ("I am not what somebody says I am") as forms of resistance. All of it turned into liturgical theologies. That means that in every beginning of our worship we come with heavy and joyful hearts, and when we see each other together, we celebrate being in the assembly and that we are living together and we stop to breath and contemplate as a sign of awe and gratitude. We are called to respond to the love of God. We rejoice! We wonder! That joy and wonder, siblings of love, are manifested in so many forms and places in and through our work with the poor and outcast. Only after rejoicing and contemplating can we start *liturgizing*[13] what we can and need to say from the happiness and wonder of God in our week of struggles.

That is why it is important to take into consideration necessary shifts, changes, and expansions of our liturgies so that they may be not versions of some past social/cultural contexts and religious dogmas but rather the very pulsing of God in the deed and in the contemplation of an assembly in their very making of their theology of worship. When manifestations of the contemplation of God and street collide, we shift the "locus of enunciation" of our faith from what we know to the knower, to the ones whose dignity is always at stake. Our commitment is first to God but by way of our work for the equality of our society. At the same time, we are committed to the poor only by way of being caught in the contemplation/worship of God.

This contemplation is also a perception that we gain from the Spirit. As Betcher suggests the work of the Spirit is a form of perception that make us believe in this world again. She writes:

> Spirit might begin as an intensity, a vibration, within the zones of social assessment, where we admit our ease at falling into desire with the powers that be, with property and propriety, with the security of identity and with the glamors of image, all of which

---

12. Gutiérrez, *On Job*, xiii.

13. *Liturgizing* is a word I coined in my book *Eucharist and Globalization*.

keep us from the freedom and responsibility of creating a new earth, if even subversively from within the belly of empire.[14]

This vibration of the Spirit helps us see that our faith has a double constitution, being what the liturgy says life should be about and then corrected by what life actually says it is about, in this place right now, so it becomes liturgy next Sunday. In other words, liturgy is past corrected by the present, tradition enlivened by the potentialities of the lives of the outcasts, transcendence corrected by immanence, God's glory shaped by the work of solidarity with the immigrants, Muslims, disabled, indigenous peoples, and the poor. Liturgy then, as a double consciousness of God and the poor, is always in flux. This intense movement of the Spirit turns our desires for God to radically change our realities as our realities turn us to God.

In this circularity, a new and old glory always cuts through and enfolds our faith! The altar is always juxtaposed with the streets, the glory of God in the vivid situations of the poor, the moment of silence and contemplation in worship with the swollen feet and tired knees, the singing to God with the racism that takes the air out of our ungs. From this double movement, i.e., from the altar to the streets and from the streets to the altar, we hear and shout a liturgical prophetic call to action, a potent glory to rebuke demons and ritual actions that keep us from what John B. Cobb calls "spiritual bankruptcy."[15]

However, this spiritual bankruptcy always looms large! The devil hovers around us trying to make us live in fear of scarcity, losing our awe in God's love, relying more on budgets and buildings or pre-ordered liturgies that sometimes are no more than stale rituals of repetition without motion. The devil is hovering around trying to de-form our shouts of "Glory!," disfiguring our love of God and making our glorias an embarrassing, self-referential, self-destroying sound of "irrelevant transcendence or a cozy immanence."[16] The disfigured half-blown glorias we are tempted to sing time and again are the ones covered with Western universal, a-historical liturgies, with patriarchal overtones, denying racism and detached from faith, all of it reiterating different/same "locus of enunciations"[17] that are grounded as I said before, more in the known than the knower.

However, as the Holy Text says, "Discipline yourselves; keep alert. Like a roaring lion your adversary the devil prowls around, looking for someone

---

14. Betcher, *Politics of Disablement*, xii.

15. Cobb, *Spiritual Bankruptcy*.

16. Brueggemann, *Practice of Prophetic Imagination*, 3.

17. Mignolo, "Epistemic Disobedience, Independent Thought," 4.

to devour."[18] We need to watch! We need to keep loving this world and creating a new earth for the sake of God! The demon is getting ahead of us and deterring our singing of glorias. So we must be alert to get our praise and glorias grounded in the *imago Dei*, equality, solidarity, and being our brother's keepers. For the attacks of the powers that be are everywhere, trying to vanquish our own people.

The white-supremacy foundation of this nation-state hasn't changed. The colonizing project hasn't ended. The new Jim Crow is in full swing, having shifted only its words: before there were slaves, now they are criminals. These threats to God's glory continue to demand praise/thinking/singing from us, today, debunking God's glory in community life into the belief that it is the efforts of the individuals and what one alone can do that gives worth to his/her life. This reasoning, organized by the economic neoliberal market with its think tanks creating alternative facts, trying to shape our realities by turning wolves into lambs, and bringing forth emotions drenched in fears, hatreds, blind passions, and the desire to eliminate those who are different from us. The disguise of God's glory is a dangerous event, for it protects the powerful and annihilates the disenfranchised. The genuine gloria of God that promises life for all and demands us to care for one another is being fast replaced by a new spirit, a new contemporary *geist* that hovers over us by saying, "You are solely responsible for yourself and nobody else, you have to manage yourself alone in the market, making your individual life a form of business in order to sell yourself as a product so you can be included in the market."

No! We have the Holy Spirit to keep our faith pulsing, alive! It is the Holy Spirit, the communal holy spirit of full equality that will sustain the singing of our glorias to God! It is the Holy Spirit of God who gives us the possibility of a new society. The ongoing work of the Holy Spirit in our communities, in our localities, in the midst of differences between people with whom we share our daily lives, is the preservation/inauguration of an Ubuntu village. In this village, God's gloria comes from the archives found within these localities, and has the potency to create forms of circularity and connectivity between people and sources that can flow within "temporary global circulation forms"[19] and imagine new forms of living and survival. The gloria of God works within these systems of globalization but does not

---

18. 1 Pet 5:8 NRSV.

19. As Arjun Appadurai says, "I stress locality because, in the end, this is where our vitally important archives reside. Localities—in this world, and in this argument—are temporary negotiations between various globally circulating forms. They are not subordinate instances of the global, but in fact the main evidence of its reality." Appadurai, *Future as Cultural Fact*, 69; see also 81–82.

depend on their exclusive forms of flow, imagination and power. Globalization forces can be somewhat altered, reshaped, and redirected by the glory of God lived in communities. The glory of God is a ritual action situated in people's contexts, enmeshed in larger systems of oppression!

This ritual action can be a force! Tom Driver, Professor Emeritus at Union Theological Seminary, and one of the best ritual thinkers, once said this:

> The tendency in modern churches and organizations is to conceive of a ritual as some kind of communication device—either to give information or to give people some kind of experience. We need to dispense with this notion. A ritual is an action, not a thought; and it is not an emotion factory. You must figure out what you are trying to bring about in the total situation: not just something to bring about immediately, when the people are right there, nor a change in their feelings. but a change in the situation in which you and they exist. . . . We can only go so far with the analogy between ritual and theater . . . People who attend a ritual are not its audience. Maybe it doesn't even have an audience. Both the people who lead it and those who otherwise take part in it are actors (meaning doers). They must be brought to the point at which they are all actors; and this means the leaders must figure out what to do and why and how to carry the action through. The most deadly thing is to think that you are delivering something to the people! Instead the task is to evoke their wholehearted participation.[20]

Our liturgies will be actions filled with the Spirit and done with wholehearted participation. In this way, liturgy becomes truth-telling, and the glory of God the ongoing stretch of the universal moral arc towards justice. The actions to be carried through are the daily liturgical theological work for the dignity of the most vulnerable. In the midst of loss and violence, we discover that the glory of God is about the togetherness of a "tenuous 'we' of us all."[21] This *we* is the discovery of common commitments, common compassion, common grounding, and common allegiances in the midst of racial, sexual, class, and cultural multiplicities. In this action, our theologies of worship will always be the messy work of the people and the singing of God's glory filled with interruptions, paradoxes, and inconsistencies.

It is with this acute self-awareness that we can perceive the glory of God in our lives and in our midst and we can celebrate it together. It is the

20. Tom Driver, from a workshop with Richard Schechner and Ronald Grimes at Union Theological Seminary. Quoted from a video. Not published.

21. Butler, *Precarious Life*, 20.

gracious work of the Holy Spirit in our midst that will put fresh air in our lungs so we can resist and even increase our singing of glorias and our commitment to the poor! For it is the worship of God and the singing of glorias that keep us from sinking!

We sing Gloria because God is with us!

We sing Gloria because our memory is in God, our "sweet light!"

We sing Gloria because there is always a promise of new life!

We sing Gloria because we feel that a new earth is about to come!

We sing Gloria because this community will take care of me and my family!

We sing Gloria because we have made it through another week!

We sing Gloria because we will make it to another week!

We sing Gloria because God will deliver us from bondage and suffering!

We sing Gloria because we feel empowered not to rely on ourselves to make it on our own, or to gain success, or to make things change, but to work together in communities beyond the partisan political structure, by organizing local assemblies with local neighbors with platforms of popular power!

We sing Gloria because women and children will lead the way.

We sing Gloria to undo local policies that destroy marginalized people.

We sing Gloria so we can pay attention to the patterns and pace of the earth!

We sing Gloria because we must bring soul back to the world so that it reveals the glory of God.

We sing Gloria to learn to desacralize the notion of economic growth and deaccelerate the buying patterns that shape who we are as human beings.

We sing Gloria when we learn other songs of glory from other people and other religions.

We sing Gloria because every shout of "Glory!" is another step towards the restoration of the humanity of those made into beasts and the garbage of our society.

We twist our tongues and queer our Glorias when we live within multiplicities of sexualities.

We gain a new song of Gloria when we pay attention to people with disabilities, and fight for their support.

We sing a new Gloria when we sing with angels and along with people with mental illness.

We are blessed with a new incandescent Gloria every time a child makes a loud sound in our worship.

We sing Gloria when beauty visits us from within and a thousand other places, showing us that our humanity is always more than we imagine.

We sing Gloria because we are able to listen to the birds singing their own glorias!

We sing Gloria because we hear the leaves dancing and the plants springing up!

We sing Gloria when rivers flow throughout the earth and we weep with the lack of Glorias then they run dirty and in death!

We sing Gloria because we await the day when God will resurrect our bodies in glory!

We sing Gloria because we know so very well; or better said, we are "convinced that neither death, nor life, nor angels, nor rulers, nor things present, nor things to come, nor powers, nor height, nor depth, nor anything else in all creation, will be able to separate us from the love of God in Christ Jesus our Lord."[22]

I end with the words of Teresa L. Fry Brown:

> Keep in mind that every tear you shed on the journey
> Every pain you feel on the journey
> Every lonely night you spend on the journey
> Every headache you experience on the journey
> Every joy you share on the journey
> Every victory you have on the journey
> Is all to the glory of God![23]

Glory be to God!

22. Rom 8:38 NRSV.

23. Fry, *Weary Throats and New Songs*, 52.

Postlude

Imagine a congregation

- where a new pastor begins as a leader only after living in the midst of the community for six months;
- where every person knows each other's names as an expectation for leading the community's prayer;
- where a congregation pays attention to "its knees," not only the experiences of our bodies, yes, that too, but also the structures of power expressed in its liturgies where authority bends to every person's worth;
- where the substance and forms of worship are shaped by those who live without enough food, medicine, work, without the essential aspects of human dignity.

To embody faith with attention to these ideals is the essence of this book.

Carvalhaes argues for change from theological, ecclesial, and political premises, with a caveat, that is, as they connect with the hearts of people's day to day lives. He does not assume one pattern fits all. Rather, he offers a myriad of examples. But there is something that does apply universally. Carvalhaes insists that authentically Christian worship begins with attention to the experiences of people who are poor.

Carvalhaes invites radical change, that is, a return to the model of Jesus. It requires thinking critically about what our worship expects us to be and to do, when love, kindness, goodness, and expanding boundaries ground our choices.

Janet R. Walton
Professor of Worship, Union Theological Seminary (New York)

Bibliography

African American Intellectual History Society. "#Charlestonsyllabus." http://aaihs.org/resources/charlestonsyllabus/.

Alexander, Michelle. *The New Jim Crow: Mass Incarceration in the Age of Colorblindness.* New York: New Press, 2012.

Allen, Theodore W. *The Invention of the White Race.* 2 vols. 2nd ed. London: Verso, 2012.

Althaus-Reid, Marcella. *Indecent Theology: Theological Perversions in Sex, Gender and Politics.* London: Routledge, 2000.

Alves, Rubem. *Creio na ressurreição do corpo.* Rio de Janeiro: Cedi, 1983.

———. *Perguntaram-me se eu acredito em Deus.* Translated by Emily Everett. São Paulo: Editora Planeta do Brasil, 2007.

———. "Sobre Política e Jardinagem." In *Melhores crônicas de Rubem Alves,* 26–30. Campinas, SP: Editora Papirus, 2012.

Anzaldúa, Gloria. *Borderlands/La Frontera: The New Mestiza.* San Francisco: Aunt Lute, 1987.

Appadurai, Arjun. *The Future as Cultural Fact: Essays on the Global Condition.* London: Verso, 2013.

Arregi, José "The Spirit Who Moans in All Beings: Notes for a Liberating Eco-spirituality." Translated by Andrés Krankerberger. *Voices: Theological Journal of EATWOT,* n.s., 37.2–3 (2014) 75–84.

Augustine. *Confessions.* Translated by Garry Wills. New York: Penguin, 2008.

———. *Sermons on the Liturgical Seasons.* Translated by Mary Sarah Muldowney. Fathers of the Church 38. Washington, DC: Catholic University of America Press, 1959.

Barber, William J., and Barbara Zelter. *Forward Together: A Moral Message for the Nation.* St. Louis: Chalice, 2014.

Barth, Karl. *Dogmática de la Iglesia, II/1.* Sal Terrae, 2000.

Bender, Harold S., et al., eds. *The Mennonite Encyclopedia.* Vol. 3. Scottdale, PA: Mennonite Publishing House, 1957.

Benjamin, Walter. "Theses on the Philosophy of History." In *Illuminations,* edited by Hannah Arendt, translated by Harry Zohn, 253–64. New York: Schocken, 1969.

Berry, Thomas. *The Great Work: Our Way into the Future.* New York: Bell Tower, 1999.

Berry, Wendell. *The Way of Ignorance: And Other Essays.* Berkeley: Counterpoint, 2006.

———. *What Matters? Economics for a Renewed Commonwealth.* Berkeley: Counterpoint, 2010.

Betcher, Sharon V. *Spirit and the Politics of Disablement*. Minneapolis: Fortress, 2007.

Boff, Leonardo. *Jesus Christ Liberator: A Critical Christology for Our Time*. Translated by Patrick Hughes. Maryknoll, NY: Orbis, 1978.

———. *Seleção de textos espirituais*. Rio de Janeiro: Vozes, 1991.

Bollain, Iciar, director. *Even the Rain*. Image Entertainment, 2012.

Bonhoeffer, Dietrich. *Discipleship*. Edited by Geffrey B. Kelly and John D. Godsey. Translated by Barbara Green and Reinhard Krauss. Minneapolis: Fortress, 2003.

Bradshaw, Paul. "Easter in Christian Tradition." In *Passover and Easter: Origin and History to Modern Times*, edited by Paul F. Bradshaw and Laurence A. Hoffman, 1–7. Two Liturgical Traditions 5. Notre Dame: University of Notre Dame Press, 1999.

———. *Eucharistic Origins*. Oxford: Oxford University Press, 2004.

Breton, André. *Mad Love*. Translated by Mary Ann Caws. Lincoln: University of Nebraska Press, 1987.

Brown, Kelly Douglas. *Stand Your Ground: Black Bodies and the Justice of God*. Maryknoll, NY: Orbis, 2015.

Brown, Teresa L. Fry. *Weary Throats and New Songs: Black Women Proclaiming God's Word*. Nashville: Abingdon, 2003.

Brueggemann, Walter. *The Practice of Prophetic Imagination: Preaching an Emancipating Word*. Minneapolis: Fortress, 2012.

Buarque, Chico, and Edú Lobo. "Salmo." Álbum de Teatro. Sao Paulo: Sony-BMG, 1996.

Buchanan, John M. "Entry Points: A Kingdom of Peace, Kindness and Justice." *Christian Century*, March 9, 2010. http://www.christiancentury.org/article/2010-03/entry-points.

Budde, Michael L. *The Borders of Baptism: Identities, Allegiances, and the Church*. Eugene, OR: Cascade, 2011.

Butler, Judith. *Excitable Speech: A Politics of the Performative*. New York: Routledge, 1997.

———. *Precarious Life: The Powers of Mourning and Violence*. New York: Verso, 2004.

Caputo, John D. *The Insistence of God: A Theology of Perhaps*. Bloomington: Indiana University Press, 2013.

Carvalhaes, Cláudio. *Eucharist and Globalization: Redrawing the Borders of Eucharistic Hospitality*. Eugene, OR: Pickwick, 2013.

———. "Multiplying the Glorias Around the Earth." *Unbound: An Interactive Journal of Christian Social Justice*, December 9, 2013. http://justiceunbound.org/carousel/multiplying-the-glorias-around-the-earth/.

———. "White Reasoning and What Is Common in Our Common Worship? A Methodological Critique to the Process of Renewal of the Book of Common Worship–Presbyterian Church, U.S.A." *Call to Worship: Liturgy, Music, Preaching, and the Arts* 49.3 (2017) 19–27.

Casaldáliga, Pedro, and Pedro Tierra; music by Milton Nascimento. "Missa dos Quilombos." PolyGram Discos 811 500-501, 1982. http://www.servicioskoinonia.org/Casaldaliga/poesia/quilombos.htm.

Castro, Eduardo Viveiros de. "Antropologia renovada." *Revista Cult*, Edições 153. https://revistacult.uol.com.br/home/antropologia-renovada/.

———. *Encontros*. Rio de Janeiro: Azougue Editorial, 2008.

Cha, Ariana Eunjung. "Spain's Crisis Spawns Alternative Economy That Doesn't Rely on the Euro." *The Guardian*, September 4, 2012. http://www.theguardian.com/world/2012/sep/04/spain-euro-free-economy.

Chupungco, Anscar J. *Shaping the Easter Feast*. Washington, DC: Pastoral Press, 1992.

Cobb, John B., Jr. *Spiritual Bankruptcy: A Prophetic Call to Action*. Nashville: Abingdon, 2010.

Comblin, José. "The Holy Spirit." In *Systematic Theology: Perspectives from Liberation Theology (Readings from Mysterium Liberationis)*, edited by Jon Sobrino and Ignacio Ellacuría, 146–64. Maryknoll, NY: Orbis, 1996.

Comissão Pastoral da Terra. "Carta Final: Faz escuro, mas cantamos!" https://www.cptnacional.org.br/index.php/publicacoes-2/destaque/2723-carta-final-faz-escuro-mas-eu-canto.

Cone, James H. *Martin & Malcolm & America: A Dream or a Nightmare?* 20th anniv. ed. Maryknoll, NY: Orbis, 2012.

Connell, Martin. "From Easter to Pentecost." In *Passover and Easter: The Symbolic Structuring of Sacred Seasons*, edited by Paul F. Bradshaw and Laurence A. Hoffman, 94–106. Two Liturgical Traditions 6. Notre Dame: University of Notre Dame Press, 1999.

Cox, Harvey. *The Future of Faith*. San Francisco: HarperOne, 2009.

Datrino, José. "Gentileza gera gentileza." *Revista Prosa Verso e Arte*. http://www.revistaprosaversoearte.com/gentileza-gera-gentileza-profeta-gentileza-jose-datrino/.

Davies, J. G. *Holy Week: A Short History*. Richmond: John Knox, 1963.

Derrida, Jacques. *The Ear of the Other: Otobiography, Transference, Translation; Texts and Discussions with Jacques Derrida*. Edited by Christie McDonald. Translated by Peggy Kamuf and Avital Ronell. Lincoln: University of Nebraska Press, 1988.

Driver, Tom F. *Liberating Rites: Understanding the Transformative Power of Ritual*. Boulder, CO: Westview, 1997.

Dworkin, Craig. *Reading the Illegible*. Evanston: Northwestern University Press, 2003.

Fanon, Frantz. *A Dying Colonialism*. Translated by Haakon Chevalier. New York: Grove, 1965.

Fitzgerald, Allan, et al., eds. *Augustine Through the Ages: An Encyclopedia*. Grand Rapids: Eerdmans, 2009.

Flatow, Nicole. "DOJ Finds Unconstitutional Solitary Confinement of Mentally Ill for Months, Years in Pennsylvania." *thinkprogress.org*, June 6, 2013. http://thinkprogress.org/justice/2013/06/06/2114821/doj-finds-unconstitutional-solitary-confinement-of-mentally-ill-for-months-years-in-pennsylvania/?mobile=nc.

Fortino, Ellyn. "'Moral Monday' Activists Engage in Civil Disobedience to Protest State Budget Cuts." *progressillinois.com*, July 13, 2015. http://progressillinois.com/posts/content/2015/07/13/moral-monday-activists-engage-civil-disobedience-protesting-state-budget.

Foster, Hal, et al. *Art since 1900: Modernism, Antimodernism and Postmodernism*. 2nd ed. London: Thames & Hudson, 2011.

Foucault, Michel. *The History of Sexuality*. Vol. 1, *An Introduction*. Translated by Robert Hurley. London: Vintage, 1990.

Galbreath, Paul. "Ash Wednesday: A Three-Act Play in Turning, Nurturing and Growing." Liturgy for Union Presbyterian Seminary Chapel, 2010.

Galeano, Eduardo. *Open Veins of Latin America: Five Centuries of the Pillage of a Continent*. Translated by Cedric Belfrage. 25th anniv. ed. New York: Monthly Review Press, 1997.

Garrigan, Siobhán. "Worship Audible Only in the Mouth, So Far." Forthcoming.

Gebara, Ivone. "Liturgia e Theologia, Uma Nota Dissonante." In *Teologia do Culto: Entre o Altar e o Mundo: Aportes Multidisciplinares da Liturgia*, edited by Cláudio Carvalhaes, 57–73. São Paulo: Fonte Editorial, 2012.

Genova, Alexandra. "'In the Old Days, He'd Be Carried Out on a Stretcher': Trump Says He'd Like to Punch Protestor 'in the Face.'" *Daily Mail*, February 23, 2016. http://www.dailymail.co.uk/news/article-3459653/I-d-like-punch-face-Trump-complains-protester-s-gentle-treatment.html#ixzz4UwuoadvU.

Gerlach, Karl. *The Ante-Nicene Pascha: A Rhetorical History*. Leeuven: Peeters, 1998.

Gibler, Linda. *From the Beginning to Baptism: Scientific and Sacred Stories of Water, Oil, and Fire*. Collegeville, MN: Liturgical, 2010.

Green, Laci. "Is Racism Over Yet?" https://www.youtube.com/watch?v=h_hx30zOi9I.

Gruzinski, Serge. *A Colonização do Imaginário: Sociedades Indígenas e Ocidentalização no México Espanhol; Séculos XVI–XVIII*. Translated by Beatriz Perrone-Moisés. São Paulo: Companhia das Letras, 2003.

Gutiérrez, Gustavo. *On Job: God-Talk and the Suffering of the Innocent*. Translated by Matthew J. O'Connell. Maryknoll, NY: Orbis, 1987.

Hall, Douglas John. *The Cross in Our Context: Jesus and the Suffering World*. Minneapolis: Fortress, 2003.

Hedges, Chris. "Let's Get This Class War Started." *commondreams.com*, October 21, 2013. http://www.commondreams.org/views/2013/10/21/lets-get-class-war-started.

Heidegger, Martin. "The End of Philosophy and the Task of Thinking." In *Basic Writings: From "Being and Time" (1927) to "The Task of Thinking" (1964)*, edited by David Farrell Krell, 307–26. New York: Harper & Row, 1993.

Heng, Geraldine. "The Invention of Race in the European Middle Ages I: Race Studies, Modernity, and the Middle Ages." *Literature Compass* 8.5 (2011) 315–31.

Hernandez, Eleazar Lopez. "Deus, tradições indígenas e globalização." In *Teologia para Outro Mundo Possível*, edited by Luiz Carlos Susin, 305–20. São Paulo: Paulinas, 2006.

Heschel, Abraham Joshua. *Moral Grandeur and Spiritual Audacity: Essays*. Edited by Susannah Heschel. New York: Farrar, Straus and Giroux, 1997.

Hoffman, Laurence. "The Passover Meal in Jewish Tradition." In *Passover and Easter: Origin and History to Modern Times*, edited by Paul Bradshaw and Laurence Hoffman, 8–26. Notre Dame: University of Notre Dame Press, 1999.

Hoffman, Paul E. *Faith Shaping Ministry*. Eugene, OR: Cascade, 2013.

———. "The Rite of Affirmation of Baptismal Vocation in the World." Presentation given at "God's Mission and Worship," Mid-winter Convocation, Luther Seminary, St. Paul, MN, January 29–31, 2014.

Horkheimer, Max, and Theodor W. Adorno. *Dialectic of Enlightenment*. Edited by Gunzelin Schmid Noerr. Translated by Edmund Jephcott. Stanford: Stanford University Press, 2007.

Hughes, Graham. *Worship as Meaning: A Liturgical Theology for Late Modernity*. Cambridge: Cambridge University Press, 2003.

Isasi-Diaz, Ada María. *La Lucha Continues: Mujerista Theology*. Maryknoll, NY: Orbis, 2004.

Jennings, Willie James. *The Christian Imagination: Theology and the Origins of Race*. New Haven: Yale University Press, 2010.

Johnson, Maxwell. *The Rites of Christian Initiation: Their Evolution and Interpretation*. Collegeville, MN: Liturgical, 1999.

Julian of Norwich. *Revelations of Divine Love*. Amazon Digital Services LLC, 2010.

Kehl, Maria Rita. *Sobre ética e psicanálise*. São Paulo: Companhia das Letras, 2004.

King, Martin Luther, Jr. "The Good Samaritan." A sermon delivered at Ebenezer Baptist Church, Atlanta, GA, August 28, 1966.

———. "Letter from Birmingham Jail." http://kingencyclopedia.stanford.edu/kingweb/popular_requests/frequentdocs/birmingham.pdf.

———. *Strength to Love*. Minneapolis: Fortress, 2010.

Lathrop, Gordon. *Holy People: A Liturgical Ecclesiology*. Minneapolis: Fortress, 2006.

———. *Holy Things: A Liturgical Theology*. Minneapolis: Fortress, 1993.

Lee, Michelle Ye Hee. "Donald Trump's False Comments Connecting Mexican Immigrants and Crime." *Washington Post*, July 8, 2015. http://www.washingtonpost.com/blogs/fact-checker/wp/2015/07/08/donald-trumps-false-comments-connecting-mexican-immigrants-and-crime/.

Leiman, Melvin. *The Political Economy of Racism*. Chicago: Haymarket, 2010.

Lipovetsky, Gilles, and Sébastien Charles. *Hypermodern Times*. Translated by Andrew Brown. Cambridge: Polity, 2005.

Lowery, Wesley. *They Can't Kill Us All: Ferguson, Baltimore, and a New Era in America's Racial Justice Movement*. Boston: Little, Brown, 2016.

Machado, Ismael. "Elas, marcadas para morrer." *CartaCapital*, July 17, 2013. http://www.cartacapital.com.br/sociedade/elas-marcadas-para-morrer-7816.html.

Maciel, Camila. "Impunidade em mortes é motor da violência no campo." April 14, 2016. http://www.mst.org.br/2016/04/14/impunidade-em-mortes-e-motor-da-violencia-no-campo.html.

Malkin, Elisabeth. "Isidro Baldenegro, Mexican Environmental Activist, Is Shot to Death." *New York Times*, January 18, 2017. https://www.nytimes.com/2017/01/18/world/americas/mexico-environmental-activist-shot-sierra-madre.html.

Malone, Jacqui. *Steppin' on the Blues: The Visible Rhythms of African American Dance*. Urbana: University of Illinois Press, 1996.

Maraschin, Jaci C. "A antecipação da liberdade do Reino de Deus." *Simpósio* 32 (1989) 349–63.

———. *Da leveza e da beleza: Liturgia na pós-modernidade*. São Paulo: ASTE, 2011.

———. "Libertação da Liturgia." In *A beleza da santidade: Ensaios de liturgia*. São Paulo: ASTE, 1996.

———. *O espelho e a transparência: O credo niceno-constantinopolitano e a teologia latino-americana*. Rio de Janeiro: CEDI/Programa de Assessoria à Pastoral, 1989.

Marx, Karl. *Capital: A Critique of Political Economy*. Vol. 1, pt. 1, *The Process of Capitalist Production*. New York: Cosimo Classics, 2013.

Mattson, Stephen. "American 'Christianity' Has Failed." *Sojourners*, January 25, 2017. https://sojo.net/articles/american-christianity-has-failed.

Mbembe, Achille. *Crítica da razão negra*. Lisbon: Ediciones Antígona, 2014.

———. "Necropolitics." Translated by Libby Meintjes. *Public Culture* 15 (2003) 11–40.

Metta, John. "I Racist." *Those People*, July 6, 2015. https://thsppl.com/i-racist-538512462265.

Metz, Johann Baptist. *Faith in History and Society: Toward a Practical Fundamental Theology*. Translated by David Smith. New York: Seabury, 1980.

———. *A Passion for God: The Mystical-Political Dimension of Christianity*. Edited and translated by J. Matthew Ashley. New York: Paulist, 1998.

Mic. "Artist Creates 'Letter from a Birmingham Jail' Memes to Stop People from Whitewashing MLK." January 16, 2017. https://mic.com/articles/165598/artist-creates-letters-from-birmingham-jail-memes-to-stop-people-from-whitewashing-mlk#.YFxrLjEaN.

Mignolo, Walter D. "Epistemic Disobedience, Independent Thought and Decolonial Freedom." *Theory, Culture & Society* 26.7–8 (2009) 159–81.

Mitchell, Nathan D. *Meeting Mystery: Liturgy, Worship, Sacraments*. Maryknoll, NY: Orbis, 1984.

Moltmann, Jürgen. *Un Nuevo estilo de vida: Sobre la libertad, la alegría y el juego*. Salamanca: Ediciones Sígueme, 1981.

Morrill, Bruce T. *Anamnesis as Dangerous Memory: Political and Liturgical Theology in Dialogue*. Collegeville, MN: Liturgical, 2000.

Morrison, Toni. "Nobel Lecture." December 7, 1993. http://www.nobelprize.org/nobel_prizes/literature/laureates/1993/morrison-lecture.html.

Nietzsche, Friedrich. *Thus Spake Zarathustra*. Translated by Thomas Common. New York: Dover, 1999.

Penn, Michael Philip. *Kissing Christians: Ritual and Community in the Late Ancient Church*. Philadelphia: University of Pennsylvania Press, 2005.

———. "On Kissing: A Q&A with Michael Penn." June 2006. https://www.mtholyoke.edu/offices/comm/news/kissing.shtml.

Pereira, Nancy Cardoso. "De todos os objetos . . . os que mais amo são os usados: Um olhar pastoral sobre os conflitos no campo e os movimentos sociais no Brasil." In "Caderno de Conflitos no Campo da Comissão Pastoral da Terra," 2012. http://www.cptnacional.org.br/index.php/component/jdownloads/viewdownload/43-conflitos-no-campo-brasil-publicacao/316-conflitos-no-campo-brasil-2012?Itemid=23.

———. "De-evangelization of the Knees: Epistemology, Osteoporosis and Affliction." In *Liturgy in Postcolonial Perspectives: Only One Is Holy*, edited by Cláudio Carvalhaes, 119–24. New York: Palgrave Macmillan, 2015.

Procter-Smith, Marjorie. *In Her Own Rite: Constructing Feminist Liturgical Tradition*. Nashville: Abingdon, 1990.

Quental, Paula. "Copavi, no Paraná: 22 anos de produção solidária." *Solidare*, March 4, 2015. http://agenciasolidare.com.br/copavi-no-parana-22-anos-de-producao-solidaria/.

Ramos, Valeriano, Jr. "The Concepts of Ideology, Hegemony, and Organic Intellectuals in Gramsci's Marxism." *Theoretical Review* 27 (March-April 1982). https://www.marxists.org/history/erol/periodicals/theoretical-review/1982301.htm#fw12.

Rasmussen, Larry L. *Earth-Honoring Faith: Religious Ethics in a New Key*. Oxford: Oxford University Press, 2015.

Ribeiro, Darcy. "Duas Leis Reitoras." *Folha de São Paulo*, October 2, 1995. http://www1.folha.uol.com.br/fsp/1995/10/02/opiniao/8.html.

Richardson, Cyril C., ed. *Early Christian Fathers*. Philadelphia: Westminster, 1953.

Rivera, Mayra. "Glory: The First Passion of Theology?" In *Polidoxy: Theology of Multiplicity and Relation*, edited by Catherine Keller and Laurel C. Schneider, 167–85. London: Routledge, 2011.

Ruíz, Samuel. "Monseñor Óscar Arnulfo Romero: Mártir de la justicia y de la opción por los pobres." Sermon given on the 30th anniversary of the martyrdom of Archbishop Romero, San Salvador, El Salvador, March 24, 2010.

Rumi, Jalal al-Din. *The Essential Rumi*. Translated and edited by Coleman Barks. New expanded ed. New York: HarperOne, 2004.

Russell, Letty M. *Church in the Round: Feminist Interpretation of the Church*. Louisville: Westminster John Knox, 1993.

Safatle, Vladimir. "Por um colapso do indivíduo e de seus afetos." Instituto CPFL, September 29, 2015. http://www.institutocpfl.org.br/cultura/2015/09/29/por-um-colapso-do-individuo-e-de-seus-afetos-com-vladimir-safatle-versao-na-integra/.

Saliers, Don. "Afterword: Liturgy and Ethics Revised." In *Liturgy and the Moral Self: Humanity at Full Stretch before God; Essays in Honor of Don Saliers*, edited by E. Byron Anderson and Bruce T. Morrill, 209–24. Collegeville, MN: Liturgical, 1998.

Satterlee, Craig. *Ambrose of Milan's Method of Mystagogical Preaching*. Collegeville, MN: Liturgical, 2002.

Sifton, Elisabeth. *The Serenity Prayer: Faith and Politics in Times of Peace and War*. New York: Norton, 2005.

Smith, Dennis. *From Symposium to Eucharist: The Banquet in the Early Christian World*. Minneapolis: Fortress, 2003.

Smith, Dennis, and Hal E. Taussig. *Many Tables: The Eucharist in the New Testament and Liturgy Today*. London: SCM, 1990.

Sobrino, Jon. "A Igreja costuma se distanciar de Jesus para que ele não incomode." Interview with Jon Sobrino. Instituto Humanitas Unisinos, December 21, 2010. http://www.teleios.com.br/a-igreja-costuma-se-distanciar-de-jesus-para-que-ele-nao-incomode-entrevista-com-jon-sobrino/.

Solnit, Rebecca. *A Paradise Built in Hell: The Extraordinary Communities That Arise in Disaster*. New York: Penguin, 2010.

Spinks, Bryan D. *Early and Medieval Rituals and Theologies of Baptism: From the New Testament to the Council of Trent*. Aldershot, UK: Ashgate, 2006.

Stanford Center on Poverty and Inequality. "20 Facts about U.S. Inequality That Everyone Should Know." 2011. http://inequality.stanford.edu/publications/20-facts-about-us-inequality-everyone-should-know.

Stein, Ben. "In Class Warfare, Guess Which Class Is Winning." *New York Times*, November 26, 2006. http://www.nytimes.com/2006/11/26/business/yourmoney/26every.html?_r=0.

Stevenson, Kenneth. *Jerusalem Revisited: The Liturgical Meaning of Holy Week*. Washington, DC: Pastoral Press, 1988.

Stiglitz, Joseph E. *The Price of Inequality: How Today's Divided Society Endangers Our Future*. New York: Norton, 2013.

Stuart, Elizabeth. "Criminalizing Poverty: During Economic Crisis, New Laws Crack Down on America's Poor, Homeless." *Deseret News*, August 13, 2011. http://www.deseretnews.com/article/700170566/Criminalizing-poverty-During-economic-crisis-new-laws-crack-down-on-Americas-poor-homeless.html?pg=all.

Swaine, John, et al. "Young Black Men Killed by US Police at Highest Rate in Year of 1,134 Deaths." *The Guardian*, December 31, 2015. https://www.theguardian.com/us-news/2015/dec/31/the-counted-police-killings-2015-young-black-men.

Taussig, Hal. *In the Beginning Was the Meal: Social Experimentation and Early Christian Identity*. Minneapolis: Fortress, 2009.

Taussig, Michael. *Defacement: Public Secrecy and the Labor of the Negative*. Stanford: Stanford University Press, 1999.

Taylor, Barbara Brown. *The Preaching Life*. Cambridge, MA: Cowley, 1993.

Taylor, Mark C. *About Religion: Economies of Faith in Virtual Culture*. Chicago: University of Chicago Press, 1999.

———. *Altarity*. Chicago: University of Chicago Press, 1987.

———. "Retracings." In *The Craft of Religious Studies*, edited by Jon R. Stone, 258–76. New York: St. Martin's, 1998.

———. *Rewiring the Real: In Conversation with William Gaddis, Richard Powers, Mark Danielewski, and Don DeLillo*. New York: Columbia University Press, 2014.

Thomas, Linda E. "The Social Sciences and Rituals of Resilience in African and African American Communities." In *The Cambridge Companion to Black Theology*, edited by Dwight N. Hopkins and Edward P. Antonio, 44–57. Cambridge: Cambridge University Press, 2012.

Townes, Emilie M. *Womanist Ethics and the Cultural Production of Evil*. New York: Palgrave Macmillan, 2006.

Untener, Ken. "A Future Not Our Own." http://www.journeywithjesus.net/PoemsAndPrayers/Ken_Untener_A_Future_Not_Our_Own.shtml.

Veloso, Caetano. "O Quereres." Track 3 of *Personalidade*. PolyGram Discos 514137-2, 1993, compact disc.

Waldrop, Rosmarie. *Lavish Absence: Recalling and Rereading Edmond Jabès*. Middletown, CT: Wesleyan University Press, 2005.

Walton, Janet R. *Feminist Liturgy: A Matter of Justice*. Collegeville, MN: Liturgical, 2000.

"Wealth Inequality in America." https://www.youtube.com/watch?v=25FNm8lRvoM.

Wilkinson, John, ed. *Egeria's Travels to the Holy Land*. Rev. ed. Jerusalem: Ariel, 1981.

Williams, Delores S. "Black Theology and Womanist Theology." In *The Cambridge Companion to Black Theology*, edited by Dwight N. Hopkins and Edward P. Antonio, 58–72. Cambridge: Cambridge University Press, 2012.

Wilmore, Gayraud S. "Historical Perspective." In *The Cambridge Companion to Black Theology*, edited by Dwight N. Hopkins and Edward P. Antonio, 19–32. Cambridge: Cambridge University Press, 2012.

Wilson, Robert L. *The First Spanish Methodist Church and the Young Lords*. New York: United Methodist Church, 1970.

Wrathall, Mark A. "Introduction: Metaphysics and Onto-theology." In *Religion After Metaphysics*, edited by Mark A. Wrathall, 1–6. Cambridge: Cambridge University Press, 2003.

Žižek, Slavoj. "Love as a Political Category." Lecture delivered at the 6th Subversive Festival, Zagreb, Croatia, May 16, 2013. http://www.youtube.com/watch?v=b44IhiCuNw4.

Name/Subject Index

Scripture Index